Landlord's Legal Guide in New York

Second Edition

Brette McWhorter Sember
Mark Warda
Attorneys at Law

SPHINX® PUBLISHING
AN IMPRINT OF SOURCEBOOKS, INC.®
NAPERVILLE, ILLINOIS
www.SphinxLegal.com

For Kathleen and Thomas,

who gave me my rights and duties

Contents

Forms
Signatures
Backing Out of a Lease

Using Self-Help Law Books

Before using a self-help law book, you should realize the advantages and disadvantages of doing your own legal work and understand the challenges and diligence that this requires.

The Growing Trend

Rest assured that you will not be the first or only person handling your own legal matter. For example, in some states, more than 75% of the people in divorces and other cases represent themselves. Because of the high cost of legal services, this is a major trend, and many courts are struggling to make it easier for people to represent themselves. However, some courts are not happy with people who do not use attorneys and refuse to help them in any way. For some, the attitude is, "Go to the law library and figure it out for yourself."

We write and publish self-help law books to give people an alternative to the often complicated and confusing legal books found in most law libraries. We have made the explanations of the law as simple and easy to understand as possible. Of course, unlike an attorney advising an individual client, we cannot cover every conceivable possibility.

Cost/Value Analysis

Whenever you shop for a product or service, you are faced with various levels of quality and price. In deciding what product or service to buy, you make a cost/value analysis on the basis of your willingness to pay and the quality you desire.

When buying a car, you decide whether you want transportation, comfort, status, or sex appeal. Accordingly, you decide among choices such as a Neon, a Lincoln, a Rolls Royce, or a Porsche. Before making a decision, you usually weigh the merits of each option against the cost.

When you get a headache, you can take a pain reliever (such as aspirin) or visit a medical specialist for a neurological examination. Given this choice, most people, of course, take a pain reliever, since it costs only pennies; whereas a medical examination costs hundreds of dollars and takes a lot of time. This is usually a logical choice because it is rare to need anything more than a pain reliever for a headache. But in some cases, a headache may indicate a brain tumor, and failing to see a specialist right away can result in complications. Should everyone with a headache go to a specialist? Of course not, but people treating their own illnesses must realize that they are betting, on the basis of their cost/value analysis of the situation, that they are taking the most logical option.

The same cost/value analysis must be made when deciding to do one's own legal work. Many legal situations are very straightforward, requiring a simple form and no complicated analysis. Anyone with a little intelligence and a book of instructions can handle the matter without outside help.

But there is always the chance that complications are involved that only an attorney would notice. To simplify the law into a book like this, several legal cases often must be condensed into a single sentence or paragraph. Otherwise, the book would be several hundred pages long and too complicated for most people. However, this simplification necessarily leaves out many details and nuances that would apply to special or unusual situations. Also, there are many ways to interpret most legal questions. Your case may come before a judge who disagrees with the analysis of our authors.

Therefore, in deciding to use a self-help law book and to do your own legal work, you must realize that you are making a cost/value analysis. You have decided that the money you will save in doing it yourself outweighs the chance that your case will not turn out to your satisfaction. Most people handling their own simple legal matters never have a problem, but occasionally people find that it ended up costing them more to have an attorney straighten out the situation than it would have if they had hired an attorney in the beginning. Keep this in mind while handling your case, and be sure to consult an attorney if you feel you might need further guidance.

Local Rules The next thing to remember is that a book which covers the law for the entire nation, or even for an entire state, cannot possibly include every procedural difference of every jurisdiction. Whenever possible, we provide the exact form needed; however, in some areas, each county, or even each judge, may require unique forms and procedures. In our state books, our forms usually cover the majority of counties in the state or provide examples of the type of form that will be required. In our national books, our forms are sometimes even more general in nature but are designed to give a good idea of the type of form that will be needed in most locations. Nonetheless, keep in mind that your state, county, or judge may have a requirement, or use a form, that is not included in this book.

You should not necessarily expect to be able to get all of the information and resources you need solely from within the pages of this book. This book will serve as your guide, giving you specific information whenever possible and helping you to find out what else you will need to know. This is just like if you decided to build your own backyard deck. You might purchase a book on how to build decks. However, such a book would not include the building codes and permit requirements of every city, town, county, and township in the nation; nor would it include the lumber, nails, saws, hammers, and other materials and tools you would need to actually build the deck. You would use the book as your guide, and then do some work and research involving such matters as whether you need a permit of some kind, what type and grade of wood is available in your area, whether to use hand tools or power tools, and how to use those tools.

Before using the forms in a book like this, you should check with your court clerk to see if there are any local rules of which you should be aware or local forms you will need to use. Often, such forms will require the same information as the forms in the book but are merely laid out differently or use slightly different language. They will sometimes require additional information.

Changes in the Law

Besides being subject to local rules and practices, the law is subject to change at any time. The courts and the legislatures of all fifty states are constantly revising the laws. It is possible that while you are reading this book, some aspect of the law is being changed.

In most cases, the change will be of minimal significance. A form will be redesigned, additional information will be required, or a waiting period will be extended. As a result, you might need to revise a form, file an extra form, or wait out a longer time period. These types of changes will not usually affect the outcome of your case. On the other hand, sometimes a major part of the law is changed, the entire law in a particular area is rewritten, or a case that was the basis of a central legal point is overruled. In such instances, your entire ability to pursue your case may be impaired.

Introduction

New York's landlord/tenant laws are like a double-edged sword. If a landlord does not know about them, or ignores them, he or she can lose thousands of dollars in rent, penalties, and attorney's fees. However, a landlord who knows the law can use the procedures to simplify life and save money. Knowledge is power, and knowing the laws governing rentals will give you the power to protect your rights and deal with problems effectively.

Laws are written to be precise, not to be easily readable. This book explains the law in simple language so that New York landlords can know what is required of them and know their rights under the law. If you would like more detail about a law, you can check the statutes in Appendix A or research the court cases as explained in Chapter 1.

Nearly every year the New York legislature passes new laws regulating landlord/tenant relations and the New York courts write more opinions defining the rights of landlords and tenants. Laws and regulations regarding rent control and stabilization in New York City and surrounding counties also change frequently. Check **http://public.leginfo.state.ny.us** periodically for such updates in state law.

No book of this type can be expected to cover every situation that may arise. Laws change and different judges have different interpretations of what the laws mean. Only a lawyer, reviewing the unique characteristics of your situation, can give you an opinion as to how the laws apply to your case; however, this book can give you the legal framework to avoid costly mistakes.

This book contains valuable information and step-by-step procedures for handling your property and evicting tenants. It includes easy-to-use forms that will assist you in handling the entire eviction process on your own or in simply starting it yourself.

When following the procedures in this book, it should be kept in mind that different counties have different customs and some judges have their own way of doing things, so the requirements in your area may differ somewhat from those outlined in this book. Court clerks and judges' law clerks cannot give you legal advice, but often they can tell you what is required in order to proceed with your case. Before filing any forms, ask if your court provides its own forms or has any special requirements.

Laws that Govern Rental Property

New York landlord/tenant law consists of statutes passed by the legislature, various municipal codes, and legal opinions written by judges. The statutes and municipal codes usually address specific issues that have come up repeatedly in landlord/tenant relations. The judicial opinions interpret the statutes and codes, and decide what the law is in areas not specifically covered by statutes and codes.

Since the statutes and codes were written at different times by different legislators, they sometimes conflict. There are also administrative regulations that conflict with those laws, and judges do not always interpret them in the same way. Consequently, a landlord can be caught in a situation of uncertainty, in which even an experienced lawyer cannot find an easy solution.

Fortunately, this is a rare situation. If it happens to you, your two choices are to fight the issue in a higher court or to give in and do what is demanded. Most small landlords cannot afford a long court battle, so the only practical solution is to relent. For this reason, it is usually better to work out a settlement with a tenant than to let an issue go to a building inspector or before a judge. This is explained in more detail later in the book.

When reading the law contained in judges' opinions, be sure to note from which court the opinion originated. If it is not from your district, it might not be binding on your case. New York Court of Appeals opinions apply to all courts in New York, but appellate division opinions only apply to the department in which they sit. Supreme court appeals of county court cases are only binding in the district in which that court sits, and county court opinions are not binding in other courts, but they may be used as rationale by other county courts.

NEW YORK STATE LAWS

There is no one place where landlord/tenant law in New York can be located. The laws governing landlords and tenants can be found in various parts of the Consolidated Laws of New York, including the Real Property Actions and Proceedings, the Real Property Law, the Multiple Residence Law, and the Multiple Dwelling Law. There are other state laws that have an impact on the landlord/tenant relationship, such as the Mobile Home Owners Bill of Rights, the Lien Law, the General Obligations Law, and the General Business Law. Many of these New York state laws are referred to throughout this book, and Appendix A contains some of the important New York state laws to which you may need to refer. Be sure to read the section on "Legal Research" on page 3 for more information on finding these laws.

LOCAL LAWS

Some local governments have passed laws governing landlords and tenants. You should check for both city and county laws that may apply to you. Rent control laws apply to New York City and parts of Nassau, Rockland, and Westchester counties. Chapter 4 discusses these rent control laws. There are also administrative regulations that may affect landlords.

FEDERAL LAWS

The *Civil Rights Act* and the *Americans with Disabilities Act*, which deal with discrimination, are just two examples of the federal laws that apply to rental property. There are other applicable federal laws, such as the rules of the Environmental Protection Agency (specifically the rules about lead paint), and the rules of the Department of Housing and Urban Development (HUD). A handbook with public housing rules and other HUD rules is available from HUD. Check the United States Government pages of your phone book for your local office.

LEGAL RESEARCH

Obviously, entire cases and statutes cannot be included in this book; however, you will find summaries of laws and statutes. If you would like to read a full case opinion (or decision) or an entire statute, or if you would like to look for other cases that may apply to your situation, you will need to do some legal research.

Law Libraries   Each county in New York has a law library in the county or supreme court courthouse. Look in your phone book for county listings. Law schools also have law libraries that can be used.

New York Statutes   The *New York Statutes* (i.e., the laws passed by the New York legislature) may be found in a large set of books titled *McKinney's Consolidated Laws of New York Annotated*. The statutes are divided according to the subject, and there may be one or more volumes for each subject. Find the New York Statutes, go to the appropriate subject area, and look up the section number of the law you need. The following is a list of the titles of the various statutes that are used in this book, as well as their abbreviations.

- ✪ Civil Practice Law and Rules (CPLR)

- ✪ Civil Rights Law (CRL)

- ✪ Energy Law (Ener. L.)

- ✪ Executive Law (Exec. L.)

✧   General Obligations Law (GOL)

✧   Lien Law (LL)

✧   Multiple Dwelling Law (MDL)

✧   Multiple Residence (MRL)

✧   New York Military Law (NY Mil. L.)

✧   Penal Law (PL)

✧   Public Service Law (PSL)

✧   Real Property Actions and Proceedings Law (RPAPL)

✧   Real Property Law (RPL)

✧   Unconsolidated Laws (Unconsol. L.)

Municipal Laws

If you have rental property in New York City, there are various code provisions of which you should be aware, such as the New York City Administrative Code (NYC Admin. Code) and the New York City Health Code (NYC Health Code). If you have property outside of New York City, you should check with the city, county, or other municipality where the property is located to find out if there are any local laws you should know about.

Researching Court Cases

To look up a particular case, you will need to be able to decipher citation abbreviations. For example, if you find the citation "*Brainard Mfg. Co. v. Dewey Garden Lanes, Inc.*, 78 A.D.2d 365, 435 N.Y.S.2d 417 (4th Dept. 1981)," you would look in volume 78 of the Appellate Division Reports, Second Series, on page 365, or in volume 435 of the New York Supplement, Second Series, on page 417. This case was decided in 1981 by the Appellate Division in the Fourth Department.

Internet Research

You may also do research on the Internet by visiting the following governmental and legal websites.

- ✪ http://public.leginfo.state.ny.us

- ✪ www.findlaw.com/11stategov/ny

- ✪ www.megalaw.com/ny/nycode.php

- ✪ www.nyccouncil.info

- ✪ www.tenant.net

To learn more about legal research, refer to the book *Legal Research Made Easy*, available at your local bookstore or directly from Sphinx Publishing at **www.sphinxlegal.com**.

FICTITIOUS NAMES

If you are operating a business under a name other than your own, you must register that name with the county clerk in the county where you are doing business. Go to a legal stationery store and purchase a DBA (doing business as) form. Fill it out and file it with the county clerk. There is a filing fee. Corporations doing business under fictitious names must register the name with the secretary of state in Albany. For more information, see the books *How to Start a Business in New York*, by Paul W. Barnard and Mark Warda; and *How to Form a Corporation in New York*, by Brette McWhorter Sember and Mark Warda. Both are available from your local bookstore or directly from Sphinx Publishing at **www.sphinxlegal.com**.

Creating the Landlord/Tenant Relationship

The best way to avoid problems with tenants is to make the right decisions when creating the relationship. This means choosing the right tenant, using the right lease, and avoiding any violations of the laws that apply to your situation.

SCREENING PROSPECTIVE TENANTS

The first step in avoiding legal problems with tenants is to carefully choose who will be your tenant. As long as you do not discriminate based on categories such as race, sex, and age, you can be selective as to whom you rent your property. A tenant who had the same apartment and job for the last five years will probably be a better tenant than one who has been evicted several times.

You should get a written application from all prospective tenants. Besides allowing you to check their past records as tenants, the information can be helpful in tracking them down if they disappear owing you rent or damages. Be sure that the form you use does not ask illegal questions, such as those concerning an applicant's nationality.

You should check the *defendant index* of the court records (not just the *official records*) of your county or the last county the applicants lived in to see if they have ever been evicted or sued. It would also be wise to check the *plaintiff index* to see if they have ever sued a landlord. In some counties these indexes are combined.

You should check with a prior landlord to see if he or she would rent to these tenants again. Do not bother checking with their present landlord. He or she may lie just to get rid of them. Be sure the people you talk to are really landlords. Some tenants use friends who lie for them.

There are some companies that, for a fee, will investigate tenants, including employment, previous landlords, court cases, and their own files of bad tenants. Some landlords require a nonrefundable application fee to cover such an investigation. Equifax offers a Tenant Apartment Protection Service. Call 800-685-1111, or check your phone book under Credit Reporting Agencies.

Information from Tenant

Additionally, you should obtain the prospective tenant's checking and savings account numbers, Social Security number, and credit card information. You may wish to see a pay stub, last year's W-2 or 1099 tax form, or last year's income tax return. You should call the prospective tenant's employer and verify the salary and time on the job. Be mindful that when providing employers' names and other references, some deceitful tenants may give the number of a friend who poses as a reference.

Whatever is done to check on one prospective tenant must be objective and done for all prospective tenants. Fair housing laws prohibit landlords from doing extensive prospective tenant checks on just one person or one type of person. The steps used in prospective tenant checks should be listed on a checklist that you fill out for each prospective tenant and keep with the tenant file. Remember, the checks should be objective and done for every prospective tenant.

DISCRIMINATION LAWS

Since Congress passed the Civil Rights Act of 1968, it has been a federal crime for a landlord to discriminate in the rental or sale of property on the basis of race, religion, sex, or national origin. In 1988, the United States Congress passed an amendment to the Civil Rights Act that bans discrimination against both the disabled and families with children. Except for apartment complexes that fall into the special exceptions, such as those designated as senior living facilities, all rentals must now allow children in all units.

Civil Rights Act of 1968   Under the *Civil Rights Act of 1968*, any policy that has a discriminatory effect is illegal. (United States Code (U.S.C.), Title 42, Section 3631.) This means that even if you do not intend to discriminate, if your policy (such as requiring a certain income level) has the effect of discriminating, you can be liable. Failure to attend a hearing or to produce records can subject you to up to a year in prison or a $1,000 fine.

Penalty. A victim of discrimination under this section can file a civil suit or a HUD complaint, or request the U.S. Attorney General to prosecute. Damages can include actual losses and punitive damages of up to $1,000.

Limitation. The complaint must be brought within 180 days of a violation of the Act.

Exemptions. This law does not apply to single-family homes if:

- ❂ the owner owns three or fewer such homes;

- ❂ there is no more than one sale within twenty-four months;

- ❂ the owner does not own any interest in more than three such homes at one time; and,

- ❂ no real estate agent or discriminatory advertisement is used.

It also does not apply to a property that the owner lives in if it has four or less units.

Coercion or intimidation. If coercion or intimidation is used to effectuate discrimination, there is no limit to when the action can be brought or the amount of damages that can be awarded. For example, firing a real estate agent who rented to African-Americans was found to be intimidating enough to warrant unlimited damages.

Civil Rights Act, Section 1982

The *Civil Rights Act, Section 1982* is similar to the previously discussed statute, but whereas Section 3631 applies to any policy that has a discriminatory effect, this law applies only when it can be proven that the person had an intent to discriminate. (U.S.C., Title 42, Section 1982.)

Penalty. The penalty for a violation of this Act is actual damages plus unlimited punitive damages.

In 1992, a jury in Washington, D.C. awarded civil rights groups $850,000 in damages against a developer who only used Caucasian models in rental advertising. The *Washington Post* now requires that 25% of the models in the ads it accepts be African-American, in order to reflect the percentage of African-Americans in the Washington area.

Limitation. There is no limitation on when a complaint can be brought.

Exemptions. There are no exemptions to this law.

Civil Rights Act 1988 Amendment

The 1988 Amendment to the Civil Rights Act, also known as the *Fair Housing Act*, bans discrimination against the disabled and families with children. (U.S.C., Title 42, Sec. 3601.) Unless a property falls into one of the exemptions, it is illegal under this law to refuse to rent to persons because of age or to people with children. While landlords may be justified in feeling that children cause damage to their property, Congress has ruled that the right of families to find housing is more important than the rights of landlords to safeguard the condition of their property and to ensure the peace and quiet of other tenants.

Regarding the disabled, the law allows them to remodel the unit to suit their needs as long as they return it to the original condition upon leaving. It also requires new buildings of four units or more to have electrical facilities and common areas accessible to the disabled.

Penalty. The penalty for violation of the Fair Housing Act is $10,000 for the first offense; $25,000 for second violation within five years; and, up to $50,000 for three or more violations within seven years. There are unlimited punitive damages in private actions.

✪   A federal appeals court ruled that if a party who is discriminated against because of his her race does not have any actual monetary damages, he or she is not entitled to punitive damages. Punitive damages can be awarded without monetary damages when a person is denied constitutional rights, but not under the Fair Housing Act. (*Louisiana Acorn Fair Housing v. LeBlanc*, 211 F.3d 298 (5th Cir. 2000).)

Limitation. A complaint must be brought within two years for private actions.

Exemptions. This law does not apply to single-family homes if the owner owns three or fewer such homes; if there is no more than one sale within twenty-four months of the action; if the person does not own any interest in more than three such homes at one time; and, if no real estate agent or discriminatory advertisement is used. A condominium unit is not a single-family home, so it is not exempt. The law also does not apply to a property that the owner lives in if it has four or fewer units. There are also exemptions for dwellings in state and federal programs for the elderly, for complexes that are solely used by persons age 62 or older, and for complexes where at least 8% of the units are rented to persons age 55 or older.

Americans with Disabilities Act

The *Americans with Disabilities Act* (ADA) requires that *reasonable accommodations* be made to provide the disabled with access to commercial premises and forbids discrimination against disabled people. This means that the disabled person must be able to get to, enter, and use the facilities in commercial premises. It requires that if access is readily achievable without undue burden or undue hardship, changes must be made to the property to make it accessible.

The law does not clearly define important terms like *reasonable accommodations*, *readily achievable*, *undue burden*, or *undue hardship*, and does not even explain exactly who will qualify as disabled or disabled. The law includes people with emotional illnesses, AIDS, dyslexia, and past alcohol or drug addictions, as well as hearing, sight, and mobility impairments.

Under the ADA, if any commercial premises are remodeled, then the remodeling must include modifications that make the premises accessible. All new construction must also be made accessible.

What is "reasonable" will usually depend upon the size of the business. Small businesses will not have to make major alterations to their premises if the expense would be an undue hardship. Even large businesses would not need shelving low enough for people in wheelchairs to reach so long as there is an employee to assist the person.

However, there are tax credits for those businesses of less than thirty employees and less than one million dollars in sales that make modifications to comply with the ADA. For more information on these credits, obtain IRS forms 8826 and 3800 and their instructions online at **www.irs.gov**.

Some of the changes that must be made to property to make it more accessible to the disabled are:

- installing ramps;

- widening doorways;

- making curb cuts in sidewalks;

- repositioning shelves;

- repositioning telephones;

- removing high pile, low-density carpeting; and,

- installing a full-length bathroom mirror.

Both the landlord and the commercial tenant can be liable if the changes are not made to the premises. Most likely, the landlord would be liable for common areas and the tenant for the area under his or her control.

Penalty. Injunctions and fines of $50,000 for the first offense or $100,000 for subsequent offenses exist.

Exemptions. Private clubs and religious organizations are exempt from this law, and the ADA does not apply to residential property.

New York Discrimination Laws

New York has its own discrimination law, which is similar to the federal law. This gives people who have been discriminated against both federal and state ways to seek remedies. You will find the New York law in Executive Law Section 296. Under this law, it is illegal to discriminate based on marital status or because someone is disabled. The Real Property Law (Secs. 237 and 237-A) makes it illegal to discriminate against people with children (except where the landlord resides in single or duplex housing, or if the housing is designed for the elderly) and to refuse to allow tenants to have children during the lease.

New York State Human Rights Law

The New York State Human Rights Law (Exec. Law Sec. 292 (21)) gives the term *disability* a definition similar to the federal law. Reasonable accommodations are required as long as they do not create undue hardships for the landlord.

Local Laws

The New York City Administrative Code (NYC Admin. Code) provides the definition of *disability* for New York City purposes. The New York City Human Rights Law prohibits discrimination on the basis of actual or perceived sexual orientation in housing and commercial property. For residential purposes, discrimination is also prohibited based on the tenant's occupation. Alienage or citizenship are also protected categories. (NYC Admin. Code Sec. 8-107(5)(a,b,c).) Landlords should check their local city and county ordinances regarding discriminatory practices to be sure they are not in violation.

Cases

It is difficult to always know what is illegal discrimination. The following cases can give some guidance as to what types of actions are considered discriminatory by the courts.

✪ It is considered sex discrimination to not include child support and alimony in an applicant's income. (*U.S. v. Reese*, 457 F.Supp. 43 (D. Mont. 1978).)

✪ It is legal to require a single parent and a child of the opposite sex to rent a two-bedroom rather than a one-bedroom unit. (*Braunstein v. Dwelling Managers*, Inc., 476 F.Supp. 1323 (S.D.N.Y. 1979).)

✪ It is legal to limit the number of children allowed in a unit. (*Fred v. Koknokos*, 347 F.Supp. 942 (E.D.N.Y. 1972).) (However, there may be a different interpretation under the 1988 amendment. Also, be sure to check local ordinances.)

✪ It is illegal to segregate the people in an apartment complex. (*Blackshear Residents Organization v. Housing Authority of the City of Austin*, 347 F.Supp. 1138 (W.D.Tex. 1972).)

✪ A company that used only Caucasian models in its housing ads was ordered to pay $30,000 in damages. (*Ragin v. Macklowe*, 870 F.Supp. 510 (S.D.N.Y. 1994).)

DISCRIMINATION AGAINST PETS

Tenants may keep pets in their apartments if their lease permits pets or is silent on the subject. A landlord has the right to forbid a tenant to have pets. However, under the New York Civil Rights Law Sec. 47, guide dogs for the hearing and vision impaired must be permitted. New York City law states that if a tenant keeps a pet openly for at least three months and the landlord does not object, the landlord forfeits the right to object to the pet. The only exception is if the pet creates a nuisance to other tenants or causes damage. (NYC Admin. Code Sec. 27-2009.1.) This rule has been applied by judges in other parts of the state. If you are going to allow pets, use the **PET AGREEMENT**. (see form 3, p.179.)

AGREEMENTS TO LEASE

What are your rights if a tenant agrees to rent your unit but reneges? An agreement to enter into a lease may be a valid and binding contract even if a lease has not yet been signed. A lease can be implied by the intentions of the parties, the negotiations, and the conduct of the parties.

✪ A lease was found to exist where the landlord sent a letter with the proposed terms of the lease as an offer and the tenant accepted, but no lease was ever signed. (*Kalker v. Columbus Properties, Inc.*, 111 A.D.2d 117, 489 N.Y.S.2d 495 (1st Dept. 1985).)

✪   A tenant paid rent and moved in, and a lease was found to exist. (*Galante v. Hathaway Bakeries, Inc.*, 6 A.D.2d 142, 176 N.Y.S.2d 87 (4th Dept. 1958).)

New York law requires that a contract to lease for more than one year be written, indicate the amount of the rent, and be signed by both parties.

When two parties enter into a landlord/tenant relationship without a written lease, this arrangement is known as a *month-to-month tenancy*. In this type of tenancy, the tenant continues to maintain possession of the property for successive monthly periods, beginning on a specific calendar day. If either the landlord or the tenant gives one calendar month's notice of termination of the arrangement on the day beginning the arrangement, the arrangement will terminate at the beginning of the next monthly period. If, however, notice of termination is given to the tenant less than one calendar month before the beginning of the next month-to-month period, the tenant may remain in the apartment for an additional month. For example, if a landlord terminates a month-to-month tenancy on June 15, the tenant may remain on the premises until August 1.

As a practical matter, it will probably not be worth the time and expense to sue someone for breaching an oral agreement to lease. Whether a landlord could keep a deposit after a prospective tenant changed his or her mind would depend upon the facts of the case and the understanding between parties. Writing "nonrefundable" on the deposit receipt would work in the landlord's favor.

LEASES AND RENTAL AGREEMENTS

There are different opinions as to whether a landlord should use a lease with a set term, such as one year, or an open-ended rental agreement. Some argue that they would rather not have a lease, so they can get rid of a tenant at any time. The disadvantage is that the tenant can also leave at any time, which means the unit may be vacant during winter months, when fewer people move.

Rental Agreements   In all cases, even month-to-month tenancies, there should be a written agreement between the parties. If you do not want to tie up the property for a long period of time, you can use a **Rental Agreement** stating that the tenancy is month-to-month that also includes rules and regulations that protect the landlord. (see form 6, p.189.)

Leases   A lease is a rental agreement that is for a set term. The term can be as short as a few weeks or as long as several years. Sample **Lease** forms are provided for houses or duplexes (form 4, p.181) and apartments (form 5, p.185). Additional forms for rent-stabilized units will be discussed later in this book. A *vacancy lease* is a lease signed by a new tenant. A *renewal lease* is a lease signed by a current tenant who is renewing the lease. These terms are generally used in regard to rent-stabilized units. (see Chapter 4.)

Requirements   The minimum elements that a lease must contain to be valid are:

- name of lessor (landlord) or lessor's agent;

- name of lessee (tenant);

- description of the premises;

- rental rate;

- starting date; and,

- granting clause (i.e., "Lessor hereby leases to Lessee...").

(There have been cases in which a lease has been held to be valid when one or more of these terms has been omitted if there was an objective means to determine the missing term, but such exceptions are beyond the scope of this book.) Most leases also state the length of the rental period. If it is not stated, then by law it is month-to-month.

New York leases must have clear and legible print in at least eight-point font, include appropriate captions on the paragraphs or sections, and use words with common, everyday meanings. (CPLR Sec. 4544; GOL Sec. 5-702.)

When using one of the leases provided in this book, you may delete any clauses that do not apply, or add any of the suggested clauses in this chapter. Just make sure that you keep the legally required provisions.

Rent Receipts   A tenant must be given a written receipt for rent paid in any form other than the tenant's personal check. Even if payment is by personal check, the tenant is entitled to a written receipt upon request. The receipt must indicate the payment date, the amount paid, the rental period covered by the payment, and if applicable, the apartment number. The receipt must be signed by the person who received the payment, and must indicate that person's title, if any (such as manager). (RPL Sec. 235-e.)

Lead-Based Paint Disclosure   In 1996, the Environmental Protection Agency (EPA) and the Department of Housing and Urban Development (HUD) issued regulations requiring notices to be given to tenants of rental housing built before 1978 that there may be lead-based paint present and that it could pose a health hazard to children. This applies to all housing except housing for the elderly or zero-bedroom units (efficiencies, studio apartments, etc.). It also requires that a pamphlet about lead-based paint, titled "Protect Your Family From Lead in Your Home," be given to prospective tenants. The recommended **LEAD-BASED PAINT DISCLOSURE** form is included in this book as form 7. (see p.193.)

More information and copies of the pamphlet can be obtained from the National Lead Information Center at 800-424-5323. The information can also be obtained at **www.nsc.org/issues/lead**. You are also required to make disclosures to the tenants when you do any work on the property that disturbs more than two square feet of paint.

New York City's Lead Paint Hazard Reduction Law. Local Law 1 of 2004 (Local Law 1) is a comprehensive law concerning the prevention of childhood lead poisoning through the remediation of lead paint hazards in housing and day care facilities. This legislation repeals the former lead law, Local Law 38 of 1999.

The law covers all pre-1960 multiple dwellings. The law also places certain responsibilities on owners in post-1960 to pre-1978 buildings where the owner knows there is lead-based paint. Owners whose buildings fall into this category should consult the law. The provisions of Local Law 1 do not apply where title to a multiple dwelling unit is held by a cooperative or condominium and the shareholder of record or his or her family occupies the unit. The law does, however, apply to cooperative or condominium units occupied by a tenant or subtenant.

As an owner of property located in New York City, it is your responsibility to familiarize yourself with Local Law 1 and to comply with its requirements. The law imposes a number of property owner responsibilities, including the following.

○ The law requires annual notifications by owners to all occupants, as well as to occupants upon lease-up, lease renewal, and agreement to lease or commencement of occupancy inquiring if there are children under 6 years of age residing in the unit. Owners must include a notice about owner responsibilities under the law with each lease and must provide a pamphlet informing occupants about lead. There is also a requirement that owners physically inspect units whose occupants do not respond to determine if there is a child under age 6 residing in the unit.

○ Owners must investigate units where children under age 6 reside, as well as common areas in the property, to find peeling paint, chewable surfaces, deteriorated subsurfaces, and friction and impact surfaces. This investigation must be conducted at least annually, or more often if the owner knows about a condition that may cause a lead hazard, or the occupant complains about such a condition.

○ Owners must remediate lead hazards, using safe work practices and trained workers.

○ Owners must make apartments lead safe on turnover.

○ Owners must use safe work practices for all repairs and renovations performed in a unit where a child under age 7 resides, and in the common areas of buildings with such units.

Owners should also be aware that under the law, not only lead violations, but also any repairs or renovations that are performed in dwelling units with children under age 6, must be undertaken by trained workers and followed by lead-contaminated dust clearance tests upon completion. Any such work performed after August 2, 2004 is subject to the new requirements under Local Law 1. For information on types of training and certified training providers, go to the website of the U.S. Environmental Protection Agency at **www.epa.gov/lead**.

Between January 1 and January 15 annually (or with the January rent bill if issued before January 1), owners must send a lead notice to all tenants in pre-1960 multiple dwellings and in multiple dwellings built between 1960 and 1978 if owners know there is lead paint in the building. Since owners must also send out window guard notices, this is the only joint window guard/lead approved form. An **ANNUAL NOTICE TO TENANT OR OCCUPANT IN BUILDINGS WITH 3 OR MORE APARTMENTS** is provided in Appendix C. (see form 49, p.281.)

Window Guard Rider

In New York City, a **WINDOW GUARD RIDER** (form 45, p.273) must be attached to the lease. See the discussion in Chapter 5 for more information about window guards.

Suggested Clauses

The following types of clauses are not required by any law, but are suggested by the authors to avoid potential problems during the tenancy:

✪   security and/or damage deposit;

✪   last month's rent;

✪   use clause (limiting the way the property is to be used);

✪   maintenance clause (spelling out who is responsible for what maintenance);

✪   limitation on landlord's liability;

✪   limitation on assignment of the lease by tenant;

✪   clause granting attorney's fees for enforcement of the lease;

✪   clause putting duty on the tenant for his or her own insurance;

✪   late fee and bounced check fee;

✪   limitation on number of persons living in the unit;

✪   in a condominium, a clause stating that the tenant must comply with all the rules and regulations of the condominium;

✪   requirement that if locks are changed, the landlord is given a key (forbidding tenants to change locks may subject the landlord to liability for theft);

✪   limitation on pets (see form 3, **Pet Agreement**);

✪   limitation on where cars may be parked (not on the lawn, etc.);

✪   limitation on storage of boats on the property;

✪   in a single-family home or duplex, a landlord should put most of the duties for repair on the tenant;

✪   in commercial leases, there should be clauses regarding the fixtures, insurance, signs, renewal, eminent domain, and other factors related to the business use of the premises; and,

✪   the landlord's right to dispose of any property left behind or abandoned by the tenant after the end of the tenancy without liability. (see form 9, **Agreement Regarding Abandoned Property**.)

For an explanation of each of the different clauses used in residential and commercial leases, and suggestions on how to negotiate, see *Essential Guide to Real Estate Leases*, by Mark Warda, available through your local bookstore or directly from Sphinx Publishing **www.sphinxlegal.com**.

Oral Leases   A lease for less than one year does not have to be in writing to be valid. Oral leases have been held up in court. It just depends upon who sounds more believable to the judge and what actions the parties took.

✪ An oral lease of more than a year was upheld because there was partial performance of the lease. (*Rosen v. 250 West 50 St. Corp.*, 270 A.D.2d 171, 59 N.Y.S.2d 33 (1st Dept. 1945).)

✪ An oral agreement to lease property for more than one year will be upheld if there is a written note or memorandum signed by the parties. (GOL Sec. 5-701.)

PROBLEM CLAUSES

If a judge determines that a rental agreement or lease is grossly unfair, he or she may rule that it is *unconscionable*. It is therefore unenforceable. (RPL Sec. 235-c.) In such a case, the judge may ignore the entire lease or may enforce only parts of it. Therefore, making your lease too strong may defeat your purpose.

A provision requiring a tenant to pledge household furniture as security for the payment of rent is void. (RPL Sec. 231.) Otherwise, there is not much guidance as to what may or may not be unconscionable, so the judge may use his or her discretion.

✪ The mere fact that a rental term is far below market value does not make it unconscionable. (*Bay Ridge Federal Sav. and Loan Ass'n v. Morano*, 199 A.D.2d 354, 605 N.Y.S.2d 377 (2d Dept. 1993).)

Waivers of Liability Rights

If any of the following types of clauses are included in a lease, the clause is void and unenforceable. A party suffering damages because of the clause may recover money from the landlord for any losses so caused.

Warranty of habitability. A tenant cannot be required to waive the warranty of habitability. (RPL Sec. 235-b.)

Security deposit. A clause in which the tenant waives the right to have the security deposit held in an interest-bearing account is not valid. (GOL Sec. 7-103.)

Negligence waiver. The tenant cannot waive the landlord's liability for negligence. (GOL Sec. 5-321; RPL Sec. 259-c.)

Jury trial. Neither party may waive the right to a jury trial. (GOL Sec. 5-321; RPL Sec. 259-c.)

Attorney's fees. If the contract gives the landlord the right to collect attorney's fees from the tenant if the landlord wins, the tenant is also entitled to collect attorney's fees from the landlord if the tenant wins. (RPL Sec. 234.)

Rent regulation. A rent-regulated tenant cannot waive rent regulation protections.

Bankruptcy prohibition. A tenant cannot be prohibited from filing for bankruptcy. (11 U.S.C.A. Sec. 365(e)(1).)

Subletting. A clause waiving the tenant's right to sublet the property with the reasonable consent of the landlord is unenforceable. The tenant has the right to sublet with the reasonable consent of the landlord, and to terminate the lease if the landlord unreasonably withholds consent. (RPL Sec. 226-b.)

Tenants' association. A landlord cannot include a provision in a lease prohibiting a tenant from forming or joining a tenants' association. (RPL Sec. 230.)

Waivers in Commercial Leases

In a commercial lease, a tenant may waive rights that may not be waived in a residential lease. A commercial lease spells out nearly all of the rights and obligations of the parties. The parties to a commercial lease may waive any right not prohibited by the statutes.

Limiting Similar Businesses

Provisions in a lease that limit the landlord's right to lease to similar businesses should be strictly construed. It is permissible for a lease to limit the landlord's right to lease to similar businesses.

OPTIONS

Both residential and nonresidential leases may contain clauses that grant the tenant an option to extend the lease for another term or several terms. Often these options provide for an increase in rent during the renewal periods. If there is no option in the contract, the tenancy expires at the end of the term. In a rent-regulated tenancy, the tenant may choose either a one-year or two-year renewal option. (See Chapter 4 for more information about rent-regulated tenancies.)

✪ An automatic renewal provision is unenforceable unless the landlord gives the tenant written notice fifteen to thirty days before the end of the term of the tenancy. (GOL Sec. 5-905.)

✪ The amount of rent in the renewed lease must be clearly specified in the option to renew and cannot be left "to be negotiated." If it is too hard to specify an amount, it is permissible to state a formula or guideline that will be used to determine the amount. (*Seiden v. Francis*, 184 A.D.2d 904, 585 N.Y.S.2d 562 (3d Dept. 1992); *Sunrise Mall Associates v. Import Alley of Sunrise Mall, Inc.*, 211 A.D.2d 711, 621 N.Y.S.2d 662 (2d Dept. 1995).)

✪ If there is to be a change in the terms of the lease in the renewed lease, those terms must be stated in the option. (*Kay-Bee Toy and Hobby Shops, Inc. v. Pyramid Company of Plattsburgh*, 126 A.D.2d 703, 511 N.Y.S.2d 308 (2d Dept. 1987).)

Options to Purchase

If a lease contains an option to purchase, it is usually enforceable exactly according to its terms. An *option to purchase* gives the tenant the irrevocable right to purchase the property. This is different from a *right of first refusal*, in which the landlord never has to sell, but if he or she does decide to sell, the property must be offered to the tenant before anyone else.

✪ The terms of an option to purchase must be clear and definite, and the purchase price, or a guideline for determining one, must be specified. (*Cobble Hill Nursing Home, Inc. v. Henry and Warren Corporation*, 548 N.Y.S.2d 920 (1989).)

✪   The lease and the option to purchase are considered to be separate, and even if the lease is breached, the option still exists. (*Curry Road Ltd. v. Rotterdam Realties Inc.,* 195 A.D.2d 780, 600 N.Y.S.2d 339 (3d Dept. 1994).)

FORMS

Forms 4, 5, and 6 in this book are leases or rental agreements developed and used by the authors. They are free of legalese and intended to be easily understandable by both parties.

Be careful to choose a good lease form. Some forms on the market do not comply with New York law and can be dangerous to use. Blumberg, a company that sells legal forms, has forms for residential and commercial leases that contain most of the above clauses and conform to New York law. They can be purchased at legal stationery stores and are also available on CD-ROM and disk. You can also obtain some forms from the New York State Division of Housing and Community Renewal. (See Chapter 4 for information about how to contact this agency.)

SIGNATURES

If you do not have the proper signatures on the lease, you could have problems enforcing it or evicting the tenants.

Landlord   If the property is owned by more than one person, it is best to have all owners sign the lease.

Tenant   In most cases, it is best to have all adult occupants sign the lease so that more people will be liable for the rent. However, in inexpensive rentals where evictions are frequent, having just one person sign will save a few dollars in fees for service of process.

Initials   Some landlords have spaces on the lease for the tenant to place his or her initials. This is usually done next to clauses that are unusual or strongly pro-landlord. However, even initials might not help if a judge really does not like a clause.

Witnesses   Signatures of the parties to New York leases need not be witnessed.

Notary   A lease does not need to be notarized to be valid. A landlord should not allow his or her signature on a lease to be notarized, because the lease could then be recorded in the public records, which would be a cloud on his or her title and could cause a problem when the property is sold.

Agents   Landlords may appoint an agent to collect rent on his or her behalf, and to handle all dealings with tenants. Use **NOTICE OF APPOINTMENT OF AGENT** (form 16, p.211) or a **NOTICE OF TERMINATION OF AGENT** (form 15, p.209).

BACKING OUT OF A LEASE

There are circumstances in which a party can back out of a lease. However, these circumstances are limited and subject to misconceptions.

Rescission   Contrary to the beliefs of some tenants, there is no law allowing a rescission period for a lease. Once a lease has been signed by both parties, it is legally binding on them.

Fraud   If one party fraudulently misrepresents a material fact concerning the lease, the lease may be unenforceable. There must be an allegation that a party knew the truth and concealed it for fraud to exist. A real mistake made by a party is not fraud. (*Barclay Arms, Inc. v. Barclay Arms Associates,* 74 N.Y2d 644, 542 N.Y.S. 512 (1989).)

Impossibility   If the lease states that the premises are rented for a certain purpose and it is impossible to use the premises for that purpose, the lease may not be enforceable.

> ✪   A landlord's failure to obtain a certificate of occupancy is not enough to void a lease. The landlord must violate a law that concerns public health, safety, and welfare, or that precludes or restricts the use of the premises. (*Kosher Konveniences, Inc. v. Ferguson Realty Corp.*, 171 A.D.2d 650, 567 N.Y.S.2d 131 (2d Dept. 1991).)

✪ An intended use of the premises as a shop was illegal under residential zoning law and this voided the lease. (*Hartsin Const. Corp. v. Millhauser*, 136 Misc. 646, 241 N.Y.S. 428 (1930).)

If a lease is entered into for an illegal purpose, it is void and unenforceable by either party.

Under Real Property Law Sec. 231(1), a lease is void if the premises are used for illegal trade, manufacture, or business.

A rental unit must be available at the beginning of the term of the lease (unless the lease contains a different date for the beginning of occupancy). If the unit is not available at the beginning of the term of the lease, the tenant may cancel the lease and receive a full refund of any deposit. (RPL Sec. 223-a.)

Handling Security Deposits

A tenant may be required by the landlord to pay a security deposit at the beginning of the lease to insure the landlord against potential damages and unpaid rent. The landlord may request up to one month's rent to be held in security during the term of the lease. If the apartment is in a building with six or more units, the landlord is required by law to place the security deposit in a separate interest-bearing bank account in New York State and notify the tenant concerning the bank in which it is being held.

If the security deposit is put into an interest-bearing account, the landlord may keep 1% of the amount deposited per year for administrative expenses, the remaining interest to be paid annually to the tenant or left to accumulate at the tenant's option. If, at the end of the lease, the tenant does not owe any rent and the apartment is in good condition except for normal wear and tear, the landlord must return the security deposit with interest within a reasonable time. If the security deposit is withheld without reason, the tenant may sue in small claims court for return of the disputed amount.

The laws governing security deposits in New York apply to all rentals, including commercial, residential, mobile home, and hotel, unless otherwise specified.

AMOUNT

Security deposit amounts are regulated only in some rent control situations. In all other instances, landlords are free to determine the amount. This decision must be made based on the practical consideration of what is the most you can get without scaring away desirable tenants.

BANK ACCOUNT

Residential security deposits (except in some rent control situations) must be held in a separate interest-bearing bank account. This does not apply to rental properties with less than six units. (GOL Sec. 7-103(2).) However, if a landlord with less than six units does place security deposits in an interest-bearing account, the landlord must comply with the same requirements as for six or more units. The landlord may not commingle any of his or her personal funds in this account.

- ✪ If commingling occurs, courts have allowed the landlord to correct it and have not required an immediate return of the deposit to the tenant. (*Purfield v. Kathrane*, 73 Misc.2d 194, 341 N.Y.2d 376 (Civ.Ct. N.Y. City, 1973).)

- ✪ A tenant breached the lease and the landlord was still required to maintain a separate account and not commingle funds. (*In re Perfection Svcs. Press, Inc.*, 18 N.Y.2d 644, 273 N.Y.S.2d 71 (1966).)

The above provisions will probably be a surprise to most landlords. Very few landlords or tenants are aware of these rules and even fewer understand them. However, it makes sense—when tenants come and go and the deposit is several hundred dollars, the bank would not be pleased with the opening and closing of accounts with each new tenant.

Technically, the landlord cannot commingle even $10 of his or her own money in the account to keep it open. As a practical matter, a $5 or $10 deposit of a landlord's own money to keep an account open during periods when there are no security deposits on hand would probably not be considered an actionable violation of the statute. It appears that most small New York landlords do not keep the funds separate, and the issue is seldom brought up by tenants.

NOTICE

When a security deposit has been taken and is required to be deposited in an account, the landlord must notify the tenant in writing as to the name and location of the bank and the amount of the deposit. (GOL Sec. 7-103(2).) Use the **NOTICE OF HOLDING SECURITY DEPOSIT**. (form 8, p.195.)

- ✪ Writing "for deposit only" on the back of the tenant's check along with the bank's stamp is not considered sufficient notice. (*LeRoy v. Sayers,* 217 A.D.2d 63, 635 N.Y.S.2d 217 (1st Dept. 1995).)

- ✪ A landlord's failure to notify the tenant of the name and location of the bank was held to be inconsequential and did not entitle the tenant to a return of the deposit. (*Purfield v. Kathrane*, 73 Misc.2d 194, 341 N.Y.S.2d 376 (Civ.Ct., N.Y. City, 1973).)

INTEREST

The interest that accrues on the account belongs to the tenant and must be held in trust and paid to the tenant at the end of the tenancy. In the alternative, the tenant can request that the interest be paid to the tenant or applied to rent annually. The landlord is entitled to keep 1% of the security deposit as an annual administrative fee. (GOL Sec. 7-103(2).)

Most tenants do not even know they are entitled to interest on their deposit, but occasionally a vacating tenant will demand interest. A landlord who has not followed the separate account rule is better off paying it and avoiding a suit, which could cost attorney's fees.

KEEPING THE DEPOSIT

A security deposit (and the interest minus 1% of the deposit) is always the property of the tenant and must be refunded to the tenant at the end of the tenancy if the tenant paid all the rent and left the property in acceptable condition. (*Kaplan v. Shaffer*, 112 A.D.2d 369, 491 N.Y.S.2d 821 (2d Dept. 1985).) Offsets may be taken against the security deposit according to provisions in the lease, which usually include unpaid rent and damage to the premises. (*Rivertower Associates v. Chalfen*, 153 A.D.2d 196, 549 N.Y.S.2d 719 (1st Dept. 1990).) Damage can only be offset if it is beyond normal wear and tear. This may be a difficult distinction to make. A broken window or a missing sink is not normal wear and tear, but a few scuff marks on the wall are. Obviously, much damage falls in between these two examples, and you should consult an attorney if you are not sure.

If there has been any damage to your rental property, you should take photographs of the damage and keep all receipts for any repairs. If you do any of the repairs yourself, you should keep a record of them. If you do the repairs yourself, you are entitled to keep what is equal to a reasonable amount you would have paid to have the repairs done. Of course, it would be helpful to get a written estimate from a specialist before doing the work yourself.

- ✪ Whatever remains of the security deposit after the unpaid rent or repairs must be returned to the tenant. (*Prudential Westchester Corp. v. Tomasino*, 5 A.D.2d 489, 172 N.Y.S.2d 652 (1st Dept. 1958).)

- ✪ An Illinois court allowed a landlord to deduct $40 for cleaning a stove and refrigerator himself. (*Evans v. International Village Apts.*, 520 N.E.2d 919 (Ill.App. 1988).)

- ✪ A Florida court allowed a landlord to charge a tenant for the cost of a real estate agent's fee for finding a new tenant for a rental unit. (*McLennan v. Rozniak*, 15 Fla.Supp.2d 42 (Palm Beach 1985).)

Some leases have clauses that allow a landlord to keep the entire deposit or a certain portion of it if the tenant leaves before the end of the lease. When the clause has been considered a liquidated damages clause, it has usually been upheld, but when it has been considered a penalty, it has been dismissed. It is not possible to say for certain whether a clause will be considered one or the other, because judges have wide leeway in their rulings. Usually, the decision depends upon who the judge considers the good guy and the bad guy in the case.

- ✪   In one case, an automatic $200 re-rental fee was considered acceptable. (*Lesatz v. Standard Green Meadows*, 416 N.W.2d 334 (Mich.App. 1987).)

- ✪   In another case, an automatic $60 cleaning fee was considered a penalty, and therefore, illegal. (*Albregt v. Chen*, 477 N.E.2d 1150 (Ohio App. 1985).)

- ✪   In a California case, an additional $65 fee in a lease resulted in a civil penalty against the landlord of $271,000, plus $40,000 in attorney's fees. (*People v. Parkmerced Co.*, 244 Cal.Rptr. 22 (Cal.App.Div. 1988).)

SPECIAL RULES

In addition to all of the rules previously discussed in this chapter regarding security deposits, there are some special rules of which you should be aware.

Renewals   When a lease is renewed, the landlord remains in possession of the security deposit, and it becomes the security deposit for the new lease.

Sale of Property   If the property is sold during a tenancy, the security deposit and an accounting must be transferred to the new owner within five days of the sale. The tenant must be notified of the transfer in writing by certified or registered mail. The notice must include the new owner's name and address. Failure to provide such notice is a misdemeanor. (GOL Sec. 7-105.)

If you purchase a rent-controlled or rent-stabilized building, or one with at least six units where tenants have written leases, you are responsible to the tenants for their security deposits even if the seller never transferred the deposits to you.

Prepaid Rent   If a tenant prepays rent, the advance rent must be held in trust like a security deposit. (*In re Pal-Playwell, Inc.*, 334 F.2d 389 (2d Cir. 1964).)

Rent Regulations

Usually, a landlord is free to charge whatever rent he or she feels is appropriate. In New York City and some parts of Nassau, Rockland, and Westchester counties, as well as some other municipalities across the state, the amount of rent a landlord can charge is regulated by law. There are two ways rent can be regulated: one is called *rent control* and the other is called *rent stabilization*.

Rent control exists in buildings built before 1947, with three or more units, in which the same tenant has lived continuously since before July 1, 1971. *Rent stabilization* exists in any rent-controlled unit that becomes vacant, as well as buildings built before 1974 with six or more units.

There are many laws governing rent control and rent stabilization. There are numerous acts with various names—too many to list and describe them all. These acts are part of larger sections of the law. Because of this, the name of each act will not be mentioned. Instead, you will be given the citation that will tell you where to find the regulation being discussed. Rent regulation laws that apply throughout the state of New York are found in New York Unconsolidated Laws (Unconsol. L.) and in New York Codes, Rules and Regulations (NYCRR). Laws that apply only to New York City are contained in the

New York City Administrative Code (NYC Admin. Code). Each of these will be followed by a section number.

Rent regulation began during a shortage of affordable housing after World War II. Since then, landlords have been very vocal in opposing a system that they see as overly regulatory. Tenants complain that rent charges are already too high and that any change would be disastrous.

The *Division of Housing and Community Renewal* (DHCR) is the state agency that regulates rent-controlled and rent-stabilized units in New York State. The DHCR has many helpful fact sheets available at no cost, as well as a Small Building Owners' Assistance Unit, which assists owners of buildings with fifty or fewer units. It provides assistance with forms, procedures, and tenant complaints and appeals. The DHCR can be reached at 718-739-6400 or at **www.dhcr.state.ny.us**. There are also several local offices, which are listed on pages 42–43.

A landlord may not take any action to unlawfully force rent-regulated tenants to vacate their apartments or to give up any rights they have under the rent laws. Landlords found guilty of harassment are subject to fines of up to $5,000 for each violation. Tenants may contact DHCR if they believe they are the victims of harassment. Under certain circumstances, harassment can constitute a class E felony. (Penal Law Article 241.)

RENT CONTROL

Rent control exists in fifty-one municipalities in New York State. In New York City, rent control applies to buildings with three or more units that were converted to residential use prior to February 1, 1947, and have been continuously occupied by the same tenant or his or her successor (a family member who has lived with the tenant for the last two years as his or her primary residence) since July 7, 1971. (9 NYCRR Sec. 2104.6.) Government housing, units used for charitable or educational purposes by not-for-profit institutions, motor courts, mobile homes, hotels, and furnished rooms are exempt from this legislation.

Most rent-controlled units are occupied by the elderly. Once the unit becomes vacant, it is governed by rent stabilization laws or becomes deregulated. Rent-controlled units are statutory tenancies. Once the lease expires, there is a statutory tenancy governed by certain laws (the Local Emergency Rent Control, beginning at Unconsol. L. Sec. 8601 for New York City; and the Emergency Housing Rent Control Law, beginning at Unconsol. L. Sec. 8581 for areas outside New York City).

Subleasing

Rent-controlled units may be subleased only if allowed in the original lease. Without a subleasing clause in the original lease, it is not allowed.

Rent Amounts

The laws governing rent-controlled units set the *maximum base rent* (MBR) that can be charged for the unit. The amount of the MBR is determined by using a formula that considers the taxes, water expense, sewer costs, and operating and maintenance expenses of the building, and deducts losses from vacancies and returns on capital. (9 NYCRR Sec. 2201.4.) The MBR can be changed every two years to reflect changes in operating costs, but cannot be raised in excess of 7.5% in New York City.

Outside New York City, the DHCR determines the maximum allowable rates of rent increase. (9 NYCRR Secs. 2201.5 and 2201.6.) A landlord must apply to the DHCR for an *Order of Eligibility* to raise rent. Contact your local DHCR office for an application. Rent may also be raised in the following circumstances, upon application to the DHCR:

- major capital improvements are made to the building that benefit all tenants, such as a new boiler (there is a 15% limit per year on increases due to this);

- improvements or enlargements are made to the unit, including increase in services, furniture, or equipment (the tenant's consent is required);

- the landlord and tenant agree to another formula due to substantial improvements to the building or unit (9 NYCRR Sec. 2202.5);

- the tenant subleases the unit without the landlord's consent;

✪   the current operating and building expenses are not being met (9 NYCRR Secs. 2202.8 through 2202.11);

✪   unique circumstances cause the maximum rent to be lower than that for comparable units (9 NYCRR Sec. 2202.7); or,

✪   the tenant agrees to a two-year lease that includes an increase of services, furniture, or equipment (9 NYCRR Sec. 2202.5).

NOTE: *A landlord may charge a surcharge that will not be considered part of the maximum rent for the installation and use of washing machines, dryers, and dishwashers, as well as when the landlord acts as the provider of a utility service (e.g., electricity, gas, cable, or telecommunications). (9 NYCRR Secs. 2202.26 and 2202.27.)*

Deregulation   Rent can be decreased by the DHCR if the tenant can show a reduction in services, such as an inoperative elevator. (*Jemrock Realty v. Anderson*, 228 A.D.2d 355, 644 N.Y.S.2d 263 (1st Dept. 1996).)

A rent-controlled unit can become *deregulated* (no longer subject to rent control) if:

✪   the tenant, or the tenant's successor, vacates the unit, or

✪   the maximum rent is $2,000 on or after July 7, 1993, and the tenant's annual income is over the statutory limit of $175,000 for each of the past two years. (Unconsol. L. Sec. 8582.2.)

Eviction   It is very difficult to evict a rent control tenant. Before the tenant can be evicted, the landlord must apply to the DHCR for a *Certificate of Eviction* and properly notify the tenant. The only grounds for eviction of a rent control tenant are:

✪   the tenant fails to pay rent (9 NYCRR Sec. 2104.1);

✪   the tenant commits nuisance or objectionable conduct (Unconsol. L. Sec. 8585.1);

❂   the tenant's occupancy is illegal under law (Unconsol. L. Sec. 8585.1);

❂   the tenant uses the unit for illegal or immoral use (Unconsol. L. Sec. 8585.1);

❂   the tenant refuses to provide access for necessary repairs or improvements (Unconsol. L. Sec. 8585.1);

❂   the landlord needs the unit for him- or herself, or for his or her immediate family (this must be an immediate and compelling need) (Unconsol. L. Sec. 8585.2);

❂   the landlord needs the property for a charitable or educational purpose and the landlord is a not-for-profit institution;

❂   the landlord wishes to demolish the building or withdraw it from the rental market;

❂   the landlord wishes to subdivide or substantially alter the unit or building; or,

❂   the tenant refuses to renew at the end of the rental period.

The landlord may evict the tenant without applying for a Certificate of Eviction if:

❂   the tenant did not use the unit as his or her primary residence (9 NYCRR Sec. 2504.4), or

❂   the tenant breached the lease (Unconsol. L. Sec. 8585.1).

RENT STABILIZATION

Rent stabilization is much more common than rent control, with over one million units in New York State subject to it. Rent stabilization applies to the following buildings.

In New York City, rent stabilization applies to:

○ buildings of six or more units built between February 1, 1947 and January 1, 1974;

○ buildings of six or more units that were built before February 1, 1947, and whose current tenant moved in after June 30, 1971; and,

○ buildings of thirty or more apartments built or substantially renovated since 1974, and that are receiving special tax benefits.

Outside of New York City, rent stabilization applies to:

○ buildings of six or more units built before January 1, 1974, in localities that adopted the Emergency Tenant Protection Act (ETPA);

○ apartments in areas that adopted the ETPA; and,

○ rent-controlled apartments vacated after June 30, 1971.

The following units are excluded from rent stabilization:

○ rent-controlled units;

○ government housing;

○ buildings completed or substantially rehabilitated after 1974;

○ units owned or operated by charitable or educational institutions;

○ hotel rooms; and,

○ units not used by the tenant as his or her primary residence.

In New York City, a *Rent Stabilization Lease Rider* must be attached to any new lease for a unit subject to rent stabilization, and a Renewal Lease Form must be used whenever a current tenant renews a lease on a rent-stabilized unit. Both of these forms may be obtained from the Division of Housing and Community Renewal (see the list of DHCR offices beginning on page 42 to find the nearest office). In addition, a **WINDOW GUARD RIDER** (form 45, p.273) must also be attached to all New York City leases (even for units not subject to rent stabilization). The lease must state the beginning and ending dates. The tenant is entitled to receive a copy of the signed lease within thirty days after the landlord receives the lease that has been signed by the tenant.

Rent Amount   Rent-stabilized units must be registered initially and yearly with the DHCR, and a copy of the registration must be provided to the tenant. This registration contains the legal regulated rent or base rent, which is the rent that has been charged for the past four years. All increases and adjustments are added to this amount. A new tenant has ninety days to appeal the base amount and prove that it exceeds the *fair market value* of the unit. There can be no appeal if the first rent-stabilized tenant moved in between 1971 and 1974. (Unconsol. L. Sec. 8629.b.) *Fair market value* is equal to the average of the maximum controlled rent or the maximum base rent, whichever is higher, and the rents of qualifying comparable apartments, with an addition for any new equipment.

Tenants have a choice of a one-year or two-year lease under either a vacancy or renewal lease. There is a vacancy bonus of 20% of two years' rent under a vacancy lease. Renewal increases may be collected when a lease is renewed. Additional rent increases are set yearly by the local rent guidelines boards in New York City and Nassau, Westchester, and Rockland counties.

In New York City, there is a fuel cost adjustment that may be added to the rent, depending on the increase or decrease of fuel costs. (NYC Admin. Code Sec. 26-405(n).) (Fuel refers to oil or gas used for heating.) Adjustments may only be made upon application to the DHCR. It is necessary to maintain essential services to qualify.

Rent increases can also occur when major improvements or enlargements have been made to the unit. Consent of the tenant is required unless the work is done during vacancy. Ordinary maintenance and repairs do not qualify for a rent increase. (*Linden v. New York State Div. Of Housing and Community Renewal*, 217 A.D.2d 407, 629 N.Y.S.2d 32 (1st Dept. 1995).)

Major capital improvements (MCI) to the entire building, which benefit all the tenants, also warrant a rent increase. An installation of something like a new boiler would qualify. (Unconsol. L. Sec. 8584.3, NYCRR Sec. 2522.4.) There is a limit of 6% per year in New York City on MCI increases. Outside New York City, there is a 15% limit. Rent may also be increased due to an increase in building services if 75% of the tenants consent. Consent by 55% percent is required if the addition is part of an overall improvement. (9 NYCRR Sec. 2102.3.b.)

An increase may also occur when normal increases do not offset increased operating expenses. (Unconsol. L. Sec. 8626.d.) Provisions for New York City are contained in 9 NYCRR 2522.4, and provisions for outside New York City are contained in 9 NYCRR Sec. 2502.4. There is a limit of 6% per year for this type of increase.

Landlords are not required to raise rents, and if you choose to make a rent concession for a tenant, be careful to specify in the vacancy lease whether the concession is intended for a particular vacancy or renewal lease term. If this is not specified, you will be required to offer this concession with each renewal. (*Century Operating Corp. v. Popolizio*, 90 A.D.2d 731, 455 N.Y.S.2d 7789 (1st Dept. 1982).)

Deregulation   A rent-stabilized unit is deregulated (no longer subject to rent stabilization) if the rent reaches $2,000 per payment period (usually a month) and the tenant's income for the past two years exceeds $175,000, or if the unit becomes vacant and the rent reaches $2,000.

Eviction   It is difficult to evict a rent-stabilized tenant. The standards are the same as for rent control tenants. Refer to the section on page 36 regarding eviction of rent control tenants.

LOFTS

Lofts, or *interim multiple dwellings* (IMDs), are units made out of large spaces that were first used for manufacturing or commercial purposes, and then occupied by residential tenants before renovations were made to convert the units to residential use and before a Certificate of Occupancy was obtained. Lofts were another answer to the housing crisis in New York City, and first became popular during the 1970s. Lofts in New York City are governed by the Multiple Dwelling Law and are regulated by the Loft Board.

Improvements to lofts made and paid for by tenants are owned by the tenants. Rent increases are not permitted until the unit is in compliance with the safety requirements in the Multiple Dwelling Law. Once there is compliance, rent may be raised based on the owner's costs involved in meeting the requirements. When the Certificate of Occupancy is obtained, another increase is permitted. At this point, a lease must be offered to the tenant, the rent stabilization guidelines apply, and the unit becomes regulated by the rent guidelines board. (MDL Sec. 286.)

NOTE: *Parts of the Multiple Dwelling Law are set to repeal on May 31, 2007 unless extended by the legislature.*

Rent regulation does not apply if the space is used for commercial or manufacturing purposes again or if the owner buys the tenant's improvements when the tenant vacates.

SINGLE ROOM OCCUPANCY

A *single room occupancy* (SRO) is a single room with a kitchen or bathroom, but not both. These are governed by the Emergency Tenant Protection Act (ETPA). Buildings with six or more SROs are rent-stabilized unless they are used for transients. There is no regulation of rent charged to transients. Transient residents cannot be denied the right to become permanent residents.

Eviction   The eviction rules for rent regulation apply to permanent residents, but there is no eviction for the tenant's refusal to sign a renewal lease.

Division of Housing and Community Renewal
District Rent Offices

Bronx Borough Rent Office
One Fordham Plaza
2ⁿᵈ Floor
Bronx, NY 10458
718-563-5678

Brooklyn Borough Rent Office
55 Hanson Place
7ᵗʰ Floor
Brooklyn, NY 11217
718-722-4778

Buffalo Rent Office
Statler Towers
107 Delaware Avenue
Suite 600
Buffalo, NY 14202
716-842-2244

Central Office for Rent Administration
Queens Rent Office
Gertz Plaza
92–31 Union Hall Street
4ᵗʰ Floor
Jamaica, NY 11433
718-739-6400

Harassment Unit
Gertz Plaza
92–31 Union Hall Street
Jamaica, NY 11433
718-480-6239

Lower Manhattan Borough Rent Office

(South Side of 110th Street and below)

25 Beaver Street

5th Floor

New York, NY 10004

212-480-6238

212-480-6239

Upper Manhattan Borough Rent Office

(North Side of 110th Street and above)

Adam Clayton Powell, Jr. Office Building

163 West 125th Street

5th Floor

New York, NY 10027

212-961-8930

Nassau County Rent Office

50 Clinton Street

6th Floor

Hempstead, NY 11550

516-481-9494

Rockland County Rent Office

94–96 North Main Street

Spring Valley, NY 10977

845-425-6575

Staten Island Borough Rent Office

60 Bay Street

7th Floor

Staten Island, NY 10301

718-816-0278

Westchester County Rent Office

55 Church Street

3rd Floor

White Plains, NY 10601

914-948-4434

Responsibility for Maintenance

Responsibility for maintenance is another area in which the landlord needs to spell out exactly what is expected from each party and make sure that the law is being followed.

NONRESIDENTIAL RENTALS

In commercial rentals, the landlord's responsibility for maintenance is governed by the provisions of the lease. There is no statutory obligation of maintenance. The *warranty of habitability* (explained on page 51) does not apply to commercial property in New York. However, a landlord has a duty to use reasonable care to maintain the premises over which he or she retains control in a suitable condition. (*Polak v. Bush Lumber Co.*, 170 A.D.2d 932, 566 N.Y.S.2d 757 (3d Dept. 1991).)

A commercial landlord must maintain essential services (*Union City Suit Co., Ltd. v. Miller*, 162 A.D.2d 101, 556 N.Y.S.2d 864 (1st Dept. 1990)) and take minimal precautions to protect the tenant from foreseeable harm. (*Juarez v. Wave Crest Management Team Ltd.*, 88 N.Y.2d 628, 649 N.Y.S.2d 115 (1996).)

RESIDENTIAL APARTMENTS

The Multiple Dwelling Law (applying to buildings with three or more units in cities with a population of 325,000 or more (MDL Sec. 3)) and the Multiple Residence Law (applying to smaller cities (MRL Sec. 3)) set out some maintenance requirements for the landlord. Other requirements are described in cases and other statutes or regulations. Landlords must provide basic services, which include garbage removal, locks and keys, clean and safe conditions in common areas, extermination of vermin, heat in the winter, and hot and running water. Other requirements include the following.

✪ The landlord must install and maintain self-closing and self-locking doors in buildings built or converted to such use after January 1, 1968, and in buildings built before 1968 if the majority of tenants request or consent (if there is no consent, minimal precautions must be taken). Doors must be kept locked at all times unless there is an attendant. (MDL Sec. 50-a.)

✪ The landlord must maintain the premises free of any known defects or any that would be reasonably known. (MDL Sec. 78, RPL Sec. 235-b.)

✪ The landlord must comply with all health, housing, and building codes. Check with your local building inspector.

✪ Two-way intercoms with buzzers to open the main door must be installed and maintained in buildings built or converted to such use after January 1, 1968, and in buildings built before 1968 if the majority of tenants request or consent. The cost of providing this equipment may be recovered from the tenants. (MDL Sec. 50-a.)

✪ There is no requirement to remove snow or ice from sidewalks, unless it is bumpy or rough. (*Greenstein v. Springfield Development Corp.*, 22 Misc.2d 740, 204 N.Y.S.2d 518 (Civ.Ct., New York County, 1960).) In New York City, snow must be removed four hours after snow stops falling. (NYC Admin. Code Secs. 16-123 & 19-152.)

✪ Smoke detectors must be installed and maintained in each unit. (MDL Sec. 68; MRL Sec. 15; NYC Admin. Code Secs. 27-2045 & 2446.) In New York City, tenants may be charged up to $10 for the landlord's purchase and installation of each smoke detector.

✪ Exterior lighting must be provided above the front entrance in cities with populations of 325,000 or more (MDL Sec. 35), and interior lighting must be provided in the vestibule, halls, and stairs. (MDL Sec. 37.)

✪ Lead-based paint that is peeling must be removed or covered in New York City. (NYC Admin. Code Sec. 27-2023h1; NYC Health Code Sec. 173.14.) See page 17 for more information.

✪ The landlord must observe the restrictions on the removal and handling of asbestos. (12 NYCRR Sec. 56-1.7.)

✪ In New York City, government-approved window guards must be installed in units with children age ten and under, and on windows in public hallways. They must also be installed upon the request of any tenant. Windows accessing fire escapes are excluded. Tenants must be given an annual notice of their right to window guards (see form 45, p.273), and a lease rider must be provided. Tenants in rent-controlled and rent-stabilized units may be charged for the guards. (NYC Admin. Code Sec. 17-123; NYC Health Code Sec. 131.15.)

✪ In New York City, apartments must be painted at least every three years (sooner if the lease requires), unless the owner never provided this service. (See DHCR Fact Sheet #28 for more details. The fact sheet is available from the DHCR—see Chapter 4 for offices and phone numbers.)

✪ United States Postal regulations require that buildings with three or more units have secure mailboxes for each unit, unless management distributes the mail to the tenants. The mailboxes must be kept in good repair.

✪ Elevators must have mirrors that allow people to see who is on the elevator before entering it. (MDL Sec. 51-b; and NYC Admin. Code Sec. 27-2042.)

✪ Peepholes and door chains are required in New York City. (MDL Sec. 51-c; NYC Admin. Code Sec. 27-2041.)

✪ In New York City, between October 1 and May 31, apartments must be heated to at least 68° Fahrenheit between 6 a.m. and 10 p.m. if the outside temperature falls below 55° Fahrenheit, and they must be heated to at least 55° Fahrenheit between 10 p.m. and 6 a.m. if the outside temperature falls below 40° Fahrenheit. (MDL Sec. 79.)

✪ Electrical, plumbing, sanitary, heating, ventilating systems, and appliances installed by landlords must be maintained in safe and working order. (MDL Secs. 78 & 80; MRL Sec. 174.)

Carbon Monoxide Detectors

Building owners have several responsibilities under New York City's law on carbon monoxide detectors. Landlords must provide and install at least one approved carbon monoxide alarm within each dwelling unit. The carbon monoxide alarms must be installed within fifteen feet of the primary entrance to each sleeping room. This applies to all multiple dwellings and one- and two-family homes. In addition, a landlord must do the following.

✪ File (in person or by mail) a **CARBON MONOXIDE DETECTOR— CERTIFICATE OF INSTALLATION** within ten days from the date of installation, with Department of Housing Preservation and Development's (HPD) Borough Code Enforcement office in the borough in which the dwelling is located. (see form 46, p. 275.) This applies to all multiple dwellings.

✪ Post a notice in a form approved by HPD in a common area informing occupants of Local Law 7 requirements. This applies to class "A" multiple dwellings, which are dwellings used, as a rule, for permanent residences. The typical residential apartment is an "A" unit. A sample notice is found in Appendix C. (see form 47, p. 277.)

✪ Provide a notice in a form approved by HPD informing occupants of Local Law 7 requirements. This applies to non-owner-occupied units in private one- and two-family homes. The notice sample in Appendix C can be used for this requirement as well. (see form 47, p. 277.)

✪ Provide written information regarding the testing and maintenance of carbon monoxide alarms, including general information concerning carbon monoxide poisoning and what to do if a carbon monoxide alarm goes off, to at least one adult occupant of each dwelling unit. This applies to class "A" multiple dwellings and non-owner-occupied units in one- and two-family homes.

✪ Keep all records relating to the installation and maintenance of carbon monoxide alarms and make them available upon request to the Department of Housing Preservation and Development (HPD), the Department of Buildings (DOB), the Fire Department, and the Department of Health and Mental Hygiene (DOHMH). Records for all multiple dwellings must be kept on the premises unless HPD grants permission to keep them elsewhere; records for non-owner-occupied units in private dwellings may be kept by the owner.

✪ Keep and maintain the carbon monoxide alarms or systems in good repair. This applies to class "B" multiple dwellings, which are dwellings used, as a rule, on a temporary basis. For example, single-room occupancies are typically B units.

✪ Some units in buildings without fossil fuel burning furnaces or boilers may be exempt (see Department of Buildings regulations at **www.nyc.gov/buildings** for more info). Carbon monoxide detectors are also required in dormitories, nursing homes, and schools.

Approved carbon monoxide detectors must be marked "UL." For existing buildings, carbon monoxide detectors can be battery-operated, or can plug into an electrical outlet as long as it has a battery back-up in case of power interruption. New buildings or substantially improved buildings must have detectors that are hard-wired to the building's electrical systems. The installation of a combination smoke alarm/carbon monoxide detector is allowed (in which case, use form 48, p.279).

Local Law 7 requires the owner of the dwelling to provide and install at least one approved and operational carbon monoxide alarm. If building owners and tenants are in agreement in allowing the tenant to install the carbon monoxide alarm, it is strongly suggested that the owner be provided access to confirm that an approved carbon monoxide alarm is properly installed and operational. The owner of the multiple dwelling must file (in person or by mail) the certificate of installation with HPD.

The law places responsibility for maintaining the detectors with the tenant; however, building owners must replace any detectors that are lost, stolen, or become inoperable. The owner has to replace, within thirty calendar days after the receipt of written notice, any such device that becomes inoperable.

Failure to provide or maintain a carbon monoxide detector is a class B violation. Civil penalties can range from $25 to $100 and $10 per day for each violation until the violation is certified as corrected. In addition, failure to provide proper notices to occupants or certification of installation is a class A violation, which can carry civil penalties of up to $50.

With prior notice to the tenant, a landlord is entitled to enter the premises to make repairs, to show the unit to prospective buyers or tenants, and under any other circumstances where entry is allowed by the lease. Use the **INSPECTION REQUEST** (form 10, p.199) to notify a tenant of your need to enter the premises to make repairs or for other reasons. In an emergency, such as fire, the landlord can enter without prior notice to, or consent of, the tenant.

SINGLE-FAMILY HOMES AND DUPLEXES

The only requirements for single-family homes and duplexes in New York State are that all applicable laws, codes, and regulations be met, and that the warranty of habitability be met.

CODE VIOLATIONS

Landlords should be aware that governmental bodies can levy fines of hundreds of dollars a day for minor violations. Ignoring notices of violation can be expensive.

Whenever you receive a governmental notice, you should read it very carefully and follow it to the letter. One landlord who sold his property and thought the problem was solved was fined $11,000 ($500 a day for the last twenty-two days he owned the property) for a violation. After you correct a violation, be sure that the governmental body that sent the notice gives you written confirmation that you are in compliance.

WARRANTY OF HABITABILITY

In recent years, the centuries-old theories of landlord/tenant law have been replaced with new obligations on landlords to protect their tenants. One of these is the *implied warranty of habitability*, which has been accepted in over forty states. Under this doctrine, any time a dwelling unit is turned over to a tenant, the tenant is automatically given a warranty by the landlord that the premises are in safe and habitable condition and will remain so during the term of the lease.

Every lease contains an implied warranty of habitability, regardless of whether it is written in the lease, that cannot be waived by the tenant. (RPL Sec. 235-b.) The warranty applies to each unit, as well as all common areas. The warranty of habitability requires:

✪   that the premises be fit for human habitation (the unit must have essential services and features that a tenant would reasonably expect to have, including not only heat and water, but services such as garbage collection, working smoke detectors, and existing elevators in working order);

✪   that the premises be fit for uses reasonably intended by the parties; and,

✪   that the tenant not be subjected to conditions that are dangerous, hazardous, or detrimental to life, health, or safety.

Breaches of the warranty of habitability are often found by courts when there is an ongoing pattern of defects, or one very substantial defect. For example, a breach was found when a tenant was without hot water for eighteen consecutive days (*Romanov v. Heller*, 121 Misc.2d 469, N.Y.S.2d 876 (Civ.Ct., New York County, 1983)), but not when a tenant was without hot water for seven days in one month. (*Toomer v. Higgins*, 161 A.D.2d 347, 554 N.Y.S.2d 921 (1st Dept. 1990).)

A landlord is not liable for breach of the warranty of habitability if the uninhabitable condition was caused by the misconduct of the tenant. Landlords are also not responsible when essential services are lost due to strikes or other labor disputes, unless a court finds that the landlord did not make a good faith attempt to provide the services. However, if the landlord saved money by not having to pay for services during a strike, the tenant may be awarded a portion of that savings.

If the warranty is breached, the tenant can sue and recover an amount equal to the rent charged minus the reasonable rent for the unit with the defect. If a landlord fails to fix a defect that breaches the warranty, the tenant can do the repair and recover the cost of the repair from the landlord. However, landlords are not required to rebuild or make huge repairs from things such as fires, tornadoes, and so on. If damage such as this occurs, the tenant has the option to terminate the lease. (*Smith v. Kerr*, 108 N.Y. 31 (1888).) If a breach by the landlord is malicious or intentional, the tenant can recover punitive damages.

Landlords should also be aware that failure to comply with local housing codes can constitute a breach of the warranty of habitability. (*Park West Management Corp. v. Mitchell*, 47 N.Y.2d 316 (1979).)

The following cases have examined certain types of breaches:

✪   common areas (*Solow v. Wellner*, 154 Misc.2d 737, 595 N.Y.S.2d 619 (1st Dept. 1992));

✪   garbage and maintenance services (*Park West Management Corp. v. Mitchell*, 47 N.Y.2d 316, 418 N.Y.S.2d 310 (1979));

✪ heat and hot water (*Park West Management Corp. v. Mitchell*, 47 N.Y.2d 316, 418 N.Y.S.2d 310 (1979));

✪ noise (*Justice Court Mutual Housing Cooperative, Inc. v. Sandow*, 50 Misc.2d 541, 270 N.Y.S.2d 829 (Sup.Ct., Queens County, 1966));

✪ defective plumbing lines and fixtures (*Spatz v. Axelrod Management Co., Inc.*, 165 Misc.2d 759, 630 N.Y.S.2d 461 (City Ct., Yonkers, 1995));

✪ security (*Carp v. Marcus*, 112 A.D.2d 546, 491 N.Y.S.2d 484 (3d Dept. 1985));

✪ vermin (*Town of Islip Community Development Agency v. Mulligan*, 130 Misc.2d 279, 496 N.Y.S.2d 195 (Dist.Ct., Suffolk County, 1985));

✪ odor (*Keklass v. Saddy*, 88 Misc.2d 1042, 389 N.Y.S.2d 756 (Dist.Ct. 1974));

✪ lack of building services (*111 East 88th Partners v. Simon*, 106 Misc.2d 693 (1980));

✪ ventilation (*Department of Housing Preservation and Development of the City of New York v. Sartor*, 109 A.D.2d 665 (1985)); and,

✪ lack of air-conditioning (*Whitehouse Estates, Inc. v. Thomson*, 87 Misc.2d 813 (1976).)

If a landlord violates the warranty of habitability to the point where a tenant has been forced to abandon the premises, or a portion of it, it is known as *constructive eviction.* (*Lincoln Plaza Tenants Corp. v. MDS Properties Development Corp.*, 169 A.D.2d 509, 564 N.Y.S.2d 729 (1st Dept. 1991).)

TENANT'S RIGHTS AND RESPONSIBILITIES

The tenant's duties are not set out in any statute, but are usually specified in the lease. However, courts have found that tenants have a duty to make any repairs necessary to prevent further damage. For example, a tenant should cover a broken window to prevent further water damage until the landlord can repair it. (*Starpoli v. Starpoli*, 180 A.D.2d 727, 580 N.Y.S.2d 369 (2d Dept., 1992).) The tenant who fails to do so may be liable for damage resulting from the failure to make a temporary repair. A tenant is also expected to keep the premises free of defects and in a reasonably safe condition. (*Zito v. 241 Church Street Corp.*, 223 A.D.2d 353, 636 N.Y.S.2d 40 (1st Dept. 1996).) This may make a tenant liable for failure to notify the landlord of a needed repair.

A tenant may install his or her own lock in addition to the landlord's locks, but the lock may not be more than three inches in circumference and the landlord must be provided with a duplicate key upon request. (MDL Sec. 51-c; NYC Admin. Code Sec. 27-2043.)

A commercial tenant has a duty to its customers and employees to keep the premises safe. One court held that a commercial tenant who knows, or should know of, a condition creating an unreasonable risk of harm to employees or patrons has a duty to make it safe or to warn of the danger. (*Hinkel v. R.H. Macy, Inc.*, 201 N.Y.S.2d 211 (Sup.Ct., New York County, 1960).)

Tenants in a multiple dwelling with eight or more units are entitled to maintain a lobby attendant whenever one provided by the landlord is not on duty. (MDL Sec. 50-c.)

Tenants in multiple dwellings heated by oil may contract for oil delivery if the landlord fails to supply sufficient fuel, and may deduct the cost of the oil from the rent. (MDL Sec. 302-c; MRL Sec. 305-c.) Before signing a lease that requires the tenant to pay for heating and cooling bills, the tenant is entitled to receive (for free, upon a written request to the landlord) either a summary or complete set of bills for the past two years. (Energy Law Sec. 17-103.)

If utility service in a multiple dwelling is terminated because of the landlord's failure to pay the utility bill, the tenants may recover damages from the landlord. When the landlord of a multiple dwelling pays the utility bills, public utilities must notify tenants in writing in advance of a shut-off. The tenants may then pay the bill, and deduct the amount from their rent. (RPL Sec. 235-a; PSL Sec. 33.)

Tenants have the right to privacy within their apartments. A landlord, however, may enter a tenant's apartment with reasonable prior notice, and at a reasonable time:

✪   to provide necessary or agreed-upon repairs or services;

✪   in accordance with the lease; or,

✪   to show the apartment to prospective purchasers or tenants.

In emergencies, such as fires, the landlord may enter the apartment without the tenant's consent. A landlord may not abuse this limited right of entry or use it to harass a tenant. A landlord may not interfere with the installation of cable television facilities. (Public Service Law Sec. 228.)

LEAD PAINT NOTICE

Under rules of the Environmental Protection Agency, if any repairs are done to the property during a tenancy and more than two square feet of lead paint is disturbed, notice must be given to the tenants and the landlord must obtain a receipt from the tenant for the notice. The following rules also apply:

✪   any work by plumbers, painters, electricians, and others is included;

✪   the tenants must be given the pamphlet *Protect Your Family From Lead in Your Home*;

✪   if the work is done on common areas of the building, all tenants must be notified; and,

✪   emergency renovations and repairs are excluded.

In New York City, an **Annual Notice to Tenant or Occupant in Buildings with 3 or More Apartments—Protect Your Child from Window Falls and Lead Poisoning** must be given to tenants. (see form 49, p.281.) Instructions for completing and filing the form are included with the form in Appendix C.

Landlord Liability

The law of responsibility for injuries and crime on rental property has changed considerably over the last couple of decades. Landlords are now often liable, even for conditions that are not their fault. This change was not made by elected legislators representing their constituents, but by appointed judges who felt tenants needed protection and landlords should give it to them.

INJURIES ON THE PREMISES

Landlords are liable for injuries or damages only when the landlord has a duty to make repairs under the Multiple Dwelling Law (MDL), the Multiple Residence Law (MRL), other laws and regulations, warranty of habitability, or when the landlord is negligent.

Negligence is a complicated legal theory and occurs when a landlord violates a duty to keep the premises in a reasonably safe condition. The legal definition basically states that *negligence* is a failure to exercise the degree of care that would be exercised by a reasonably prudent person under the circumstances, which causes injury or damage that was reasonably foreseeable.

What this boils down to is that a landlord must be careful not to cause a defect or fail to repair a defect that any reasonable person would know could cause damage or injury. In other words, make sure the premises is reasonably safe. This includes defects of which a landlord is unaware, but should know.

Areas Not Under the Landlord's Control

A landlord is liable for injury or damage that occurs in areas not under his or her control as follows:

- ✪ where the landlord is negligent;

- ✪ where a danger exists that is or should be known to the landlord;

- ✪ where there is a preexisting defect in construction;

- ✪ where the condition of the premises violates a law or regulation;

- ✪ where the landlord is required under the lease to make repairs or where the landlord does or begins repairs; and,

- ✪ where the premises is a nuisance or could become one under the expected use of the premises.

Cases Holding a Landlord Not Liable

The following are cases that held that a landlord would not be liable for injuries. Keep in mind that the holdings in some of the earlier cases may have been modified by the rulings in later cases.

- ✪ A landlord was not liable when a tenant was injured after knocking boiling water off a hot plate. This injury was not a foreseeable result of not providing a stove. (*Wells v. Finnegan*, 177 A.D.2d 893, 576 N.Y.S.2d 653 (3d Dept. 1991).)

- ✪ A landlord who failed to provide adequate heat was not liable when an infant fell into the bathtub that the tenant had filled with hot water to provide heat. This injury was not a foreseeable result of not providing heat. (*Lam v. Neptune Assoc.*, 203 A.D.2d 334, 610 N.Y.S.2d 538 (2d Dept. 1994).)

- ✪ A landlord was not liable when a child fell off a cliff on the property because there is no duty to fix natural, open conditions, even though the injury was foreseeable. (*Diven v. Village of Hastings-on-Hudson*, 156 A.D.2d 538, 548 N.Y.S.2d 807 (2d Dept. 1989).)

✪ A landlord was not liable for a fall on the slippery waxed floor of a commercial rental. The landlord's retention of the right to reenter and make repairs makes the landlord liable only for structural or design defects and not for maintenance. (*Levy v. Daitz*, 196 A.D.2d 454, 601 N.Y.S.2d 294 (1st Dept. 1993).)

✪ A landlord was not liable for injury when the lease made the tenant responsible for all repairs. The landlord did not reserve any control over the premises, and thus, the tenant was liable for the injury. (*Fresina v. Nebush*, 209 A.D.2d 1004, 619 N.Y.S.2d 447 (4th Dept. 1994).)

Cases Holding a Landlord Liable

The following cases are examples of when a landlord was held liable for injuries to a tenant or a guest.

✪ A landlord was liable when a child was injured falling on exposed metal from a broken window screen that the landlord should have repaired. (*Contento v. Albany Medical Center Hospital*, 57 A.D.2d 691, 394 N.Y.S.2d 74 (3d Dept. 1977).)

✪ A landlord was liable for a malfunctioning elevator, despite a contract for maintenance with an elevator repair company. The landlord's duty to keep the premises safe cannot be delegated. (*Camaj v. East 52nd Partners*, 215 A.D.2d 150, 626 N.Y.S.2d 110 (1st Dept. 1995).)

✪ A commercial landlord was liable for a malfunctioning elevator that caused injury, because the landlord retained the right to enter the premises to make elevator repairs. (*Cassuto v. Broadway 86th Street Associates*, 243 A.D.2d 263, 664 N.Y.S.2d 721 (1997).)

✪ A landlord who had provided a lobby attendant was liable for assault when the attendant was absent. When a landlord voluntarily provides a service, even if there is no obligation to do so, the tenant may rely on that service and hold the landlord liable if the service is discontinued. (*Nallan v. Helmsley-Spear, Inc.*, 50 N.Y.2d 507, 429 N.Y.S.2d 606 (1980).)

✪   Landlords can be liable to third-party persons who are patrons or guests of the tenant, because their presence is foreseeable. (*Fitzsimmons v. State*, 34 N.Y.2d 739, 357 N.Y.S.2d 498 (1974).)

LANDLORD'S WARRANTY OF HABITABILITY

In 1975, the New York legislature reversed centuries of landlord/tenant law by adopting the theory of the landlord's warranty of habitability for residential property. The warranty of habitability requires the landlord to provide a safe and habitable property, and is explained in more detail in Chapter 5. The landlord's warranty of habitability does not apply to nonresidential rentals.

A landlord was liable for a tenant's repeatedly overflowing sink (caused by the tenant) that flooded a neighbor's apartment, causing damage to personal belongings. The court found that the landlord should have evicted the tenant with the sink when the overflowing continued to happen. (*Benitez v. Restifo*, 167 Misc.2d 967, 641 N.Y.S.2d 523 (1996).)

PROTECTION FROM LIABILITY FOR INJURIES

The basis for liability in the previously discussed cases is that the landlord breached a duty to keep the premises safe. If a landlord puts the duty to keep the premises safe on the tenant, there will be less likelihood that the landlord can be held liable. However, under GOL Sec. 5-321, a provision in the lease that waives a landlord's liability for his or her negligence is not enforceable.

The result of all this is that the landlord is the insurer of the safety of tenants, and must therefore carry adequate insurance to cover any liability. Rent can be raised to compensate for this additional insurance expense.

Be sure to read Chapter 5 for more details about what is legally required to maintain safe premises.

LIABILITY FOR CRIMES ON THE PREMISES

Another area where liability of landlords has been greatly expanded is in the area of crimes against tenants. The former theory of law was that a person cannot be held liable for deliberate acts of third parties. This had been the theory for hundreds of years, but has recently been abandoned in favor of a theory that a landlord must protect his or her tenants from crimes.

Basis for Liability

In New York, a landlord can be held liable for criminal acts against a tenant if the landlord could have or should have foreseen a risk of harm. Past identical incidents are not necessary. The landlord, based upon all of the circumstances, must have reason to anticipate the general type of crime, not its exact details. This liability for crime, unlike the warranty of habitability, applies to both residential and commercial tenancies, but it has not been extended to single-family homes yet.

Cases Holding Landlord Liable

The following are examples of cases in which a landlord was determined to be liable.

- A landlord was liable for the rape of a tenant when the rapes occurred in other buildings of a housing project, even though none had occurred in that building. (*Jacqueline S. v. The City of New York*, 81 N.Y.2d 288, 598 N.Y.S.2d 160 (1993).)

- A landlord who failed to provide locks on outer doors was liable for a break-in. (*Dawson v. New York City Housing Authority*, 203 A.D.2d 55, 610 N.Y.S.2d 28 (1st Dept. 1994).) Recent cases have followed this conclusion, and indicated that the landlord will be liable for physical injuries to the tenant even if the person who committed the crime is never identified.

Cases Holding Landlord Not Liable

The following cases have held that the landlord was not liable.

○ When there was no prior evidence of criminal activity on the premises, a landlord was not liable for a tenant who was stabbed by an ex-lover. (*Camacho v. Edelman*, 176 A.D.2d 453, 574 N.Y.S.2d 356 (1st Dept. 1991).)

○ A landlord was not liable for injuries caused by arson when the landlord was unaware the premises was being used for gambling activities or that there had been any threats of violence. (*Rodriguez v. Mohr*, 174 A.D.2d 382, 571 N.Y.S.2d 221 (1st Dept. 1991).)

Protection from Liability for Crimes

The law is not clear as to just how far courts will go in holding landlords liable for crimes against tenants. A clause in a lease that makes a tenant responsible for locks and security may provide some protection to landlords in some situations, especially in single-family homes and duplexes.

However, in some inner-city apartment complexes, where crime is common, landlords may be required to provide armed guards or face liability. Again, insurance is a must, and this additional cost will have to be covered by rent increases.

STRICT LIABILITY

Landlords can also be held liable for things that are not their fault. It is not necessary that the landlord knew or should have known about the defect, nor is it necessary that the harm was foreseeable. The New York legislature and the U.S. Congress have passed laws making landlords responsible for damage or injury caused by the following items:

○ improper operation of sprinklers and other fire prevention equipment (MRL Secs. 15, 52, 54, 58, & 61; MDL Secs. 68 & 284);

NOTE: *MDL Sec. 284 is set to repeal on May 31, 2007 if not extended by legislature.*

✪ injuries to construction workers while they are working on the premises (Labor Law Sec. 240);

✪ leakage of home heating oil and other petroleum products, including underground gas storage tanks on the premises (*Leone v. Leewood Service Station, Inc.*, 212 A.D.2d 669, 624 N.Y.S.2d 610 (2d Dept. 1995); *State v. N.Y.Cent. Mut. Fire Ins. Co.*, 147 A.D.2d 77, 542 N.Y.S.2d 402 (3d Dept. 1989));

✪ injury or death of a firefighter or police officer in the line of duty on the premises as a result of violation of any statute or ordinance that causes the death or injury (GOL Secs. 11-106);

✪ failure to provide window guards in New York City (NYC Admin. Code Sec. 17-123); or,

NOTE: *There are two separate laws contained in the New York City Administrative Code with the reference number of the section.*

✪ environmental damage in violation of:

• Comprehensive Environmental Response, Compensation and Liability Act of 1980 (42 U.S.C.A. 9607);

• Solid Waste Disposal Act (42 U.S.C.A. 6973);

• Air Pollution Prevention and Control Act (42 U.S.C.A. 7401); or,

• Water Pollution Control Act (33 U.S.C.A. 1251).

Changing the Terms of the Tenancy

chapter 7

During the course of a tenancy, circumstances can change for either the landlord or the tenant. While it is not possible to cover every possible change that may arise, there are some common situations of which you should be aware.

ASSIGNMENT OR SUBLEASE BY TENANT

In an *assignment*, a tenant assigns (transfers) all of his or her interest in a lease to another party, who takes over the tenant's position. This party becomes responsible for rent and all of the other obligations of the tenant. The original tenant is no longer responsible to the landlord.

Unless the lease specifies otherwise, a tenant may not assign a lease without prior written consent from the landlord. The landlord may not withhold consent *without cause* (in other words, without a good reason). (RPL Sec. 226-b(1).) Commercial tenants may always assign, unless the lease states otherwise.

In a *sublease*, the tenant enters into a new agreement with a third party who deals solely with the tenant. The original tenant is then the *sublessor* and the new tenant is the *sublessee*. The original tenant remains responsible to the landlord. A tenant is free to sublease the unit or a portion of the unit. However, in a building with four or more units the landlord's prior written consent is required. The landlord may not unreasonably withhold consent. If consent is unreasonably withheld, the tenant may sublet without permission. (RPL Sec. 226-b(2).) Commercial tenants may always sublet, unless the lease states otherwise.

Liability   If a lease contains a covenant to pay rent and the landlord does not release the tenant upon the assignment, the landlord may sue the original tenant if the new tenant defaults. (*Gillette Bros. v. Aristocrat Restaurant*, 239 N.Y. 87 (1924).)

Waiver   If a landlord knowingly accepts rent from an assignee or a sublessee of a lease, then the landlord waives the right to object to the assignment. However, if the landlord was unaware of the assignment, it does not constitute a waiver. (*Brentson Realty Corp. v. D'Urso Supermarkets, Inc.*, 182 A.D.2d 604, 582 N.Y. 5.2d 216 (2d. Dept. 1992).)

SALE OF PROPERTY BY LANDLORD

A landlord has the right to sell property covered by leases, but the new owner takes the property subject to the terms of the existing leases.

The new owner cannot cancel the old leases or raise the rent while the leases are still in effect (unless the leases have provisions allowing the landlord to do so). The new owner must perform any repairs to the property that the old owner would have been required to do under the terms of the lease. In most cases, a landlord is relieved of his or her obligations under a lease upon sale of the property. (*Kilmer v. White*, 254 N.Y. 64 (1930).)

When selling property, a landlord must specify in the sales contract that the sale is subject to existing leases. Otherwise, the buyer may sue for failure to deliver the premises free and clear of other claims. At closing, the leases should be assigned to the buyer.

Foreclosures   When property is purchased at a foreclosure sale, the leases of the tenants are terminated if they were signed after the date of the mortgage and if the tenants were joined as parties to the suit. (*United Security Corp. v. Suchman*, 307 N.Y. 48 (1954); *Lincoln First Bank, N.A. v. Polishuk*, 86 A.P.2d. 652, 446 N.Y.5.2d. 399 (2d. Dept. 1982).)

Otherwise, the purchaser takes subject to the lease and is not entitled to possession until the expiration of the lease. (*Lewis v. Rodriguez*, 155 Misc.2d 12, 587 N.Y.S.2d 121 (Sup. Ct., Bronx County, 1992); *Metropolitan Life Ins. Co. v. Childs Co.*, 230 N.Y. 285 (1921).)

RAISING THE RENT

If a tenancy is for a set term (such as a one-year lease) at a specified rent, the landlord cannot raise the rent until the term ends unless such a right is spelled out in the lease. If the tenancy is month to month, the landlord would be able to raise the rent if he or she gives notice at least thirty days prior to the end of the month. This is based upon the law that the landlord can cancel the tenancy by giving thirty days' notice. To raise the rent in a month-to-month tenancy, you can use the **NOTICE OF CHANGE OF TERMS**. (see form 12, p.203.)

In such a case, the tenant would probably not have to give thirty days' notice if he or she decided not to stay at the end of the month. This is because by raising the rent, the landlord would be terminating the previous tenancy and making the tenant an offer to enter into a new tenancy at a different rental rate. See Chapter 4 for the special rules that apply to rent-stabilized and rent-controlled properties.

MODIFYING THE LEASE

You should put it in writing if you agree to modify the terms of your lease with a tenant. If you do not put it in writing and you allow a tenant to do things forbidden in the lease, you may be found to have waived your rights. To modify the terms, you can use the **AMENDMENT TO LEASE/RENTAL AGREEMENT**. (see form 13, p.205.)

RENEWING THE LEASE

When a lease expires, you are not obligated to renew it. There are exceptions for rent-regulated units (see Chapter 4), or if the lease itself gives the tenant an option to renew. If you do not want to renew, use the **NOTICE OF NON-RENEWAL**. (see form 17, p.213.) If you wish to renew, you can either renew on the same terms as the original lease and use the **LETTER—CONTINUATION OF TENANCY** (form 14, p.207) or renegotiate the terms and use a new lease.

chapter 8

Problems During the Tenancy

During the course of a tenancy, any number of problems can arise. Some of these problems are caused by the tenant, but some are caused by the landlord. You should be aware of some of the common problems that can arise and know what to do to lessen their impact.

LANDLORD'S ACCESS TO THE PREMISES

Under the historic principles of landlord/tenant law, which still apply to nonresidential tenancies, the landlord has no right to enter the premises unless it is given to the landlord in the lease. However, a landlord may enter in an emergency to protect the landlord's or the tenant's property.

A residential landlord may enter the premises:

✪ when permitted by the lease;

✪ to make repairs; or,

✪ to show the premises for the purpose of renting or selling it.

A tenant is entitled to reasonable notice of the planned entry. No notice is necessary if there is an emergency or an emergency repair.

VIOLATIONS BY THE TENANT

Often the biggest problems during the tenancy are ones caused by tenants.

Rent Due Date

Rent is due on the date specified in the lease. If it is not specified in the lease, it is not due until after it is earned, at the end of the term. (*DeSimone v. Canzonieri*, 246 A.D. 735, 283 N.Y.S. 860 (2d Dept. 1935).)

If a landlord enters to make repairs after the tenant vacates early, he or she is not considered to have taken possession on his or her own account. (*Sammis v. Day*, 48 Misc. 327, 96 N.Y.S. 777 (County Ct. 1905).)

Vacating Early

If the tenant breaches the lease by vacating the property before the expiration of the lease, the landlord may do one of three things: 1) terminate the lease and take possession of the property for his or her own account (relieving the tenant of further liability); 2) take possession of the premises for the account of the tenant and hold the tenant liable for the difference in rent due under the lease and the rent eventually received; or, 3) let the unit sit vacant and sue the tenant for the full rent as it comes due.

The law in this area is very complicated. The decisions by the courts are confusing and contradictory in New York as well as other states. Many landlords have lost in their attempts to collect damages from tenants. Before taking action regarding large sums of money, a landlord should consult an attorney and request that the attorney review the latest cases in this area, as well as the latest publications on landlord/tenant law.

Problems. The problem in most of the cases where landlords have lost their suits against tenants is that they have tried to terminate the lease and sue for the rent, combining option (1) with option (2). When this is done, the courts have usually found that the landlord accepted a surrender of the premises and lost all rights to sue for damages.

❂   If a tenant vacates the premises before expiration of the lease, and the landlord enters and re-leases the premises without the tenant's permission, the landlord does so on his or her own account and is considered to have accepted the tenant's surrender. The tenant is no longer liable for rent. (*Schnee v. Jonas Equities, Inc.*, 442 N.Y.S.2d 342 (1981).)

If the landlord wishes to sue the tenant for rent for the period up to the point when a new tenant is found or for future rent, the landlord should not terminate the tenancy, but should use option (2) and take possession for the account of the tenant.

Possible solutions. The usual problem in the court cases is a misinterpretation of the landlord's intent. To avoid this, the landlord should analyze his or her options and make his or her intent clear, either in the form of a certified letter to the tenant or in the allegations of the complaint.

❂   When the landlord has many vacant units, he or she can elect option (3) and just sue the tenant for the rent due without trying to rent the unit.

❂   If the landlord expects to rent the unit out at a lower rate, he or she should make clear that he or she is taking possession for the account of the tenant and will hold the tenant liable for the difference.

Acceleration   The lease may provide that all the rent for the rest of the rental term becomes due when there is a default (nonpayment of rent). (*Fifty States Management Corp. v. Pioneer Auto Sales, Inc.*, 46 N.Y.2d 573, 415 N.Y.S.2d 800 (1979).) Such a lease provision requiring rent acceleration when the landlord terminates the lease was found to be enforceable in *Holy Properties Ltd. v. Kenneth Cole Productions*, 87 N.Y.2d 130, 637 N.Y.S.2d 964 (1995).

Bad Checks   If a tenant pays with a bad check, the landlord can collect double the amount of the check, up to $750, if the tenant did not have an account at that bank. If the tenant did have an account, the limit is $400. Notice must be sent by regular and certified mail. (GOL Sec. 11-104(8).) (See the **DEMAND FOR PAYMENT OF DISHONORED CHECK**, form 19, p.217.)

However, if a tenant cannot immediately make good on a check, the landlord would be better advised to immediately start the eviction rather than sue on the bad check.

There is also a criminal law that prohibits writing a bad check. (Penal Law Secs. 190.00 through 190.15.) You may get your sheriff to prosecute the tenant. However, the tenant might have a defense if he or she makes payment on the check within ten days.

Damage to the Premises If the tenant does intentional damage to the premises, the landlord can terminate the tenancy (see Chapter 10) and can also get an injunction against the tenant. This can be done by filing a complaint with the appropriate court. Damages can also be requested.

Lease Violations If the violation is not curable or if the tenant repeats a noncompliance after receiving notice, the landlord may terminate the tenancy. (see page 84.)

Apartment Sharing Tenants are permitted to share their apartment with their spouse and children. If only one tenant is named on the lease, the tenant's immediate family, one additional person, and the additional person's children are allowed. At least one tenant named in the lease, or the spouse of a named tenant, must occupy the shared apartment as his or her primary residence. If there is no named tenant or spouse of a named tenant living in the unit, other occupants do not have any right to occupy the unit unless the landlord consents. (RPL Sec. 235-f.)

Death of a Tenant If a tenant dies during the term of a lease, the lease becomes part of his or her estate, and the estate is liable for the rent due for the rest of the lease term. (*MacDonald v. Rosenblum*, 150 Misc. 556, 269 N.Y.S. 562 (1934).)

RETALIATORY CONDUCT BY THE LANDLORD

Retaliation by a landlord against a tenant in prohibited. (RPL Sec. 223-b.) It can be argued that the law is too vague, but it would be expensive to take the argument to court. The best strategy is to read the following rules carefully and avoid any conduct that might look like a violation.

Under Real Property Law Sec. 223-b(2), a landlord must not *discriminatively* do any of the following acts in retaliation against a tenant:

✪   evict the tenant;

✪   refuse to renew a lease; or,

✪   substantially alter the terms of the tenancy (which may include raising the rent).

The key word here is *discriminatively*. It is okay to raise the rents of all tenants, but you can not raise one tenant's rent in retaliation against him or her.

Under Real Property Law Sec. 233b-1, the conduct of a tenant that a landlord may not retaliate for is unlimited, but specifically includes instances in which:

✪   the tenant, in good faith, complains to a governmental agency about code violations;

✪   the tenant participates in tenants' organizations; and,

✪   the tenant complains to the landlord about maintenance and the warranty of habitability, or takes actions to secure or enforce the tenant's rights under the lease.

A tenant can defend an eviction by saying that the landlord is retaliating. However, the law states that it is not a defense to a good faith action for nonpayment of rent by the landlord, violation of the rental agreement, or violation by the tenant of the landlord/tenant laws.

If a landlord is found to have used retaliatory eviction, he or she can be subject to civil damages. (Real Property Law Sec. 223-b(3) and (4).)

DESTRUCTION OF THE PREMISES

If a premises is severely damaged or destroyed to the point of being uninhabitable, and the tenant did not cause the damage, the tenant has the right to immediately terminate the lease. (RPL Sec. 227.) This right may be waived by a lease provision. (*Johnson v. Oppenheim*, 55 N.Y. 28 (1873).)

Problems at the End of the Tenancy

Just as there can be problems during a tenancy, problems can also occur at the end of a tenancy.

TENANT HOLDING OVER

Holding over occurs when a tenant or other person wrongfully occupies the premises, such as a tenant whose lease has expired or a *squatter* (a person with no legal right to occupy the premises).

With a holdover tenant, the landlord has three options.

1.   Remove the tenant by instituting a *holdover proceeding*. (see Chapter 10.) A tenant who holds over is liable to the landlord for the reasonable value of the use and occupancy of the premises. (RPAPL Sec. 749(3).)

2.   Collect double rent. If the tenant gave notice of his or her intent to vacate the premises, but then failed to do so, the landlord may collect double the rent normally due for the period of time the tenant remains. (RPL Sec. 229.) The landlord may also remove the tenant by way of a holdover proceeding.

3. Convert to a month-to-month tenancy. If a tenant holds over and the landlord accepts at least one rent payment after the expiration of the lease, the tenancy becomes a month-to-month tenancy. A month-to-month tenancy may be terminated upon thirty days' notice. (*Tubbs v. Hendrickson*, 88 Misc.2d 917, 390 N.Y.S.2d (1976); RPL Secs. 232-a & 232-b.)

A landlord can remove any remaining property and store it at the tenant's expense. A landlord can also charge the tenant for the cost of removing the property. (*Ide v. Finn*, 196 A.D. 304, 187 N.Y.S. 202 (1st Dept. 1921).)

Notice to Terminate   No notice is required at the end of a lease, but a letter to the tenant expressing an intention to terminate or to renew is a good idea. Where trouble is expected, a **LETTER—CONTINUATION OF TENANCY** (form 14, p.207) can be used.

Public Housing   In public housing, Section 8 housing, and Section 236 housing, a landlord cannot refuse to renew a lease without good cause.

Rent Regulation   Rent-regulated tenants must be offered a renewal.

DAMAGE TO THE PREMISES
If the landlord finds damage at the end of a tenancy, the expenses of repairing the damage may be deducted from the security deposit. (see Chapter 3.)

If the damages exceed the amount of the security deposit, the landlord may sue the tenant, and if the amount is under $5,000, the landlord can file a case in small claims court.

PROPERTY ABANDONED BY TENANT
Property left behind by a tenant may constitute holding over if the amount and value of the property is very large. (*Canfield v. Elmer E. Harris and Co.*, 222 A.D. 326, 225 N.Y.S. 709 (4th Dept. 1927).)

It is advisable for a landlord to notify the tenant of the remaining property and his or her intent to dispose of it if the tenant does not remove it within a certain time period.

It may also be advisable to include the following provision in the lease.

By signing this rental agreement, the tenant agrees that upon surrender or abandonment, the landlord shall not be liable or responsible for storage or disposition of the tenant's personal property.

Terminating a Tenancy

A tenancy may be terminated in several ways. It is important to understand that terminating the tenancy is only one step in getting the tenant out of the property. The tenancy must be terminated properly before the tenant may be evicted. (Eviction is discussed in Chapter 11.) New York has very specific procedures to follow to terminate a tenancy. It is important to be careful and thorough—otherwise, evictions can be delayed in the court system.

New York tenancies can be terminated with written notice (unless otherwise indicated). The amount of notice required varies with the type of tenancy and the reason for termination. All notices must contain the termination date and the landlord's intent to commence a summary proceeding should the tenant fail to vacate. Different types of tenancies require other information to be included. All notices must be clear, definite, and unequivocal, and they may not contain conclusory or misleading language.

Unless otherwise indicated, all notices referred to in this chapter must be served on the tenant in one of the following three ways:

1. by personally delivering it to the tenant;

2. by leaving it with a person of suitable age or discretion residing at or employed at the premises; or,

3. by affixing a copy to the door of the tenant's residence.

If there is a subtenant, be sure to list him or her as a party, and have the subtenant served as well. Subtenants not listed and served cannot be included in eviction proceedings.

TENANCIES WITH NO SPECIFIC TERM

A *tenancy at will* (also called a *tenancy at sufferance*) has either an indefinite term or no term at all. It may be terminated on thirty days' written notice. (RPL Sec. 228.)

A *month-to-month tenancy* is created when a tenant rents on a monthly basis, or when a tenant with a term longer than one month holds over and the landlord accepts rent. (RPL Sec. 232-c.) Using the **NOTICE OF TERMINATION** (form 22, p.223), the tenancy can be terminated as follows.

✪   In New York City: with thirty days' written notice (for example, a notice served on October 1 is sufficient to terminate the tenancy on October 31).

✪   Outside New York City: with one full calendar month written or oral notice (for example, notice on July 31 terminates the tenancy on August 31; notice on August 1 does not terminate the tenancy until September 30). A written notice can be served by mail.

EXPIRATION OF RENTAL TERM

Month-to-month tenancies are presumed to continue until one of the parties gives notice terminating the tenancy. For all other tenancies, when the term of a lease ends, the tenant is expected to vacate the property without notice, unless the parties agree to renew or extend the lease. This is different from some states, where a lease is presumed to be renewed unless the tenant gives the landlord notice that he or she is leaving. If you believe that a tenant may not be expecting to leave at the end of the lease, you can use the **NOTICE OF NON-RENEWAL**. (see form 17, p.213.)

EMPLOYMENT RENTALS

When occupancy is a benefit of, or payment for, employment (such as a building superintendent), there is no tenancy created and occupancy ends when employment ends. There are no notice requirements. Once employment has ended, eviction procedures can be used to remove the former employee. (RPAPL Sec. 713 (11).)

EARLY TERMINATION BY TENANT

Unless certain circumstances exist, a tenant who vacates the property before the end of the lease term is liable for any unpaid rent through the end of the lease term. The following situations will allow a tenant to end the lease early without such liability.

Damage or Destruction of Premises

If the premises are damaged or destroyed other than by wrongful or negligent acts of the tenant, and if the premises are untenantable and unfit for occupancy, the tenant may immediately vacate the premises and terminate the rental. (For more information, see "Destruction of the Premises" on page 74.)

Breach by Landlord

If the landlord materially fails to comply with his or her maintenance obligations or with the terms of the lease, including failing to provide essential services, the tenant may terminate the rental and vacate the premises. The word *materially* means that the noncompliance must be in a fairly serious or important way. If the tenant fails to leave promptly, this may waive the right to terminate early. (RPL Sec. 227.) It can occur when the warranty of habitability is breached, although it is not limited to this.

In nonresidential rentals, there is no warranty of habitability. When the landlord of nonresidential property wrongfully commits acts that deprive the tenant of the use and enjoyment of the premises such that the tenant is forced to leave the premises, it is known as *constructive eviction*. (*Rockrose Associates v. Peters*, 81 Misc.2d 971, 366 N.Y.S.2d 567 (City Civ. Ct. 1975).)

Senior Citizens If a tenant, or a tenant's spouse, is at least 62 years old (or will turn 62 during the rental term), the tenant has the right to terminate the lease if the tenant or spouse relocates to an adult care facility, residential care facility, subsidized low-income housing, or other senior citizen housing. The tenant must give written notice and provide documentation of admission or pending admission to one of the above-mentioned types of facilities. The termination is effective no earlier than thirty days after the next rental payment due date. (RPL Sec. 227-a.)

Military Service A tenant may terminate a lease to serve in the military if the tenant executed the lease before entering the military service, and the property has been occupied by the tenant or his or her dependents. Written notice is required. When rent is paid monthly, the lease will terminate thirty days after the date the next rental payment is due. For all other leases, the lease will terminate on the last day of the next month. (NY Military Law Secs. 309 & 310.)

EARLY TERMINATION BY LANDLORD

A landlord may terminate a tenancy before the end of the term for two reasons: nonpayment of rent or breach of the lease other than nonpayment of rent. The rules are the same for terminating residential and nonresidential tenancies.

The laws are very strict about terminating a tenancy, and if they are not followed, the landlord may lose the case and be required to pay the tenant's damages and attorney's fees. Be sure to read all of these instructions carefully and follow them exactly. The notice should use the exact wording shown.

Nonpayment of Rent

If either the landlord accepts rent or if the tenant pays rent after a known violation by the other party, that person has waived the right to terminate the rental for that rental period, but may terminate it the next time rent comes due if the violation continues.

Demand for rent. If the tenant fails to pay the rent, the landlord must either make an oral demand or send a **DEMAND FOR RENT**. A **DEMAND FOR RENT** must be served before any court can have jurisdiction over the case. There is no required form, although you may use the **DEMAND FOR RENT** in Appendix C. (see form 18, p.215.) A **DEMAND FOR RENT** need only include a good faith statement of the rent due, the period it is claimed for, and a demand for the tenant to pay the rent due or surrender possession. A nonpayment proceeding cannot be commenced unless this notice is sent. (RPALPL Sec. 711(2).) Nonpayment proceedings are discussed in Chapter 11, as are the methods you must use to have a tenant evicted and to obtain a judgment for back rent.

The rent demand must give the tenant at least three days to *cure* (fix) the nonpayment. If the tenant fails to pay, the landlord can commence a nonpayment proceeding and recover the rent due and/or evict the tenant. The written notice must be personally served upon the tenant or affixed to the door or other place where the tenant will easily see it. In a nonpayment proceeding, the tenancy is not legally terminated until a court declares it to be.

Attempts to pay. If a tenant attempts to pay the rent before the three-day notice is up, then the landlord must accept it. If the landlord wants to evict the tenant anyway, the only way to do it is if the tenant violates another clause in the lease. (See the subsection on "Breach of Lease" on page 84.) If the tenant attempts to pay the rent after the tenancy has been terminated (after the three days are up), the landlord does not have to accept it. The landlord has the option of executing a written agreement allowing the tenant to remain and waiving the right to evict the tenant during the period the agreement covers. (RPAPL Sec. 711(2).)

Acceptance of rent. If the landlord accepts rent with the knowledge that the tenant is not complying with some aspect of the lease, the landlord waives the right to evict for that noncompliance. (*Silverstein v. Empire State Shoe Co.*, 20 A.D.2d 735, 246 N.Y.S.2d 832 (3d Dept. 1964).) A lease provision stating that acceptance of rent with knowledge of a breach of the lease does not constitute a waiver of the breach has been upheld as enforceable. (*Jefpaul Garage Corp. v. Presbyterian Hosp. In City of New York*, 61 N.Y.2d 442, 474 N.Y.S.2d 458 (1984).)

Timing of notice. The **DEMAND FOR RENT** must be made after the rent becomes delinquent, but before a nonpayment proceeding is commenced. (*Meyers v. Knights of Pythias Bronx Temple Ass'n.*, 194 App.Div. 405, 185 N.Y.S. 436 (1st Dept. 1920).)

If the rent demanded in the notice is paid and the tenant becomes delinquent for rent for another period, a new notice must be served.

Breach of Lease

If the lease provides, it may be cancelled if the tenant violates a substantial obligation of the lease. A substantial violation is:

✪ something defined in the lease as a substantial violation or

✪ a violation of the lease that would cause harm or injury to the landlord or the premises. (*Park East Land Corp. v. Finkelstein*, 299 N.Y. 70 (1949).)

Some examples of violations of substantial obligations include:

✪ altering the premises (*Rumiche Corp. v. Eisenreich*, 40 N.Y.2d 174, 386 N.Y.S.2d 208 (1976));

✪ subletting or assigning without permission (RPL Sec. 226-a);

✪ failing to provide a duplicate key (*Lavanant v. Lovelace*, 71 Misc.2d 974, 337 N.Y.S.2d 962 (1st Dept. 1973));

✪ failing to pay rent (*National Shoes, Inc. v. Annex Camera*, 114 Misc.2d 751, 452 N.Y.S.2d 537 (Civ. Ct., N.Y. County 1982)); and,

✪ failing to give a security deposit. (*Park Holding Co. v. Johnson*, 106 Misc.2d 834, 435 N.Y.S.2d 479 (Civ. Ct., N.Y. County 1980).)

Immoral or illegal use. A landlord is allowed to terminate a lease if the tenant uses the premises for prostitution or other illegal or immoral activities, such as:

- ✪ selling drugs (*City of New York v. Wright*, 222 A.D.2d 374, 636 N.Y.S.2d 33 (1st Dept. 1995));

- ✪ operating a sex club (*31 West 21st Street Assoc. v. Evening of the Unusual*, 125 Misc.2d 661, 480 N.Y.S.2d 816 (Civ. Ct., N.Y. County, 1984)); or,

- ✪ engaging in illegal trade. (RPL Sec. 231(1).)

Nuisance or objectionable conduct. A lease may be terminated for the tenant creating a *nuisance*, defined as a continuous or pervasive condition that threatens the health, safety, or comfort of neighbors or other building occupants. (*1021-27 Avenue St. John Housing Dev. Fund Corp. v. Hernandez*, 154 Misc.2d 141, 584 N.Y.S.2d 990 (Civ. Ct., Bronx County 1992).) *Objectionable conduct* includes profanity, nudity, and other offensive acts that cause a nuisance. (*Frank v. Park Summitt Realty Corp.*, 175 A.D.2d 33, 573 N.Y.S.2d 655 (1st Dept. 1991).)

Rent-regulated tenancies. Rent-regulated tenancies may also be terminated for other reasons, as discussed in Chapter 4.

Notice of default. When a tenant breaches the lease, and the breach could cause harm or damage to the landlord or the premises, the landlord may terminate the tenancy. To do so, first the landlord must serve the tenant with a **NOTICE OF DEFAULT**. (see form 20, p.219.) This notice tells the tenant the lease has been breached, and must include:

- ✪ the nature of the violation;

- ✪ direction to the tenant to cure the violation within a specific period; and,

- ✪ the consequence of the failure to cure (the consequence is termination of the tenancy).

The **NOTICE OF DEFAULT** gives the tenant a certain number of days to fix the violation or the landlord will take steps to terminate the tenancy. The lease specifies how many days are required for a **NOTICE OF DEFAULT**. In rent-regulated units, ten days' notice is required.

Notice of termination. If the tenant fails to cure the violation, the landlord must serve the tenant with a **NOTICE OF TERMINATION**. (see form 22, p.223.) The **NOTICE OF TERMINATION** must be timely, definite, and unequivocal. (*City of Buffalo Urban Renewal Agency v. Lane Bryant Queens, Inc.*, 90 A.D.2d 976, 4456 N.Y.S.2d 568 (4th Dept. 1982).) It may not contain any conclusory, misleading, or equivocal language. (*Spencer v. Faulkner*, 65 Misc.2d 298, 317 N.Y.S.2d 374 (Civ. Ct., Kings County, 1971).) The **NOTICE OF TERMINATION** must state that the violation has continued and that the time to cure has expired. It must give facts that establish the breach. The **NOTICE OF TERMINATION** gives the tenant a certain number of days before the lease will terminate. Regardless of whether the tenant vacates by the date stated in the notice, the lease is terminated on that date. If the tenant does not leave, a holdover proceeding can be commenced (because the tenant is holding over after the lease has ended). This notice must also be served on someone who is not a tenant the landlord wishes to evict or remove.

The required number of days for notice varies, depending on the location of the property and the type of tenancy, as follows.

- ✪ Tenancy at will (indefinite term): thirty days

- ✪ No tenancy at all: ten days

- ✪ In New York City:

  - • Month-to-month tenancy: thirty days

- ✪ Outside of New York City:

  - • Month-to-month tenancy: one calendar month

  - • Rent-regulated tenancy: ten days

- ✪ New York City rent-stabilized:

    - Violation of substantial obligation (including nuisance, illegal occupancy, illegal/immoral use, illegal subletting): seven days

    - Refusal to renew: fifteen days

- ✪ Outside New York City rent-stabilized:

    - Refusal to renew: fifteen days

    - Violation of substantial obligation: one month

- ✪ Rent control weekly tenant: two days

If the unit is rent-regulated, notices must also be filed with the DHCR. A Certificate of Eviction must be obtained from the DHCR before any tenancy can be terminated. If the unit is rent-stabilized, the **NOTICE OF DEFAULT** and **NOTICE OF TERMINATION** can be combined into one form. When this is done, the tenant has ten days to cure from the date of service, or the tenancy is terminated thirty days after the service.

After serving the tenant with a **NOTICE OF TERMINATION**, a landlord must serve the tenant with a **TEN-DAY NOTICE TO QUIT** (form 21, p.221), which gives the tenant ten days to vacate the property. Next, a **NOTICE OF PETITION** and a **PETITION** must be served in order to commence a holdover proceeding. (see form 23, 24, or 25 and form 29, p.237.) (See the section in Chapter 11 on "Court Procedures.")

SPECIAL RULES FOR PUBLIC HOUSING

Public housing is governed by federal law. All statutory citations given in this section are for federal statutes.

For nonpayment of rent, the landlord must give the tenant fourteen days' notice, rather than a ten-day notice, and the notice must be mailed or hand-delivered, not posted. (24 C.F.R. 866.4(1)(2).) The notice must inform the tenant of the right to a grievance procedure. At least one court has held that both a fourteen-day notice and a three-day notice must be given. (*Stanton v. Housing Authority of Pittsburgh*, 469 F.Supp. 1013 (W.D.Pa. 1977).) However, other courts have disagreed. (*Ferguson v. Housing Authority of Middleboro*, 499 F.Supp. 334 (E.D. Ky. 1980).)

✪   The public housing authority must prove both that the tenant did not pay the rent and that the tenant was at fault for not paying it. (*Maxton Housing Authority v. McLean*, 328 S.E.2d (N.C. 1985).)

✪   A Louisiana court held that a tenant was not at fault because her former husband did not pay the child support. (*Housing Authority of City of New Iberia v. Austin*, 478 So.2d 1012 (La.App. 1986) writ denied, 481 So.2d 1334 (La. 1986).)

✪   One Florida court held that posting both a fourteen-day notice and a state-required three-day notice is too confusing. It suggested that the landlord only use a fourteen-day notice or else deliver the three-day notice so that the deadline is the same as for the fourteen-day notice. (*Broward Co. Housing Authority v. Simmons*, 4 F.L.W.Supp. 494 (Co.Ct. Broward 1996).)

Federally Subsidized Section 236 Apartments

For breach of the terms of the lease other than payment of rent, a thirty-day notice must be given, except in emergencies, and it must inform the tenant of the reasons for termination, the tenant's right to reply, and the tenant's right to a grievance procedure. (24 C.F.R. 366(4)(1).) If the tenant requests a grievance hearing, a second notice must be given, even if the tenant loses in the hearing. (*Ferguson v. Housing Authority of Middleboro*, 499 F.Supp. 432 (E.D. Ky. 1980).)

For nonpayment of rent in federally subsidized Section 236 apartments, tenants must be given the ten-day notice and be advised that if there is a judicial proceeding, they can present a valid defense, if any. Service must be by first-class mail, hand-delivered, or placed under the door of the apartment. (24 C.F.R. 450.4(a).)

For breach of the terms of the lease other than nonpayment of rent, the tenant must first have been given notice that in the future, such conduct would be grounds for terminating the lease. The notice of termination must state when the tenancy will be terminated and specifically why it is being terminated, and it must advise the tenant of the right to present a defense in the eviction suit. (24 C.F.R. 450.)

The legal provision that acceptance or payment of rent is a waiver of past noncompliance does not apply to the portion of the rent that is subsidized. However, waiver will occur if legal action is not taken within forty-five days.

Section 8 Subsidized Apartments For Section 8 housing, under 24 C.F.R. 882.215(c)(4), the landlord must notify the housing authority in writing at the commencement of the eviction proceedings. Also, the previous paragraph on acceptance of rent applies to Section 8 housing.

DEATH OF A TENANT

When a tenant dies, the tenancy does not end. The lease becomes part of the tenant's estate, which then becomes responsible for the rent. (RPL Sec. 236.)

OPTIONS TO CANCEL

It is permissible for a lease to permit the landlord or tenant to cancel the lease for certain reasons, such as the sale of the property, alterations to the premises, the happening of an agreed-upon event, or simply whenever either party wishes.

✪ A lease provision allowing termination of the lease by the landlord upon the sale of the property is permissible. (*Miller v Levi*, 44 N.Y 489 (1871).)

✪ A lease provision allowing termination by the landlord, even if the tenant has paid rent in advance, is enforceable. (*In re Szpakowski*, 166 A.D. 578, 151 N.Y.S. 211 (4th Dept. 1915).)

✪ In exercising an option to terminate, a landlord must state in the termination notice what clause is being invoked, or the option is not considered invoked. (*Perrotta v. Western Regional Off-Track Betting Corp.*, 98 A.D.2d 1, 469 N.Y.S.2d 504 (4th Dept. 1983).)

Evicting a Tenant

A tenant who fails to pay rent or otherwise violates the lease may be evicted, but only after the landlord obtains a court order. The New York eviction process works at different speeds in different parts of the state. Much depends on the judge who hears the case. In some cases tenants' lawyers have abused the system and allowed nonpaying tenants to remain in possession for months, but most of the time the system allows delinquent tenants to be removed quickly.

SELF-HELP BY LANDLORD

The only way a landlord may recover possession of a dwelling unit is if the tenant voluntarily surrenders it to the landlord or abandons it, or if the landlord gets a court order giving the landlord possession. Landlords are forbidden to use self-help methods to evict tenants, even if the lease allows it, unless the premises is occupied by a *squatter* (a person with no legal right to be on the property).

Even after the landlord gets a court order for eviction, only a sheriff, marshal, or constable can carry out that order and remove the tenant. (RPAPL Sec. 749.) As explained under "Retaliatory Conduct" on page 72, if a landlord terminates utilities such as water, electricity, gas, elevators, lights, garbage collection, or refrigeration—or if the landlord locks up the unit or takes off the doors, windows, roofs, walls, and so on—the landlord can be held liable for breaching the warranty of habitability, for triple damages, and possibly for court costs and attorney's fees. In addition, the tenant will be allowed to move back into the property. In New York City, there are also criminal penalties for using illegal methods to force out a tenant.

✪ In a Missouri case, a landlord took the refrigerator, washing machine, and stove because the tenant failed to pay rent. The tenant was awarded $10,000 in damages. (*Smiley v. Cardin*, 655 S.W.2d 114 (Mo.Ct.App. 1983).)

✪ In a District of Columbia case, purchasers of a tax deed to property kept changing the locks on the property, nailing the door shut, and nailing "for sale" signs on the property when the occupant was away, in order to force the occupant to sue, so that the government would have to defend their tax deed. A jury awarded the occupant $250,000 in punitive damages. The appeals court upheld the verdict. (*Robinson v. Sarisky*, 535 A.2d 901 (D.C.App. 1988).)

✪ In a Florida case, a landlord posted a three-day notice. When the tenant was absent from the premises, the landlord entered and removed the tenant's possessions. In a lawsuit, the tenant testified that her possessions were all heirlooms and antiques. Since the landlord had disposed of them, he could not prove otherwise. The tenant was awarded $31,000 in damages. (*Reynolds v. Towne Mgt. of Fla., Inc.*, 426 So.2d 1011 (Fla. 2 DCA 1983).)

SURRENDER OR ABANDONMENT

To surrender a dwelling, a tenant must either tell the landlord that he or she is leaving or leave the keys. Courts try to determine the tenant's intent when it is unclear if there has been abandonment. It can be presumed that a tenant abandoned the dwelling if the tenant has been absent for half of the rental term (unless the rent is current or notice is given).

NOTE: *In some cases, such as when all of a tenant's possessions are gone and the electricity has been turned off, a landlord might be safe in assuming abandonment, but in the unlikely event that it went to court, the landlord could still lose.*

SETTLING WITH THE TENANT

In most New York evictions, the tenants do not answer the complaint and the landlord wins quickly; however, some tenants can create nightmares for landlords. Clever tenants and legal aid lawyers can delay the case for months, and vindictive tenants can destroy the property with little worry of ever having to paying for it. Therefore, in some cases a landlord may be wise to offer the tenant a cash settlement to leave. For example, a tenant may be offered $200 to be out of the premises and leave it clean within a week. Of course, it hurts to give money to a tenant who already owes you money, but it could be cheaper than the court costs, vacancy time, and damage to the premises.

GROUNDS FOR EVICTION

A tenant can be evicted for violating one of the terms of the lease, for failing to pay rent, or for failing to leave at the end of the lease. The most common violation of the lease is that the tenant has failed to pay the rent, but a tenant can also be evicted for violating other terms of the lease or rental agreement, such as disturbing other tenants.

When a tenancy is terminated, it means that the legal obligations of the lease end. However, this is only the first step in removing a tenant. After the tenancy is terminated, specific eviction procedures must be followed.

There are two procedures for eviction in New York:

1. a *nonpayment proceeding*, and

2. a *holdover proceeding*.

These two procedures are explained in the following sections.

NONPAYMENT PROCEEDINGS

When a tenant has failed to pay rent, the landlord must make an oral demand for payment or serve a written **DEMAND FOR RENT** (form 18, p.215) telling the tenant to pay the rent within three days, as described in Chapter 10. After the demand has been made, if the tenant fails to pay within the three days, a landlord can serve and file a **NOTICE OF PETITION** (form 26, p.231, form 27, p.233, or form 28, p.235) and a **NONPAYMENT PETITION** (form 30, p.241).

If the landlord seeks a judgment of possession in the **NONPAYMENT PETITION** and it is granted by the court, the tenancy is terminated and the tenant can then be evicted. Back rent can also be collected in a nonpayment proceeding.

HOLDOVER PROCEEDINGS

When the tenant has breached the lease, the landlord must serve the tenant with a **NOTICE OF DEFAULT** (form 20, p.219), **NOTICE OF TERMINATION** (form 22, p.223), and **TEN-DAY NOTICE TO QUIT** (form 21, p.221). After these forms have been served properly and the date given in the **TEN-DAY NOTICE TO QUIT** has passed, a holdover proceeding may be commenced to evict the tenant. This is discussed in more detail on page 75.

USING AN ATTORNEY

If the lease provides, the loser in a landlord/tenant case can be charged with the winner's attorney's fees. Because of this, it is important to handle an eviction carefully. The tenant may just be waiting for the eviction notice before leaving the premises, and in such a case, the landlord may regain the premises no matter what kind of papers he or she files. However, in some cases, tenants with no money and no defenses retain free lawyers, paid for by tax dollars, who find technical defects in the case. This can cause a delay in the eviction and cause the landlord to be ordered to pay the tenant's attorney's fees. A simple error in a landlord's court papers can cost him or her the case.

A landlord facing an eviction should consider the costs and benefits of using an attorney compared to doing it without an attorney. One possibility is to file the case without an attorney and hope the tenant moves. If the tenant stays and fights the case, an attorney can be hired to finish the case. Some landlords who prefer to do their evictions themselves start by paying a lawyer for a half-hour or hour of the attorney's time to review the facts of the case and point out problems.

Whenever a tenant has an attorney, the landlord should also have one.

- ✪ In one case, a winning tenant was awarded $8,675 in attorney's fees, which were calculated at $150 an hour and then doubled.

- ✪ In a suit by a cooperative association against a tenant for $191.33 in maintenance fees and to enforce the association rules, the tenant won the suit and was awarded $87,375 in attorney's fees.

It is important to find an attorney who both knows landlord/tenant law and charges reasonable fees. There are many subtleties of the law that can be missed by someone without experience. Some attorneys who specialize in landlord/tenant work charge very modest fees, such as $75 or $100 to file the case, and the same amount for a short hearing, unless the case gets complicated. Others charge an hourly rate that can add up to thousands of dollars. Check with other landlords or a local apartment association for names of good attorneys, or try calling the manager of a large apartment complex in the area.

If you get a security deposit at the beginning of the tenancy and start the eviction immediately upon a default, the deposit should be enough to cover the attorney's fee.

WHO CAN SUE?

An owner can represent him- or herself in court and does not need an attorney. The landlord must bring the case him- or herself, although the landlord may, of course, hire an attorney. As a general rule, no one can represent another person in court except a licensed attorney, and only an attorney can represent a corporation. Not even a corporate officer can represent a corporation. It is a criminal offense for a non-lawyer to represent another party in court.

COURT PROCEDURES

After either a Demand for Rent (in a nonpayment proceeding) or a Notice of Default, Notice of Termination, and Ten-Day Notice to Quit (in a holdover proceeding) have been served, and the tenant has not remedied the problem in the allotted time period, the landlord must seek the assistance of the court to proceed any further. Landlord/tenant cases are called *summary proceedings* because they are meant to proceed more quickly than other civil cases. A summary proceeding is commenced by serving the tenant with a **NOTICE OF PETITION** and **PETITION**.

Notice of Petition

When the court issues the **NOTICE OF PETITION**, you must purchase an index number. Ask the clerk for that court's form to request an index number. Depending on which court you are in, you may also have to file a *Request for Judicial Intervention* (available from the clerk) and pay an additional fee. The clerk will tell you if this is necessary.

The **NOTICE OF PETITION** basically gives information about who the parties are, which court is hearing the case, and when the tenant must appear. In Appendix C, there is a **NOTICE OF PETITION** for a holdover proceeding (form 23, 24, or 25, depending upon the court), and a different **NOTICE OF PETITION** for a nonpayment proceeding (form 26, 27, or 28, depending upon the court). The Notice of Petition can only be issued by a court or an attorney (but in New York City Civil Court, it can only be issued by the court), so if you are not working with an attorney, you must fill out the form, leaving the time of the hearing blank, and go to the court clerk's office and ask them to complete it. The **NOTICE OF PETITION** will be returned to you for you to serve on the tenant with the **PETITION**.

Petition   The **PETITION** gives specifics about the location of the rental property, what the problem is, what notices have been served, and if the property is rent-regulated. There is a **HOLDOVER PETITION** (form 29, p.237) and a **NONPAYMENT PETITION** (form 30, p.241). The **PETITION** must contain the following information to be valid:

- ✪ the identities of the plaintiff (landlord) and defendants (tenants and subtenants);

- ✪ the date the lease began, date the lease expires, and date the parties signed the lease (if oral, the date they agreed);

- ✪ the full address, including apartment or unit number of the premises;

- ✪ the facts the proceeding is based on;

- ✪ when any Rent Demands, Default Notices, or Termination Notices were served (copies of the notices served and their affidavits of service should be attached to the Petition);

- ✪ whether the premises is a multiple dwelling, and if so, whether it is properly registered as one (attach a copy of the registration); and,

- ✪ whether the property is rent-regulated and whether or not it is in compliance with the applicable laws.

The petitions in this book allege that the tenant is not in the military service. If your tenant is in the military, you will need an attorney.

Verification   All petitions must be verified. Attach the **VERIFICATION** (form 31, p.245) to any petition you file with the court.

Service   The **NOTICE OF PETITION** and **PETITION** must be served on the tenant in one of the following three manners:

1. personally served on the tenant;

2. served on someone of suitable age and discretion at the residence or place of work of the tenant, and mailed by certified or registered mail and regular mail; or,

3. affixed in a conspicuous place and mailed by certified or registered mail and regular mail (this method, known as *nail and mail*, may only be used if due diligence has been used to attempt the other two methods).

You can pay your local sheriff (civil division) to serve the papers, or you can hire a process server (listed in the Yellow Pages). Whoever serves the papers must complete an *Affidavit of Service*, which must be filed with the court.

Submission to the Court   Once the papers have been served, they must be filed with the court clerk of the court you are utilizing. The Affidavit of Service must be filed as well. File one copy, and keep one copy of each document for your records. Be sure to have the clerk stamp your copy "filed" so that you have proof of the filing. Be sure to file your papers five days before the court date, or your case could be dismissed. (RPAPL Sec. 735(b).)

If the case is in New York City Civil Court and is a residential case, stamped postcards addressed to all the defendants must be submitted to the court with the papers.

Waiting Period   After the papers have been served, the defendant has five days to respond (in New York City nonpayment proceedings) or three days to respond (outside New York City in nonpayment proceedings). A defendant who responds will typically do so by filing an *answer*, which usually denies everything in the Petition. In holdover proceedings, an answer must be received three days before the court date if the Petition was served eight days before the court date, but only if the Petition requests an answer. If not, an answer may be made orally at the court appearance. Some judges may allow the tenant to give an informal answer to your petition, such as to verbally deny that the rent is owed. Normally, you should object to this and ask that the tenant provide a specific answer in writing. However, if it appears that this may turn the judge against you, it may not be a good idea. If the judge seems predisposed to help the tenant, you should seek the assistance of an attorney.

Court Appearances

If the tenant does not respond or appear—if he or she *defaults*—you must make a **MOTION FOR DEFAULT**. (see form 38, p.259.) You may do this orally by telling the judge you wish to move for default based on the tenant's failure to appear, or you may prepare it in writing and have it with you if you suspect the tenant will default. However, you must be prepared to give the judge some kind of proof that you are right. The judge will usually not grant a default motion at the initial appearance and will set a date for an *inquest* (trial), at which only you would appear and briefly explain your case. Unless you have no proof whatsoever, you will most likely win.

If the tenant does answer, you will go forward with the summary proceeding. You should always be prepared to have a hearing at the first appearance. Most courts do not do so, but it is best to be prepared. In nonpayment proceedings, the hearing date is in your papers. In holdover proceedings, you must contact the judge's secretary for a trial date. You should request about fifteen minutes of time and the secretary should be able to fit you in within a week or two. If the tenant comes with an attorney and you were not notified that he or she retained an attorney, you can request that the court date be rescheduled in order for you to hire an attorney. If the tenant has an attorney, you should get one as well, because even a small mistake by you could cost you the case and you could be liable for attorney's fees. An occasional bad tenant is a risk of investing in real property, and the cost of court appearances should be factored into your return. Screen your tenants better or get a bigger deposit next time. At any time during the proceeding, you can tell the judge you have decided you want an attorney.

Depositing rent with the court. If the tenant does appear, he or she cannot present any defenses to the case unless he or she has deposited rent with the court clerk for use and occupancy charges during the proceeding (basically, the tenant must put up the money for the rent during the time the case progresses). (RPAPL Sec. 745(2)(a).) The court may waive this requirement if the tenant can show good cause. A tenant may still make a *Motion to Dismiss* (asking the court to dismiss the case because your Petition did not contain all it should), even if rent has not been deposited.

Trial   If a trial is held, you must go through each paragraph of your Petition and prove every single fact in it. You may call witnesses, produce documents, and testify under oath yourself. Be sure to present an original copy of the lease and any notices you served on the tenant.

After you present your side, the tenant will have a chance to *rebut* (disprove) the evidence you presented by asking your witnesses questions, testifying, and presenting his or her own documents and witnesses (whom you will have a chance to question).

After you have presented your side of the case, you may wish to make a *Motion for Summary Judgment*, which states that there is no triable issue of fact and that judgment should be awarded to you. The tenant may make the same type of motion, asking that judgment be awarded to him or her. A motion for summary judgment basically says that the parties do not disagree about any of the important facts, and it is simply a matter of what the law says. A **NOTICE OF MOTION FOR SUMMARY JUDGMENT** (form 37, p.257) appears in Appendix C.

Some tenants try to buy time by requesting a hearing on the validity of the service. If this happens, you must have the process server testify and present records.

NOTE: *Occasionally, someone will write to us and say that they followed this book, but the judge gave the tenants extra time to move, or let them speak without posting rent into the court. Remember, most times a case will go smoothly, but judges do make mistakes. If your case gets complicated, you should invest in an experienced landlord/tenant attorney who can finish your case quickly.*

Seeking damages. More information about obtaining a money judgment against the tenant is contained in Chapter 12. However, you should read that section before filing your eviction, since some of the forms in the eviction will be different.

Public housing. In Section 8 housing, under the Code of Federal Regulations Sec. 882.215(c)(4), the local housing authority must be notified in writing before the tenant can be served with the eviction.

Courtroom etiquette. Always refer to the judge as "Your Honor." You should stand when speaking to the judge. Do not speak to the tenant, unless he or she is testifying and you question him or her, or if the tenant questions you. Do not argue with the tenant. Refer to the tenant as "Mr. ___" or "Ms. ___." Try not to become angry or upset in court, as it makes it more difficult to get your facts across to the judge.

Never interrupt the judge. You may interrupt the tenant only to make a legal objection. This is how you let the court know that whatever the tenant or a witness has said violates courtroom rules. One rule that is often broken is called the *hearsay rule*. A person can only testify about something he or she learned about by seeing or hearing it first-hand—not about something that someone else told him or her.

Mediation

In some areas, mediation services are recommended or required before trial. A mediator is a neutral third party who works with the parties to come to a mutually agreed-upon solution. Successful mediation results in an agreement that solves the dispute without having to go to court. The parties are encouraged to resolve their differences at mediation. This may mean a planned date of departure for the tenant or perhaps allowing the tenant to stay in the premises with a timetable for paying the back rent. In some cases, damage to the premises or animosity between the parties may make it impossible to continue the tenancy. If a settlement is reached, it should be in the form of a stipulation, which is filed with the court, as described in the following paragraphs. If you merely dismiss your case as part of the settlement, you will have to start all over from scratch if the tenant again defaults.

Stipulation

Regardless of whether mediation is used, the parties may be able to resolve the matter without going through a hearing. This will allow the landlord to recover some back rent and avoid the hassle of cleaning and re-renting the unit. If you wish to settle with the tenant and come to an agreement that the rent will be paid over time, you can enter into a *stipulation* to delay the case. You should never accept any rent from the tenant once the case is filed without signing a stipulation. A stipulation may be made orally on the record in court, or written or typed and submitted to the court. Forms to write the stipulation on are available from the court. A sample **STIPULATION** that settles a holdover proceeding with an agreement to cure is form 33, found on page 249. A sample **STIPULATION** that settles a holdover proceeding by agreeing to vacate is form 34, on page 251. Stipulations for nonpayment proceedings are also included. (see form 35, p.253 and form 36, p.255.)

A stipulation may state that the parties will return to court if there is a default, that a money judgment is due, that possession is given to the landlord, and that a warrant of eviction is stayed. It may provide that a stayed warrant of eviction be issued upon future default. When a stipulation is made, it cannot be appealed by either party.

Warrant of Eviction

If you win your case, the court may ask you to prepare the **JUDGMENT** (form 39, p.261) and submit it for the judge's signature. (In New York City, the court will prepare it.) After you get it back, send a copy to the tenant. This may be enough to get the tenant to move. If possession has been awarded to you, the court will issue a **WARRANT OF EVICTION**. (see form 41, p.265.) The warrant cancels the lease (if not already terminated by the landlord) and allows a law enforcement officer, for a fee, to take back possession for the landlord.

The law enforcement agent first serves the tenant with a **72-HOUR NOTICE OF EVICTION**. (see form 40, p.263.) After the time expires, the law enforcement agent will evict the tenant. Different counties have different procedures for the removal of the tenant's possessions. Check with your local sheriff.

STAYING THE EVICTION

Anytime before a warrant is issued, it may be stayed if the tenant pays the rent due, plus interest and costs, by depositing it with the court. (RPAPL Sec. 751(1).) The tenant may also submit an undertaking with the court, securing that the amount due will be paid in ten days. After a warrant is issued, it cannot be stayed, but can be vacated for good cause.

✪   A tenant was wrongfully denied welfare, causing rent arrears. The tenant became employed after the judgment and could pay the amount due. Good cause was found and the warrant was vacated. (*Anthony Associated v. Montgomery*, 149 Misc.2d 731, 567 N.Y.S.2d 200 (Civ. Ct., Bronx County 1991).)

✪   A tenant filed for bankruptcy after the warrant was issued. This was not good cause. (*Radol v. Centeno*, 165 Misc.2d 448, 627 N.Y.S.2d 887 (Civ. Ct., Queens County 1995).)

After a warrant is issued, do not accept rent arrears unless you and the tenant agree to reinstate the tenancy, or unless you have a written agreement with the tenant that the payment and acceptance will not impact the judgment of possession and the warrant. Use the **Stipulation After Warrant**. (see form 42, p.267.)

In New York City, a warrant must be stayed for ten days if the case was based on a breach of the lease. (RPAPL Sec. 753(4).) This gives the tenant another chance to cure. A warrant in New York City may be stayed for up to six months if the tenant cannot find a comparable new place to live after making reasonable efforts, or when extreme hardship would result to the tenant if the stay was not granted. (RPAPL Sec. 753(1).) This does not apply to a premises being demolished. (RPAPL Sec. 753(3).)

Outside New York City, the warrant may be stayed for up to four months for this reason.

Commercial tenants have no statutory entitlement to a stay, but may obtain one where when the court finds it to be just. (*Pepsi-Cola Metropolitan Bottling Co. v. Miller*, 50 Misc.2d 40, 269 N.Y.S.2d 471 (Civ. Ct., Bronx County 1966).)

Yellowstone Injunctions   A tenant can seek an injunction freezing the parties in their current positions so the tenant has extra time to cure. This is called a *Yellowstone injunction*, named after the case of *First National Stores v. Yellowstone Shopping Center*, 21 N.Y.2d 630, 290 N.Y.S.2d 721 (1968). The request for this injunction must be made before the time to cure expires. It may not be used after a demand for rent has been served.

MONEY DAMAGES AND BACK RENT

Procedures for collecting money damages and back rent from a tenant are explained in Chapter 12.

TENANT'S POSSIBLE DEFENSES

A tenant who is behind in rent usually has one objective: to stay in the property rent-free as long as possible. Tenants, and the lawyers provided to them at no charge by legal aid clinics, sometimes come up with creative, though ridiculous, defenses. Following are some arguments and case law to help defeat their arguments. Remember, the tenant should not be able to bring up any defenses unless he or she filed an answer (or gave an oral answer in New York City) and deposited rent with the court.

Constitutionality A tenant claims it is unconstitutional to have a quick eviction procedure and to require the tenant to pay the rent into the court before he or she is allowed to present any defenses. The U.S. Supreme Court says that such procedures can be constitutional. (*Lindsey v. Normet*, 465 U.S. 56 (1972).)

Security Deposit A claim by a tenant that the security deposit covers a rent default is incorrect because a security deposit is for a specific purpose at the end of the tenancy and does not cover rent.

Amount Incorrect A dispute by a tenant over the amount of rent due is not a defense, because if any rent is due, the landlord is entitled to eviction in a nonpayment proceeding. However, if the amount stated in the three-day notice is wrong, the case may be dismissed.

Title A defense that the landlord has not proved that he or she has good title to the property is not valid. A tenant who has entered into a rental agreement with a landlord is *estopped* from denying that the landlord has good title.

Fictitious Name A tenant may raise as a defense that in dealings with the tenant the landlord is using a fictitious name that has not been registered with the county. If the landlord actually is using an unregistered name, the case is abated until he or she complies with the statute, but in order to use this defense, the tenant must raise the issue no later than in his or her written answer to the petition.

Corporation Is Dissolved

Under New York corporate law, a court action may not be maintained by a corporation that is not in good standing with the New York Department of State. If your corporation has been dissolved for nonpayment of fees, it can be reinstated by paying the previous year's fees and a penalty. There are companies in Albany that will hand-deliver your payment to the secretary of state and send you a certificate of good standing immediately. (See *How to Form a Corporation in New York*, by Brette McWhorter Sember and Mark Warda, available through your local bookstore or at **www.sphinxlegal.com**.)

Corporation Not Represented by Attorney

If the landlord is a corporation, it must be represented by an attorney. If the corporation is not represented by an attorney, the suit may be dismissed.

Waiver by Refusal

A refusal by the landlord to accept rent after the three-day period has ended is not a waiver of rent. While the landlord does have to give the tenant three days to pay all past-due rent, he or she does not have to accept rent after the three-day grace period expires. If it is accepted, the acceptance is a waiver, and a nonpayment proceeding cannot continue. (*Wessenvogel v. Becker,* 79 N.Y.S.2d 526 (1948).) Usually, if a landlord accepts rent after serving a notice or filing suit, he or she waives the right to continue the lawsuit, and must serve a new notice or file a new suit.

Holdover proceeding. Acceptance of rent after termination of the tenancy and before the commencement of the summary proceeding waives the termination and reinstates the lease. (RPL Sec. 232-c.)

Jurisdiction

The tenant may challenge the jurisdiction of the court to hear the case (for example, if the premises is not in the area covered by the court, or if there is a claimed defect in the landlord's papers). If the petition is misleading and looks like a court order evicting the tenant, the case may be dismissed. (*Chalfonte Realty Corp. v. Streater*, 142 Misc.2d 501, 537 N.Y.S.2d 980 (Civ.Ct., N.Y. County, 1989).)

No Building Registration

If the landlord has failed to register the building as a multiple dwelling in New York City, the case may be dismissed. (MDL Sec. 325;

Third Avenue Corp. v. Fifth Avenue Community Center of Harlem, 164 Misc.2d 257, 623 N.Y.S.2d 1011 (Civ. Ct., N.Y. County, 1995).)

Modification of a Lease Even though most leases contain a clause prohibiting oral modification, if an oral modification is made for reduced rent, it is binding if the reduced rent has been accepted. (*Central Savings Bank v. Fashoda, Inc.*, 94 A.D.2d 927, 463 N.Y.S.2d 335 (3d Dept. 1983).)

Eviction If the tenant has actually been ousted, it is a defense. Constructive eviction (see page 53) is also a defense tenants can use (the theory being that you cannot ask a court to evict someone who has already been evicted).

Laches When the landlord waits too long to sue for back rent, the doctrine of *laches* prohibits recovery. Usually, if a landlord waits more than three months to attempt to collect, it is defense.

Violations Outside New York City, a tenant may raise violations by the landlord as a defense. In New York City it is not a defense, as the tenant can commence a Housing Part Proceeding, seeking to have the court direct the landlord to make repairs. (N.Y.C. Admin. Code 27-2001, et seq.) Other municipalities have their own housing maintenance codes that can be enforced in similar ways.

Regulation Z A claim by a tenant that the landlord has not complied with Regulation Z in the Code of Federal Regulations is not a valid defense. This is a truth-in-lending requirement, but this federal regulation does not apply to the rental of property. (12 C.F.R. Sec. 226.1(c)(1).)

Unconscionable Rent A claim that rent is unconscionable is a legal conclusion, and a tenant must state facts that would prove to the court that the rent is unconscionable before it becomes a valid defense.

Retaliatory Eviction A retaliatory eviction for some lawful action is illegal under RPL Sec. 223-b. This defense does not apply if the landlord is evicting the tenant in good cause, such as for nonpayment of rent, violation of the lease or reasonable rules, or violation of landlord/tenant law.

Discovery The tenant does not have a right to *discovery* (to ask questions of the landlord and any witnesses under oath before a court reporter) in a summary proceeding, unless court permission is granted. (CPLR Sec. 408.)

Jury Trial If a tenant makes a request for a jury trial, then he or she should be required to first post the past rent and any rent that comes due during the pendency of the suit. If there is a jury presently impaneled, then it should go to that jury, and if not, one should be immediately summoned. The tenant must pay the costs of the jury.

Attorney Busy or Unprepared The tenant's attorney may say that he or she just got on the case and needs time to prepare, or has a busy schedule and is not available for trial for a month or so. This should not delay the case. The landlord has a right to a quick procedure under the RPAPL. If the tenant's attorney is unavailable, he or she should not have taken the case. Remember, if the tenant has a lawyer, you should have one too.

Attorney's Fees for Dismissal When a tenant moves out of the property, the landlord sometimes withdraws his or her case. In some cases, the tenants have then claimed that they should have their attorneys' fees paid because they were the prevailing party in the case. A tenant may recover attorney's fees only if the lease provides for it and if a judgment is made for the tenant.

If a landlord is handling his or her own eviction, he or she should not dismiss the case after the tenant moves out. The landlord should proceed to judgment at least for the court costs and to be officially granted possession. If the landlord is represented by an attorney, he or she will have to weigh the costs.

Grievance Procedure In federally subsidized housing, the regulations require that tenants be given a grievance procedure in some evictions. However, where the tenant is a threat to the health and safety of other tenants or employees, Title 24 C.F.R., Chapter 9, Sec. 966.51(a) states that such a hearing is not required.

TENANT'S POSSIBLE COUNTERSUITS

Another way a tenant may try to delay things is by filing a counter-suit, which can be included in the answer. This should not delay the eviction.

Exceeding Jurisdiction

Different courts in New York have different jurisdictional monetary limits. For example, New York City Civil Court can only hear cases for amounts under $25,000. Check with your court for its limit. Tenants sometimes ask for damages greater than this so the case will be transferred to supreme court and will take longer.

If the tenant seeks damages over $15,000, he or she must pay an extra filing fee to transfer the case. (CPLR, Art. 81.) If the case does make it to supreme court, it is usually transferred down to a lower court.

Warrant of Habitability

Counterclaims based on the warranty of habitability are permissible in nonpayment proceedings. (*Century Apartments, Inc. v. Yalkowsky*, 106 Misc.2d 762, 435 N.Y.S.2d 627 (Civ. Ct., N.Y. County, 1980).) Courts disagree as to whether this type of counterclaim is allowed in a holdover proceeding.

A minimum of one-third of the building's tenants are permitted to institute a suit against the landlord for the correction of dangerous conditions. (RPAPL, Article 7-A.) Tenants pay the rent to the court and the court appoints an administrator who uses the funds to correct the condition. Get an attorney if you are faced with a claim based on dangerous conditions.

Rent Overcharge

Rent-regulated tenants in nonpayment proceedings may recover damages for rent overcharge. (N.Y.C. Admin. Code 26-516, Unconsol. L. Sec. 8632(a)(1)(f).)

Retaliatory Eviction

In holdover proceedings, damages may be sought for retaliatory eviction. (RPL Sec. 223-b.)

Class Action and Rent Strike

You may find yourself in a struggle with many tenants at the same time. Since the tenants' claims will probably all be different, a class action suit probably would not be heard. However, rent strikes are similar to class actions. A rent strike occurs when the tenants in a building withhold rent to try to get the landlord to make repairs or fix a violation. This is authorized if there is a violation recognized by the

Department of Housing Preservation and Development that has not been fixed in six months. (MDL Sec. 302-a.) A rent strike is used as a defense when the tenants are sued for nonpayment and the cases are consolidated.

Generally, counterclaims that would delay the summary proceeding (especially regarding negligence) are severed into a separate case.

TENANT'S APPEAL

A tenant has thirty days in which to file a notice of appeal in any case, but since the Warrant of Eviction gives the tenant only twenty-four hours to vacate the property, the tenant will have to act immediately if he or she wants to stop the eviction. The eviction should not be halted by the filing of a notice of appeal. If a tenant wants to appeal a money judgment, he or she must obtain a stay from the court to prevent the enforcement of the judgment. If the tenant files an *undertaking* (a bond), the tenant is entitled to an automatic stay of a money judgment. (CPLR Sec. 5519(a)(2).) Other stays may be granted if money is deposited into court, if payment is made for the use and occupancy during the period of the appeal, or if there is good faith prosecution of the appeal.

Order to Show Cause

A tenant may seek to have a judge sign an *Order to Show Cause*, staying the judgment. The landlord can make a motion to vacate the stay and cancel the order to show cause under CPLR Sec. 5704(b).

TENANT'S BANKRUPTCY

If a tenant files bankruptcy, all legal actions must stop immediately. This provision is automatic from the moment the bankruptcy petition is filed. (United States Code (U.S.C.), Title 11, Section 362.) If you take any action in court, seize the tenant's property, try to impose a landlord's lien, or use the security deposit for unpaid rent, then you can be held in contempt of federal court. It is not necessary that you receive formal notice. Verbal notice is sufficient. If you do not believe the tenant, then you should call the bankruptcy court to confirm the filing.

The stay lasts until the debtor is discharged, the case is dismissed, the property is abandoned, or the property is voluntarily surrendered.

Relief from Stay   The landlord may ask for the right to continue with the eviction by filing a *Motion for Relief from Stay* and paying the filing fee. Within thirty days of the Motion for Relief from Stay being filed, a hearing is held, and it may be held by telephone. The motion is governed by Bankruptcy Rule 9014, and the requirements of how the tenant must be served are contained in Rule 7004. However, for such a hearing, the services of an attorney are usually necessary.

Post-Filing Rent   The bankruptcy stay only applies to amounts owed to the landlord at the time of filing the bankruptcy. Therefore, the landlord can sue the tenant for eviction and rent owed for any time period after the filing, unless the bankruptcy trustee assumes the lease. The landlord can proceed during the bankruptcy without asking for relief from the automatic stay under three conditions:

1. the landlord can only sue for rent due after the filing;

2. the landlord cannot sue until the trustee rejects the lease (if the trustee does not accept the lease within sixty days of the Order for Relief, then it is deemed rejected); or,

3. the landlord must sue under the terms of the lease and may not treat the trustee's rejection as a breach.

In Chapter 10 reorganization bankruptcy, the landlord should be paid the rent as it comes due.

Filing after Judgment   If the tenant filed bankruptcy after a judgment of eviction was entered, there should be no problem lifting the automatic stay, since the tenant has no interest in the property.

If your tenant files bankruptcy and you decide it is worth hiring a lawyer, you should locate an attorney who is experienced in bankruptcy work. Prior to the meeting with the attorney, you should gather as much information as possible (type of bankruptcy filed, assets, liabilities, case number, etc.).

LANDLORD'S APPEAL

If the landlord loses, he or she has the right to appeal the judgment. Appeals from county court are usually made to the Appellate Term of Supreme Court. Rulings by the Appellate Term can be appealed to the Appellate Division and then to the Court of Appeals. Appeals can stretch out for over a year and are very costly. If you choose to appeal, you will need an attorney.

The U.S. legal system allows one chance to bring a case to court. If you did not prepare for your trial, or thought you would not need a witness, and you lost, you do not have the right to try again. However, in certain limited circumstances, you may be able to have your case reviewed by a higher court.

- ✪ If the judge made a mistake in interpreting the law that applies to your case, it is grounds for reversal.

- ✪ If new evidence is discovered after the trial that could not have been discovered before the trial, a new trial might be granted, but this is not very common.

- ✪ If one party lied at trial and that party was believed by the judge or jury, there is usually not much that can be done.

- ✪ There are certain other grounds for rehearing, such as misconduct of an attorney or errors during the trial, but these matters are beyond the scope of this book.

Motion Rehearing

The first way to appeal a decision is to ask the judge to hear the case again. If important new evidence has been discovered or an important court case was overlooked by the judge, this may work, but if the judge was clearly on the side of the tenant, it may be a waste of time. Where there has been a jury trial, the motion used is a Motion for New Trial, not a Motion for Rehearing. Different courts have different rules as to when these motions can be made. Neither one can be made after the thirty-day period to appeal has ended. When the motion is filed with the court, a copy is sent to the other party (or his or her attorney) with the notice of the hearing, and a hearing is scheduled before the judge.

Notice of Appeal

If the judge made an error in interpreting the law, or if he or she ignored the law, you can appeal to a higher court. This is done by serving a copy of the **NOTICE OF APPEAL** (form 43, p.269) on the other party and filing a copy with the court clerk within thirty days of the judgment. The appeal must be completed, or *perfected*, after filing this form. Each court has its own time requirements for perfection. The services of an attorney will be necessary.

SATISFACTION OF JUDGMENT

If, after a judgment has been entered against the tenant, the tenant pays the amount due, it is the landlord's responsibility to file a **SATISFACTION OF JUDGMENT** with the court. (see form 44, p.271.)

chapter 12

Money Damages and Back Rent

Trying to collect a judgment against a former tenant is usually not worth the time and expense. Most landlords are just glad to regain possession of the property. Tenants who do not pay rent usually do not own property that can be seized, and it is very difficult to garnish wages. However, former tenants occasionally come into money, and some landlords have been surprised many years later when called by a title insurance company wanting to pay off a judgment. Therefore, it is usually worthwhile to put a claim for back rent into an eviction petition.

MAKING A CLAIM

To make a claim against a tenant for back rent, you can use the paragraph in your **HOLDOVER PETITION** (form 29, p.237) asking for the rent owed. A nonpayment proceeding already includes the claim for rent.

You will need to include a copy of the rent demand and proof of service. If you failed to include a request for back rent, or if your tenant moved out without a summary proceeding and owes rent, you can file a separate case for the rent owed. If the amount is under $3,000, you should file a petition in your local small claims court (contact the court for a petition form).

Claim for Damages by Tenant

If a tenant has damaged the premises, you should first send the tenant a **Statement for Repairs** (form 11, p.201) to attempt to collect it without the expense of a court proceeding. You can also refuse to renew a lease until damages are paid (rent-regulated units are an exception). To make a claim, write in a provision in your petition describing the damage done by the tenant (photos will help as proof at the hearing), and stating how much you are seeking as recompense.

Remember, in nonpayment proceedings, the judgment is for possession as well as money damages. A holdover proceeding judgment is only for possession, but may be for money damages if requested in the Petition.

AMOUNT

In New York City Civil Court, the limit on claims is $25,000. When the tenant has breached the lease, the landlord is entitled to several types of monetary damages. However, the landlord should review his or her options on default before deciding which type of claim to make against the tenant.

Prorated Rent

If you took possession of the dwelling unit for your own benefit, the tenant would be liable for rent only until he or she vacates the premises.

Future Rent

The landlord can sue the tenant for future rent if he or she takes possession for the benefit of the tenant.

Interest

A landlord is entitled to interest on the rent from the day it is due until the date of the judgment. Check with the court for the legal rate of interest in your jurisdiction.

Double Rent

When a tenant gives a notice to quit and then holds over, the landlord can receive double the amount of rent due for as long as the tenant remains. (RPL Sec. 229.)

Damage to Premises

The landlord may sue the tenant for damage to the premises. (This does not include *normal wear and tear*.) The cost of repair may also be deducted from the security deposit.

Other Losses   A landlord may make a claim against the tenant for other losses related to the damage or breach.

LIENS

A money judgment can become a lien against any real estate owned by the tenant for up to ten years in any county in which you record a certified copy of the judgment and copy of the transcript. Go to the county clerk's office and ask to record these items. There is a recording fee.

Self-Service Storage Space

chapter 13

Self-service storage space has some particular laws applicable to its rental.

Section 182 of the Lien Law applies to any real property designed and used for renting individual storage space to tenants who have access for storing and removing personal property.

If an owner issues a warehouse receipt, bill of lading, or document of title for property in storage, the relationship of the parties is governed by the Uniform Commercial Code rather than these sections.

LIENS

A written agreement is required for self-service storage space. The agreement must contain the names and addresses of the parties, the address of the storage facility, a description of the property being stored, a statement of limitation of damages, and the applicable charges. It must also contain the following notice.

> *Notice: The monthly occupancy charge and other charges stated in this agreement are the actual charges you must pay.*

The owner of the facility has a lien on all property kept in the facility, no matter who owns it. A *lien* is a security interest in favor of the landlord. This lien is superior to most other liens or security interests. If the charges are not paid, the landlord may sell the property in a public or private block or parcel sale. The sale must be on commercially reasonable terms in a commercially reasonable manner. The property must be sold in conformity with commercially reasonable practices among dealers in the type of goods that are being sold. The landlord is permitted to buy at the sale. The tenant can stop the sale at any time by paying the amount due. The owner of the facility must return any goods stored upon request (if the charges are paid).

Any violation of the provisions of this law can result in civil penalties of up to $1,000 per violation, or three times the value of the goods plus attorney's fees.

If the items to be sold are large, expensive items, such as cars or machinery, a search should be made of the records held by the Department of Motor Vehicles, the secretary of state, and the county clerk. Any prior liens on these items would take priority over the landlord's lien.

If there is any balance remaining after the sale and its expenses, and after the landlord deducts his or her amount due, a notice must be sent to the tenant at the last known address and to any other lienholder. Either may claim the balance within five years of the date of the sale. If the money is not claimed within five years, it must be turned over to the municipality in which the storage facility is located.

Notice must be given to the tenant of the sale. The notice must include:

❂   an itemized statement of the amount due;

❂   a description of the property to be sold (which should be the same as the description in the occupancy agreement);

❂   the nature of the sale;

✪   a demand for payment with a due date no sooner than ten days after the notice is received;

✪   a conspicuous statement that unless the charges are paid by that date, the goods will be sold;

✪   the time and place of the sale; and,

✪   that the tenant (or anyone else with a claim to the property) is entitled to bring a proceeding within ten days of receiving the notice to dispute the sale.

The notice must be personally delivered, or sent by registered or certified mail with return receipt requested, to the tenant's last known address.

Mobile Home Parks

Mobile homes are called *manufactured homes* in New York laws. Most people own their mobile homes and are tenants in a mobile home park. Most mobile homes are never mobile, and remain in the same spot because it is simply too costly and too difficult to move them. The owner of the mobile home park is the mobile home owner's landlord. Several years ago, cases came to light in which owners of mobile home parks took terrible advantage of the mobile home owners who rented spaces in the parks. Because of the costs of moving and many other factors, the residents were at the mercy of the park owners. Some of the abuses were quite outrageous, and they inspired the New York Legislature to pass laws protecting the residents.

Real Property Law Section 233 governs manufactured homes. This law is often called the *Mobile Home Owner's Bill of Rights*. Any county laws are superceded by this state law. The New York State Department of Housing and Community Renewal (DHCR) regulates mobile home parks. Each year, park owners must file a registration with the DHCR.

An in-depth explanation of park owners' rights and obligations is beyond the scope of this book. A park owner in a confrontation with the residents should carefully read Real Property Law Sec. 233, and should seek the counsel of an experienced attorney. Park owners should also work together to offer each other advice and assistance.

The biggest weakness in the law is the fact that the legislature has confiscated property rights and gave them to the residents without compensating the owners. This must be left to the legislature and the courts to remedy. Mobile home park owners need to be aware of the law as it currently exists.

A brief summary of the major parts of the law is as follows.

❂   The law applies to parks of three or more lots.

❂   The park owner can issue rules and regulations, but they must not be unreasonable or arbitrary.

❂   Fees are permissible only for rent, utilities, facilities, and services available to tenants.

❂   Fees can be increased only with ninety days' written notice.

❂   The tenant cannot be required to buy the home or equipment from the park owner.

❂   The tenant may sell the home within the park on twenty days' written notice of the intent to sell, and may sell to anyone. The park owner may reserve the right to approve the purchaser, but may not unreasonably deny approval.

❂   The tenant has the right to sublease upon written consent of the park owner, and such consent may not be unreasonably withheld.

❂   Eviction of tenants is governed by RPL Sec. 233(d), and may occur only for these reasons:

    •   holding over;

    •   nonpayment of rent;

- violation of a law by the tenant that affects the safety and welfare of the other tenants;

- violation of park rules and regulations by the tenant that continues after notice of violation; or,

- the park owner proposes a change in the use of the park upon written notice (eviction can occur six months after the notice or at the end of the lease, whichever is later).

✪ A warrant of eviction will be issued after ninety days, or after thirty days if the tenant is endangering the safety of the other tenants or if there is nonpayment.

✪ The park owner cannot charge extra if the tenant installs gas or electric appliances.

✪ A one- or two-year renewal lease must be offered to the tenant.

✪ The warranty of habitability applies (the park owner warrants that the park is fit for habitation, and that no dangerous condition exists).

✪ The park owner cannot retaliate against the tenant (attorney's fees can be recovered by the tenant if retaliation occurs).

✪ Rent and fees charged must be reasonable.

✪ The park owner cannot restrict occupancy.

✪ The park owner may enter a mobile home if notice is given, unless there is an emergency, in which case, no notice is needed.

✪ The park owner must designate an agent in the park to ensure an emergency response for matters affecting health, safety, and well-being of the tenants.

✪ The park owner may be charged up to $1,500 in fines per violation, and may also be civilly liable for violating this law.

Cooperative/ Condominium Conversion

Provisions governing cooperative and condominium conversion are enacted by municipalities, and thus, are not effective throughout New York State. The law requires offering plans to be filed with the attorney general and protects eligible senior citizens and eligible disabled persons.

OFFERING PLANS

Before a rental apartment building may be converted, the owner or sponsor must present an offering plan to each tenant and the attorney general. The offering plan must disclose fully a complete description of the real estate interests. No sales or advertising may take place until the plan has been filed with the attorney general.

Acceptance of the preliminary plan by the attorney general indicates that the owner or sponsor has complied with the applicable laws. The attorney general must either accept or reject the plan between four and six months from the date of submission of the plan. If the tenant believes that important facts have been omitted from the plan, the tenant should notify the attorney general, at which point the attorney general may require further investigation.

The owner or sponsor can choose to convert the building under an eviction plan or a non-eviction plan. The sponsor may change an eviction plan to a non-eviction plan by amendment to the original plan if the sponsor is unable to obtain the requisite number of purchasing tenants to maintain the eviction plan. In this event, the purchasing tenant has the option to rescind the lease within thirty days of the amendment. The sponsor may not, however, change a non-eviction plan to an eviction plan.

EVICTION PLANS

In an eviction plan, the purchaser of his or her apartment may evict a non-purchasing tenant after a certain time period. For the plan to become effective, 51% of the tenants occupying all apartments on the date the accepted plan is presented must agree in writing to purchase within six months. Every thirty days, the sponsor must post and submit to the attorney general a list of the percentage of tenants who have signed agreements. Once an eviction plan is declared effective, a non-purchasing tenant may not be evicted for failure to purchase his or her apartment until the latter of (a) the expiration of his lease or (b) three years after the effective date of the offering plan. The owner may begin eviction proceedings after the expiration of these periods, and must give the non-purchasing tenant ninety days' notice. If the apartment is under rent control, the owner may only evict if he or she seeks in good faith to recover it for his or her family's use or occupancy.

NON-EVICTION PLANS

Under a non-eviction plan, non-purchasing tenants may not be evicted for failure to buy their apartments. They continue to be rental tenants, but their apartments may be sold, at which time the tenant must pay rent to the purchaser.

RIGHTS OF SENIOR CITIZENS AND DISABLED PERSONS

Those who exceed 62 years of age and those who are disabled may choose not to purchase their apartments, and are protected from eviction regardless of their income level or length of residency in the building. However, should senior citizens or disabled persons choose to purchase their apartments, even after they have exempted themselves, they can purchase at the price offered to other tenants in the building at the time that they decide to buy.

TENANT'S EXCLUSIVE RIGHT TO PURCHASE

Once an offering plan has been accepted and filed, the tenant has the exclusive right to purchase the apartment for ninety days. After that period, tenants have an additional six months to match the sales terms offered to outside buyers. If there is a substantial amendment to the plan, the ninety-day exclusive right to purchase must be extended for an additional thirty days.

INSPECTION OF THE BUILDING

Tenants must be informed that they may physically inspect the building, during normal business hours and upon written request to the owner, after the initial plan is submitted to the attorney general.

LEASE RENEWALS

While the initial plan is pending, the landlord may not refuse to renew the tenants lease. However, the landlord may insert a "ninety-day cancellation clause" in the new lease after an eviction plan is accepted for filing by the attorney general and presented to the tenants in occupancy. Once the plan is declared effective, the landlord may cancel the lease of a non-purchasing tenant upon ninety days' written notice. The tenant must comply with all terms in the new lease; if the landlord later cancels the lease, the tenant may recover all additional costs.

RIGHTS OF NON-PURCHASING TENANTS

Non-purchasing tenants have the right to all services and facilities required by law on a nondiscriminatory basis. Furthermore, no person may interfere with, interrupt, or discontinue any essential service that substantially disrupts the comfort or peace and quiet of any tenant in his or her use or occupancy of an apartment.

Glossary

A

abandonment. When a tenant leaves a rental unit without notice.

acceleration. When all of the future rent becomes due now.

affidavit of service. Document filed with the court that swears documents were given to a specific person.

appeal. Request to have a judge's decision reviewed by a higher court.

application. Document a prospective tenant completes that gives information about him or her.

asbestos. A material that was commonly used in the construction materials of buildings in the past, now known to cause lung damage.

assignee. The person to whom the original tenant assigns all of his or her rights in the rental property.

assignment. When a tenant gives over all of his or her rights and most of his or her responsibilities to another person who "steps into his shoes" and essentially takes his or her place as the tenant.

assignor. The original tenant who assigns his or her rights to another person.

B

bankruptcy. A court order that distributes the debtor's property among creditors and eliminates all outstanding debts.

breach. Breaking a promise, or not meeting one of the obligations in a lease.

C

cancel. To make a lease void.

case law. Decisions by courts.

certificate of occupancy. Document issued by local housing department certifying that a piece of property is fit to be rented as a residence to tenants.

common areas. Areas in an apartment building that are shared by all the tenants, such as the lobby and stairways.

credit report. A list of a person's debts that indicates their status and rates how well the person pays his or her debts.

cure. To fix something, such as a lease violation.

D

damages. Financial loss that a person can sue for in court.

default. Failing to appear in court.

defense. A legal response to a court proceeding, an explanation for something.

demand for rent. A notice served to a tenant requesting payment of late rent or eviction proceedings will be begun.

deposit. Money paid to hold an available rental unit, can also refer to security deposit.

deregulation. When a rent-regulated unit becomes unregulated and the amount of the rent is no longer controlled by law.

discovery. A period of time during a court case when the parties must share certain requested information with each other.

discrimination. Illegally treating people differently based on personal factors such as race, color, religion, etc.

dishonored check. Check that has insufficient funds or from a closed account.

Division of Housing and Community Renewal (DHCR). State agency that governs rent-regulated property.

due date. The date rent is due from the tenant to the landlord, determined by the lease or type of rental agreement.

duplex. Rental property with two units.

E

eviction. A court order telling a tenant to leave a rental property.

F

foreclosure. Action by a bank to take possession of real property when payments have not been made on a mortgage.

H

holding over. When a tenant remains in a rental property after he or she was legally required to leave.

holdover proceedings. The process a landlord must follow to evict a tenant who has breached the lease.

I

illegality. When a lease is created for an illegal purpose, it cannot be enforced.

impossibility. When circumstances make it impossible for a tenant to move into a rental unit.

improvements. Alterations to a rental unit.

inquest. A trial.

inspection. Visually checking a rental unit.

interest. A percentage that is added to money that remains in a bank account.

J

judgment. Decision by a court.

jurisdiction. A court's right to hear a specific case.

L

landlord. Property owner who allows the property to be rented.

lead. A chemical that was formerly used in paint and is now known to be hazardous.

lease. A contract between a landlord and tenant regarding the rental of a unit.

liability. Legal responsibility.

lien. An entry in county records that will hold a certain amount of money to pay a creditor when the real property it is entered against is sold.

loft. Rental unit created out of a commercial space and occupied by tenants before it was approved as housing.

M

maintenance. Work done to keep a rental property in good condition.

manager. Person hired by a landlord to manage the property and deal with tenants.

manufactured home. A trailer or mobile home.

maximum base rent. The rent that may be charged for a rent-regulated unit, determined by a formula.

mobile home. A manufactured home that is placed in a mobile home park, where land is rented to place it on.

mobile home owner's bill of rights. State law for mobile home owners found at RPL Sec. 233.

modification. A change to the original terms or condition of something.

N

nonpayment. Failure of the tenant to pay rent when it is due.

nonpayment proceedings. The process a landlord must follow to evict a tenant who has failed to pay rent.

notary. A licensed individual who can certify signatures.

notice of appeal. Document filed by the person who loses a court case, asking that a higher court review the decision.

notice of default. A form the landlord gives the tenant stating that the tenant has breached the lease and explaining how the tenant can fix the problem.

notice of petition. Form given to defendant, telling him or her when a court proceeding will be heard.

notice of termination. A form served by the landlord on the tenant that gives the tenant a number of days until the lease will be terminated.

O

option to purchase. A tenant's right to purchase the property if he or she chooses (different from right of first refusal).

option to renew. The tenant's right to extend the lease if he or she chooses.

P

petition. Legal form explaining a plaintiff's case.

premises. A rental unit.

prepaid rent. Rent that is paid before it is due.

R

renewal. Entering into another lease after the current one has expired.

rent. Money owed by a tenant for the ability to live in the landlord's property.

rent-controlled. Buildings with three or more units converted to residential use prior to 1947 and have been continuously occupied by the same tenant or his or her successor since 1971.

rent-regulated. Property that is governed by laws that limit the amount of rent and other specifics about the property, includes rent-controlled and rent-stabilized units.

rent-stabilized. Some properties that were built before 1974 with six or more units.

rental agreement. An agreement that a tenant will rent property from a landlord.

rental unit. Apartment or space being rented.

rescission. Cancellation of a lease.

retaliatory conduct. Actions taken by a landlord to get back at a tenant, a form of revenge.

right of first refusal. Tenant's right to be offered the opportunity to purchase the property first before any other potential buyer. If tenant chooses not to purchase, the owner can offer the property to others.

S

satisfaction of judgment. A document filed with the court that indicates a judgment has been paid in full.

security deposit. Money given to the landlord by the tenant to cover any damage the tenant may do to the property during the rental period.

self-help. Actions taken by a landlord to remove a tenant without assistance from the court or other authorized personnel.

self-service storage space. Storage space rented to tenants.

service. Legal term for giving someone papers pertaining to a court matter.

single room occupancy (SRO). A single room with a kitchen or bathroom, but not both, that is rented to a tenant.

statute. A law.

stay. Court order that stops an eviction.

stipulation. An agreement that settles a case.

strict liability. When someone is held legally responsible for something whether or not he or she actually caused it.

sublease. When a tenant rents the unit to someone else for a portion of the lease period.

sublessee. Person who rents the unit from the original tenant.

sublessor. Name for the original tenant when he or she subleases the property out.

summary proceeding. A court proceeding that is shorter than a full-blown proceeding.

super (or superintendent). Employee of the landlord who is the tenants' main contact for repairs, rent, etc.

surrender. Giving up possession of rental property.

T

ten-day notice to quit. Form given to person occupying unit by landlord giving him or her ten days to leave the unit or be evicted.

tenant. Person who rents property from the owner.

termination. Ending a lease or rental agreement.

U

unavailability. When a rental unit is not available to be lived in at the beginning of the lease, this gives the tenant the right to cancel the lease.

unconscionable. So outrageous it will not be enforced by a court.

V

verification.   Form attached to court papers that has the person filing it verify that everything contained in the papers is true.

violation.   A condition or act that is in opposition to a term in the lease.

W

waiver.   When a party gives up some kind of right; can occur knowingly or unknowingly. (For example, when a landlord accepts rent after a violation, the landlord waives the right to terminate the rental.)

warrant of eviction.   Document issued by a court ordering a person to be removed from a rental unit.

warranty of habitability.   Requirements about the condition of rental property.

window guards.   Bars placed on windows to prevent falls.

witness.   Person who formally sees a document being signed.

New York Statutes

This appendix includes the following New York Statutes.

The Multiple Dwelling Law and Multiple Residence Law are too long to include in this book. You can make copies at your local library or download them from the Internet.

NOTE: *Keep in mind that these laws are occasionally amended by the legislature. You should check periodically for changes.*

GENERAL OBLIGATIONS LAW (GOL)
ARTICLE 7
OBLIGATIONS RELATING TO PROPERTY RECEIVED AS SECURITY
Title 1 MONEY DEPOSITED AS SECURITY TO BE HELD IN TRUST IN CERTAIN CASES
7-101 Money deposited or advanced for use or rental of personal property; waiver void.
7-103 Money deposited or advanced for use or rental of real property; waiver void; administration expenses.
7-105 Landlord failing to turn over deposits made by tenants or licensees and to notify tenants or licensees thereof in certain cases.
7-106 Money deposited or advanced for certain installations; waiver void.
7-107 Liability of a grantee or assignee for deposits made by tenants upon conveyance of rent stabilized dwelling units.
7-108 Liability of a grantee or assignee for deposits made by tenants upon conveyance of non-rent stabilized dwelling units.
7-109 Commencement of a proceeding or action by the attorney general to compel compliance.

Sec. 7-101. Money deposited or advanced for use or rental of personal property; waiver void.
1. Whenever money shall be deposited or advanced on a contract for the use or rental of personal property as security for performance of the contract or to be applied to payments upon such contract when due, such money, with interest accruing thereon, if any, until repaid or so applied, shall continue to be the money of the person making such deposit or advance and shall be a trust fund in the possession of the person with whom such deposit or advance shall be made and shall be deposited in a bank or trust company and shall not be mingled with other funds or become an asset of such trustee, excepting, however, that such trust funds may be deposited with other funds that have been deposited or advanced to the trustee as security for performance of a contract for the use or rental of personal property or be applied to payments upon such contract when due. If the money being deposited or advanced is for the use or rental of personal property and the money deposited or advanced is seven hundred fifty dollars or more and is for the use or rental of personal property for a period equal to or greater than one hundred twenty days, the person receiving such money shall deposit it pursuant to the provisions of subdivision one-a of this section.
1-a. Whenever the money so deposited or advanced is seven hundred fifty dollars or more and is for the use or rental of personal property for a period equal to or greater than one hundred twenty days, the person receiving such money shall, subject to the provisions of this section, deposit it in an interest bearing account in a banking organization within the state

which account shall earn interest at a rate which shall be the prevailing rate earned by other such deposits made with banking organizations in such area. Such person shall not be required to keep the funds of the separate persons from whom security deposits or advances have been received in separate depository accounts, provided his books of account shall clearly show the allocation of the funds deposited in his general or special depository account. The person depositing such security money shall be entitled to receive, as administration expenses, a sum equivalent to one per cent per annum upon the security money so deposited, which shall be deducted from the interest earned on such security money from the banking organization and shall be in lieu of all other administrative and custodial expenses relating to the security deposit or advance. The balance of the interest paid by the banking organization shall be the money of the lessee making the deposit or advance and shall either be held in trust by the person with whom such deposit or advance shall be made, until repaid or applied for the use or rental of the personal property, or annually paid to the lessee making the deposit of security money.
1-b. This section shall not be applicable to any advance payment of money under or with respect to any contract for the use or rental of personal property that, in accordance with the terms applicable to such payment, either (a) is not revocable by the person making such payment and is not otherwise subject to being returned or refunded to such person, or (b) otherwise satisfies or discharges an equivalent liability under such contract when such payment is made, whether or not such liability is otherwise then due and payable under the terms of such contract.
1-c. This section shall apply to money deposited or advanced on contracts for the use or rental of personal property as security for performance of the contract or to be applied to payments upon such contract when due, only if (a) such contract is governed by the laws of this state as the result of a choice of law provision in such contract, in accordance with section 1-105 of the uniform commercial code (subject to the limitations on choice of law by the parties to a consumer lease under section 2-A-106 of the uniform commercial code), or such contract is otherwise governed by the laws of this state in accordance with applicable conflict of laws rules, and (b) the lessee under such contract is located within this state, within the meaning of the uniform commercial code (with respect to the location of debtors), except that a foreign air carrier under the Federal Aviation Act of 1958, as amended, shall not be deemed located in this state solely as a result of having a designated office of an agent upon whom service of process may be made located in this state. 2. Any provision of a contract whereby a person who has deposited or advanced money on a contract for the use or rental of

personal property as security for the performance of the contract waives any provision of this section is absolutely void. 3. This section shall not be applicable to any deposit or advance of money made in connection with the borrowing of securities for any lawful purpose.

Sec. 7-103. Money deposited or advanced for use or rental of real property; waiver void; administration expenses.

1. Whenever money shall be deposited or advanced on a contract or license agreement for the use or rental of real property as security for performance of the contract or agreement or to be applied to payments upon such contract or agreement when due, such money, with interest accruing thereon, if any, until repaid or so applied, shall continue to be the money of the person making such deposit or advance and shall be held in trust by the person with whom such deposit or advance shall be made and shall not be mingled with the personal moneys or become an asset of the person receiving the same, but may be disposed of as provided in section 7-105 of this chapter.

2. Whenever the person receiving money so deposited or advanced shall deposit such money in a banking organization, such person shall thereupon notify in writing each of the persons making such security deposit or advance, giving the name and address of the banking organization in which the deposit of security money is made, and the amount of such deposit. Deposits in a banking organization pursuant to the provisions of this subdivision shall be made in a banking organization having a place of business within the state. If the person depositing such security money in a banking organization shall deposit same in an interest bearing account, he shall be entitled to receive, as administration expenses, a sum equivalent to one per cent per annum upon the security money so deposited, which shall be in lieu of all other administrative and custodial expenses. The balance of the interest paid by the banking organization shall be the money of the person making the deposit or advance and shall either be held in trust by the person with whom such deposit or advance shall be made, until repaid or applied for the use or rental of the leased premises, or annually paid to the person making the deposit of security money.

2-a. Whenever the money so deposited or advanced is for the rental of property containing six or more family dwelling units, the person receiving such money shall, subject to the provisions of this section, deposit it in an interest bearing account in a banking organization within the state which account shall earn interest at a rate which shall be the prevailing rate earned by other such deposits made with banking organizations in such area.

2-b. In the event that a lease terminates other than at the time that a banking organization in such area regularly pays interest, the person depositing such security money shall pay over to his tenant such interest as he is able to collect at the date of such lease termination.

3. Any provision of such a contract or agreement whereby a person who so deposits or advances money waives any provision of this section is absolutely void.

4. The term "real property" as used in this section is co-extensive in meaning with lands, tenements and hereditaments.

Sec. 7-105. Landlord failing to turn over deposits made by tenants or licensees and to notify tenants or licensees thereof in certain cases.

1. Any person, firm or corporation and the employers, officers or agents thereof, whether the owner or lessee of the property leased, who or which has or hereafter shall have received from a tenant or licensee a sum of money or any other thing of value as a deposit or advance of rental as security for the full performance by such tenant or licensee of the terms of his lease or license agreement, or who or which has or shall have received the same from a former owner or lessee, shall, upon conveying such property or assigning his or its lease to another, or upon the judicial appointment and qualifying of a receiver in an action to foreclose a mortgage or other lien of record affecting the property leased, or upon the conveyance of such property to another person, firm or corporation by a referee in an action to foreclose a mortgage or other lien of record affecting the property leased if a receiver shall not have been appointed and qualified in such action, at the time of the delivery of the deed or instrument or assignment or within five days thereafter, or within five days after the receiver shall have qualified, deal with the security deposit as follows:

Turn over to his or its grantee or assignee, or to the receiver in the foreclosure action, or to the purchaser at the foreclosure sale if a receiver shall not have been appointed and qualified the sum so deposited, and notify the tenant or licensee by registered or certified mail of such turning over and the name and address of such grantee, assignee, purchaser or receiver.

2. Any owner or lessee turning over to his or its grantee, assignee, to a purchaser of the leased premises at a foreclosure sale, or to the receiver in the foreclosure action the amount of such security deposit is hereby relieved of and from liability to the tenant or licensee for the repayment thereof; and the transferee of such security deposit is hereby made responsible for the return thereof to the tenant or licensee, unless he or it shall thereafter and before the expiration of the term of the tenant's lease or licensee's agreement, transfer such security deposit to another, pursuant to subdivision one hereof and give the requisite notice in connection therewith as provided thereby. A receiver shall hold the security subject to

such disposition thereof as shall be provided in an order of the court to be made and entered in the fore- closure action. The provisions of this section shall not apply if the agreement between the landlord and tenant or licensee is inconsistent herewith.

3. Any failure to comply with this section is a misde- meanor.

Sec. 7-106. Money deposited or advanced for certain installations; waiver void.

1. Whenever any non-public moneys shall be deposited or advanced by the owner of an occupied residential dwelling on a contract for the installation of a private connection to a public sewer line as secu- rity for payments or to be applied to payments upon such contract when due, such money, with interest accruing thereon, if any, until repaid or so applied, shall continue to be the money of the person making such deposit or advance and shall be a trust fund in the possession of the person with whom such deposit or advance shall be made and shall be deposited in a bank, trust company, savings bank, savings and loan association, federal savings and loan association or federal mutual savings bank and shall not be mingled with other funds or become an asset of such trustee.

2. Any provision of a contract whereby a person who has deposited or advanced money on a contract for the installation of a private connection to a public sewer line as security for payments or to be applied to payments upon such contract when due waives any provision of this section is absolutely void.

Sec. 7-107. Liability of a grantee or assignee for deposits made by tenants upon conveyance of rent stabilized dwelling units.

1. This section shall apply only to dwelling units subject to the New York city rent stabilization law of nineteen hundred sixty-nine or the emergency tenant protection act of nineteen seventy-four.

2. (a) Any grantee or assignee of any dwelling unit referred to in subdivision one of this section shall be liable to a tenant for any sum of money or any other thing of value deposited as security for the full performance by such tenant of the terms of his lease, plus any accrued interest, if his or its predecessor in interest was liable for such funds. Such liability shall attach whether or not the successor in interest has, upon the conveyance of such dwelling unit, received the sum as deposited.

(b) The liability of a receiver for payment of any secu- rity deposit plus accrued interest pursuant to this subdivision shall be limited to the amount of such deposit actually turned over to him or it pursuant to subdivision one of section 7-105 of this chapter and to the operating income in excess of expenses generated during his or its period of receivership.

3. Any agreement by a lessee or tenant of a dwelling unit waiving or modifying his rights as set forth in this section shall be void.

Sec. 7-108. Liability of a grantee or assignee for deposits made by tenants upon conveyance of non-rent stabilized dwelling units.

1. This section shall apply to all dwelling units with written leases in residential premises containing six or more dwelling units and to all dwelling units subject to the city rent and rehabilitation law or the emergency housing rent control law, unless such dwelling unit is specifically referred to in section 7-107 of this chapter.

2. (a) In circumstances where any sum of money or any other thing of value deposited as security for the full performance by a tenant of the terms of his lease is not turned over to a successor in interest pursuant to section 7-105 of this chapter, the grantee or assignee of the leased premises shall also be liable to such tenant, upon conveyance of such leased prem- ises, for the repayment of any such security deposit, plus accrued interest, as to which such grantee or assignee has actual knowledge.

(b) For purposes of this section, a grantee or assignee of the leased premises shall be deemed to have actual knowledge of any security deposit which is (i) deposited at any time during the six months immedi- ately prior to closing or other transfer of title in any banking organization pursuant to subdivision two-a of section 7-103 of this chapter, or (ii) acknowledged in any lease in effect at the time of closing or other transfer of title, or (iii) supported by documentary evidence provided by the tenant or lessee as set forth in paragraph (c) of this subdivision.

(c) With respect to any leased premises for which there is no record of security deposit pursuant to subpara- graph (i) or (ii) of paragraph (b) of this subdivision, the grantee or assignee of the leased premises shall be obligated to notify the tenant thereof in writing no later than thirty days following the closing or other transfer of title to the fact that there is no record of a security deposit for said leased premises and that unless the tenant within thirty days after receiving notice provides him or it with documentary evidence of deposit, the tenant shall have no further recourse against him or it for said security deposit. For purposes of this subdivision, "documentary evidence" shall be limited to any cancelled check drawn to the order of, a receipt from, or a lease signed by any pred- ecessor in interest, if such predecessor's interest in the leased premises existed on or after the effective date of this section. Except as otherwise provided by subpara- graphs (i) and (ii) of paragraph (b) of this subdivision the grantee or assignee of the leased premises shall not be charged with actual knowledge of the security deposit where the tenant fails within the thirty-day period to provide said documentary evidence. Where the grantee or assignee of the leased premises fails to notify the tenant as specified in this paragraph within thirty days following the closing or other transfer of title, the tenant shall be entitled to produce documen- tary evidence at any time.

(d) The grantee or assignee of the leased premises shall have the right to demand that the grantor or assignor thereof establish an escrow account equal to one month's rent for any leased premises for which there is no record of a security deposit pursuant to paragraph (b) of this subdivision to be used for the purpose of holding harmless the grantee or assignee in any case where, at a date subsequent to the closing or other transfer of title, the tenant gives notice pursuant to paragraph (c) of this subdivision.

(e) The liability of a receiver for payment of any security deposit plus accrued interest pursuant to this subdivision shall be limited to the amount of such deposit actually turned over to him or it pursuant to subdivision one of section 7-105 of this chapter and to the operating income in excess of expenses generated during his or its period of receivership. 3. Any agreement by a lessee or tenant of a dwelling waiving or modifying his rights as set forth in this section shall be absolutely void.

Sec. 7-109. Commencement of a proceeding or action by the attorney general to compel compliance.

If it appears to the attorney general that any person, association, or corporation has violated or is violating any of the provisions of title one of this article, an action or proceeding may be instituted by the attorney general in the name of the people of the state of New York to compel compliance with such provisions and enjoin any violation or threatened violation thereof.

REAL PROPERTY ACTIONS AND PROCEEDINGS LAW (RPAPL)
ARTICLE 7
SUMMARY PROCEEDING TO RECOVER POSSESSION OF REAL PROPERTY

Sec. 701. Jurisdiction; Courts; Venue.

1. A special proceeding to recover real property may be maintained in a county court, the court of a police justice of the village, a justice court, a court of civil jurisdiction in a city, or a district court.

2. The place of trial of the special proceeding shall be within the jurisdictional area of the court in which the real property or a portion thereof is situated; except that where the property is located in an incorporated village which includes parts of two or more towns the proceeding may be tried by a justice of the peace of any such town who keeps an office in the village.

Sec. 711. Grounds Where Landlord-Tenant Relationship Exists.

A tenant shall include an occupant of one or more rooms in a rooming house or a resident, not including a transient occupant, of one or more rooms in a hotel who has been in possession for thirty consecutive days or longer; he shall not be removed from possession except in a special proceeding. A special proceeding may be maintained under this article upon the following grounds:

1. The tenant continues in possession of any portion of the premises after the expiration of his term, without the permission of the landlord or, in a case where a new lessee is entitled to possession, without the permission of the new lessee. Acceptance of rent after commencement of the special proceeding upon this ground shall not terminate such proceeding nor effect any award of possession to the landlord or to the new lessee, as the case may be. A proceeding seeking to recover possession of real property by reason of the termination of the term fixed in the lease pursuant to a provision contained therein giving the landlord the right to terminate the time fixed for occupancy under such agreement if he deem the tenant objectionable, shall not be maintainable unless the landlord shall by competent evidence

establish to the satisfaction of the court that the tenant is objectionable.

2. The tenant has defaulted in the payment of rent, pursuant to the agreement under which the premises are held, and a demand of the rent has been made, or at least three days' notice in writing requiring, in the alternative, the payment of the rent, or the possession of the premises, has been served upon him as prescribed in section 735. The landlord may waive his right to proceed upon this ground only by an express consent in writing to permit the tenant to continue in possession, which consent shall be revocable at will, in which event the landlord shall be deemed to have waived his right to summary dispossess for nonpayment of rent accruing during the time said consent remains unrevoked. Any person succeeding to the landlord's interest in the premises may proceed under this subdivision for rent due his predecessor in interest if he has a right thereto. Where a tenant dies during the term of the lease and rent due has not been paid and no representative or person has taken possession of the premises and no administrator or executor has been appointed, the proceeding may be commenced after three months from the date of death of the tenant by joining the surviving spouse or if there is none, then one of the surviving issue or if there is none, then any one of the distributees.

3. The tenant, in a city defaults in the payment, for sixty days after the same shall be payable, of any taxes or assessments levied on the premises which he has agreed in writing to pay pursuant to the agreement under which the premises are held, and a demand for payment has been made, or at least three days' notice in writing, requiring in the alternative the payment thereof and of any interest and penalty thereon, or the possession of the premises, has been served upon him, as prescribed in section 735. An acceptance of any rent shall not be construed as a waiver of the agreement to pay taxes or assessments.

4. The tenant, under a lease for a term of three years or less, has during the term taken the benefit of an insolvency statute or has been adjudicated a bankrupt.

5. The premises, or any part thereof, are used or occupied as a bawdy-house, or house or place of assignation for lewd persons, or for purposes of prostitution, or for any illegal trade or manufacture, or other illegal business.

6. The tenant, in a city having a population of one million or more, removes the batteries or otherwise disconnects or makes inoperable an installed smoke or fire detector which the tenant has not requested be moved from its location so as not to interfere with the reasonable use of kitchen facilities provided that the court, upon complaint thereof, has previously issued an order of violation of the provisions heretofore stated and, subsequent to the thirtieth day after service of such order upon the tenant, an official inspection report by the appropriate department of housing preservation and development is presented,

in writing, indicating non-compliance herewith; provided further, that the tenant shall have the additional ten day period to cure such violation in accordance with the provisions of subdivision four of section seven hundred fifty-three of this chapter.

Sec. 713. Grounds Where No Landlord-Tenant Relationship Exists.

A special proceeding may be maintained under this article after a ten-day notice to quit has been served upon the respondent in the manner prescribed in section 735, upon the following grounds:

1. The property has been sold by virtue of an execution against him or a person under whom he claims and a title under the sale has been perfected.

2. He occupies or holds the property under an agreement with the owner to occupy and cultivate it upon shares or for a share of the crops and the time fixed in the agreement for his occupancy has expired.

3. He or the person to whom he has succeeded has intruded into or squatted upon the property without the permission of the person entitled to possession and the occupancy has continued without permission or permission has been revoked and notice of the revocation given to the person to be removed.

4. The property has been sold for unpaid taxes and a tax deed has been executed and delivered to the purchaser and he or any subsequent grantee, distributee or devisee claiming title through such purchaser has complied with all provisions of law precedent to the right to possession and the time of redemption by the former owner or occupant has expired.

5. The property has been sold in foreclosure and either the deed delivered pursuant to such sale, or a copy of such deed, certified as provided in the civil practice law and rules, has been exhibited to him.

6. He is the tenant of a life tenant of the property, holding over and continuing in possession of the property after the termination of the estate of such life tenant without the permission of the person entitled to possession of the property upon termination of the life estate.

7. He is a licensee of the person entitled to possession of the property at the time of the license, and (a) his license has expired, or (b) his license has been revoked by the licensor, or (c) the licensor is no longer entitled to possession of the property; provided, however, that a mortgagee or vendee in possession shall not be deemed to be a licensee within the meaning of this subdivision.

8. The owner of real property, being in possession of all or a part thereof, and having voluntarily conveyed title to the same to a purchaser for value, remains in possession without permission of the purchaser.

9. A vendee under a contract of sale, the performance of which is to be completed within ninety days after its execution, being in possession of all or a part thereof, and having defaulted in the performance of the terms of the contract of sale, remains in possession without permission of the vendor.

10. The person in possession has entered the property or remains in possession by force or unlawful means and he or his predecessor in interest was not in quiet possession for three years before the time of the forcible or unlawful entry or detainer and the petitioner was peaceably in actual possession at the time of the forcible or unlawful entry or in constructive possession at the time of the forcible or unlawful detainer; no notice to quit shall be required in order to maintain a proceeding under this subdivision.

11. The person in possession entered into possession as an incident to employment by petitioner, and the time agreed upon for such possession has expired or, if no such time was agreed upon, the employment has been terminated; no notice to quit shall be required in order to maintain the proceeding under this subdivision.

Sec. 713a. Special Proceeding for Termination of Adult Home and Residence for Adults Admission Agreement.

A special proceeding to terminate the admission agreement of a resident of an adult home or residence for adults and discharge a resident therefrom may be maintained in a court of competent jurisdiction pursuant to the provisions of section four hundred sixty-one-h of the social services law and nothing contained in such section shall be construed to create a relationship of landlord and tenant between the operator of an adult home or residence for adults and a resident thereof.

Sec. 715. Grounds and Procedure Where Use or Occupancy is Illegal.

1. An owner or tenant, including a tenant of one or more rooms of an apartment house, tenement house or multiple dwelling, of any premises within two hundred feet from other demised real property used or occupied in whole or in part as a bawdy-house, or house or place of assignation for lewd persons, or for purposes of prostitution, or for any illegal trade, business or manufacture, or any domestic corporation organized for the suppression of vice, subject to or which submits to visitation by the state department of social services and possesses a certificate from such department of such fact and of conformity with regulations of the department, or any duly authorized enforcement agency of the state or of a subdivision thereof, under a duty to enforce the provisions of the penal law or of any state or local law, ordinance, code, rule or regulation relating to buildings, may serve personally upon the owner or landlord of the premises so used or occupied, or upon his agent, a written notice requiring the owner or landlord to make an application for the removal of the person so using or occupying the same. If the owner or landlord or his agent does not make such application within five days thereafter; or, having made it, does not in good faith diligently prosecute it, the person, corporation or enforcement agency giving the notice may bring a proceeding under this article for such removal as though the petitioner were the owner or landlord of the premises, and shall have precedence over any similar proceeding thereafter brought by such owner or landlord or to one theretofore brought by him and not prosecuted diligently and in good faith. Proof of the ill repute of the demised premises or of the inmates thereof or of those resorting thereto shall constitute presumptive evidence of the unlawful use of the demised premises required to be stated in the petition for removal. Both the person in possession of the property and the owner or landlord shall be made respondents in the proceeding.

2. For purposes of this section, two or more convictions of any person or persons had, within a period of one year, for any of the offenses described in section 230.00, 230.05, 230.20, 230.25, 230.30 or 230.40 of the penal law arising out of conduct engaged in at the same real property consisting of a dwelling as that term is defined in subdivision four of section four of the multiple dwelling law shall be presumptive evidence of conduct constituting use of the premises for purposes of prostitution.

3. For the purposes of this section, two or more convictions of any person or persons had, within a period of one year, for any of the offenses described in section 225.00, 225.05, 225.10, 225.15, 225.20, 225.30, 225.32, 225.35 or 225.40 of the penal law, arising out of conduct engaged in at the same premises consisting of a dwelling as that term is defined in subdivision four of section four of the multiple dwelling law shall be presumptive evidence of unlawful use of such premises and of the owner's knowledge of the same.

4. A court granting a petition pursuant to this section may, in addition to any other order provided by law, make an order imposing and requiring the payment by the respondent of a civil penalty not exceeding five thousand dollars to the municipality in which the subject premises is located and, the payment of reasonable attorneys fees and the costs of the proceeding to the petitioner. In any such case multiple respondents shall be jointly and severally liable for any payment so ordered and the amounts of such payments shall constitute a lien upon the subject realty.

5. For the purposes of a proceeding under this section, an enforcement agency of the state or of a subdivision thereof, which may commence a proceeding under this section, may subpoena witnesses, compel their attendance, examine them under oath before himself or a court and require that any books, records, documents or papers relevant or material to the inquiry be turned over to him for inspection, examination or audit, pursuant to the civil practice law and rules. If a person subpoenaed to attend upon such inquiry fails to obey the command of a subpoena without reasonable cause, or if a person in attendance upon such inquiry shall, without reasonable cause, refuse to be sworn or to be

examined or to answer a question or to produce a book or paper, when ordered to do so by the officer conducting such inquiry, he shall be guilty of a class B misdemeanor.

Sec. 721. Person Who May Maintain Proceeding.
The Proceeding May Be Brought By:

1. The landlord or lessor.

2. The reversioner or remainderman next entitled to possession of the property upon the termination of the estate of a life tenant, where a tenant of such life tenant holds over.

3. The purchaser upon the execution or foreclosure sale, or the purchaser on a tax sale to whom a deed has been executed and delivered or any subsequent grantee, distributee or devisee claiming title through such purchaser.

4. The person forcibly put out or kept out.

5. The person with whom, as owner, the agreement was made, or the owner of the property occupied under an agreement to cultivate the property upon shares or for a share of the crops.

6. The person lawfully entitled to the possession of property intruded into or squatted upon.

7. The person entitled to possession of the property occupied by a licensee who may be dispossessed.

8. The person, corporation or law enforcement agency authorized by this article to proceed to remove persons using or occupying premises for illegal purposes.

9. The receiver of a landlord, purchaser or other person so entitled to apply, when authorized by the court.

10. The lessee of the premises, entitled to possession.

11. Not-for-profit corporations, and tenant associations authorized in writing by the commissioner of the department of the city of New York charged with enforcement of the housing maintenance code of such city to manage residential real property owned by such city.

Sec. 731. Commencement; Notice of Petition.

1. The special proceeding prescribed by this article shall be commenced by petition and a notice of petition. A notice of petition may be issued only by an attorney, judge or the clerk of the court; it may not be issued by a party prosecuting the proceeding in person.

2. Except as provided in section 732, relating to a proceeding for non-payment of rent, the notice of petition shall specify the time and place of the hearing on the petition and state that if respondent shall fail at such time to interpose and establish any defense that he may have, he may be precluded from asserting such defense or the claim on which it is based in any other proceeding or action.

Sec. 732. Special Provisions Applicable in Non-Payment Proceeding if the Rules So Provide.

If the appropriate appellate division shall so provide in the rules of a particular court, this section shall be applicable in such court in a proceeding brought on the ground that the respondent has defaulted in the payment of rent; in such event, all other provisions of this article shall remain applicable in such proceeding, except to the extent inconsistent with the provisions of this section.

1. The notice of petition shall be returnable before the clerk, and shall be made returnable within five days after its service.

2. If the respondent answers, the clerk shall fix a date for trial or hearing not less than three nor more than eight days after joinder of issue, and shall immediately notify by mail the parties or their attorneys of such date. If the determination be for the petitioner, the issuance of a warrant shall not be stayed for more than five days from such determination.

3. If the respondent fails to answer within five days from the date of service, as shown by the affidavit or certificate of service of the notice of petition and petition, the judge shall render judgment in favor of the petitioner and may stay the issuance of the warrant for a period of not to exceed ten days from the date of service.

4. The notice of petition shall advise the respondent of the requirements of subdivisions 1, 2 and 3, above.

Sec. 733. Time of Service; Order To Show Cause.

1. Except as provided in section 732, relating to a proceeding for non-payment of rent, the notice of petition and petition shall be served at least five and not more than twelve days before the time at which the petition is noticed to be heard.

2. The court may grant an order to show cause to be served in lieu of a notice of petition. If the special proceeding is based upon the ground specified in subdivision 1 of section 711, and the order to show cause is sought on the day of the expiration of the lease or the next day thereafter, it may be served at a time specified therein which shall be at least two hours before the hour at which the petition is to be heard.

Sec. 734. Notice of Petition; Service on the Westchester County Department of Social Services.

In the county of Westchester, if the local legislative body has, by local law, opted to require such notice, service of a copy of the notice of petition and petition in any proceeding commenced against a residential tenant in accordance with the provisions of this article shall be served upon the county commissioner of social services. Such service shall be made by certified mail, return receipt requested, directed to an address set forth in the local law, or pursuant to the provisions of the civil practice law and rules. Such service shall be made at least five days before the return date set in the notice of petition. Proof of such service shall be filed with the court. Failure to serve the commissioner shall not be a jurisdictional defect, and shall not be a defense to a proceeding brought pursuant to the provisions of this article.

Sec. 735. Manner of Service; Filing; When Service Complete.

1. Service of the notice of petition and petition shall be made by personally delivering them to the respondent; or by delivering to and leaving personally with a person of suitable age and discretion who resides or is employed at the property sought to be recovered, a copy of the notice of petition and petition, if upon reasonable application admittance can be obtained and such person found who will receive it; or if admittance cannot be obtained and such person found, by affixing a copy of the notice and petition upon a conspicuous part of the property sought to be recovered or placing a copy under the entrance door of such premises; and in addition, within one day after such delivering to such suitable person or such affixing or placement, by mailing to the respondent both by registered or certified mail and by regular first class mail, (a) if a natural person, as follows: at the property sought to be recovered, and if such property is not the place of residence of such person and if the petitioner shall have written information of the residence address of such person, at the last residence address as to which the petitioner has such information, or if the petitioner shall have no such information, but shall have written information of the place of business or employment of such person, to the last business or employment address as to which the petitioner has such information; and (b) if a corporation, joint-stock or other unincorporated association, as follows: at the property sought to be recovered, and if the principal office or principal place of business of such corporation, joint stock or other unincorporated association is not located on the property sought to be recovered, and if the petitioner shall have written information of the principal office or principal place of business within the state, at the last place as to which petitioner has such information, or if the petitioner shall have no such information but shall have written information of any office or place of business within the state, to any such place as to which the petitioner has such information. Allegations as to such information as may affect the mailing address shall be set forth either in the petition, or in a separate affidavit and filed as part of the proof of service.

2. The notice of petition, or order to show cause, and petition together with proof of service thereof shall be filed with the court or clerk thereof within three days after; (a) personal delivery to respondent, when service has been made by that means, and such service shall be complete immediately upon such personal delivery; or (b) mailing to respondent, when service is made by the alternatives above provided, and such service shall be complete upon the filing of proof of service.

Sec. 741. Contents of Petition.

The petition shall be verified by the person authorized by section seven hundred twenty-one to maintain the proceeding; or by a legal representative, attorney or agent of such person pursuant to subdivision (d) of section thirty hundred twenty of the civil practice law and rules. An attorney of such person may verify the petition on information and belief notwithstanding the fact that such person is in the county where the attorney has his office. Every petition shall:

1. State the interest of the petitioner in the premises from which removal is sought.

2. State the respondent's interest in the premises and his relationship to petitioner with regard thereto.

3. Describe the premises from which removal is sought.

4. State the facts upon which the special proceeding is based.

5. State the relief sought. The relief may include a judgment for rent due, and for a period of occupancy during which no rent is due, for the fair value of use and occupancy of the premises if the notice of petition contains a notice that a demand for such a judgment has been made.

Sec. 743. Answer.

Except as provided in section 732, relating to a proceeding for non-payment of rent, at the time when the petition is to be heard the respondent, or any person in possession or claiming possession of the premises, may answer, orally or in writing. If the answer is oral the substance thereof shall be indorsed upon the petition. If the notice of petition was served at least eight days before the time at which it was noticed to be heard and it so demands, the answer shall be made at least three days before the time the petition is noticed to be heard and, if in writing, it shall be served within such time; whereupon any reply shall be served at least one day before such time. The answer may contain any legal or equitable defense, or counterclaim. The court may render affirmative judgment for the amount found due on the counterclaim.

Sec. 745. Trial.

1. Where triable issues of fact are raised, they shall be tried by the court unless, at the time the petition is noticed to be heard, a party demands a trial by jury, in which case trial shall be by jury. At the time when issue is joined the court, in its discretion at the request of either party and upon proof to its satisfaction by affidavit or orally that an adjournment is necessary to enable the applicant to procure his necessary witnesses, or by consent of all the parties who appear, may adjourn the trial of the issue, but not more than ten days, except by consent of all parties.

2. In the city of New York:

(a) In a summary proceeding upon the second request by the tenant for an adjournment, the court shall direct that the tenant post all sums as they become due for future rent and use and occupancy, which may be established without the use of expert testimony, unless waived by the court for good cause shown. Two adjournments shall not include an adjournment requested by a tenant unrepresented by counsel for the purpose of securing counsel made on the initial return date of the proceeding. Such future rent and use and occupancy sums shall be deposited with the clerk of the court or paid to such other person or entity, including the petitioner, as the court shall direct or shall be expended for such emergency repairs as the court shall approve. (b) In any adjournment of a summary proceeding, other than on consent or at the request of the petitioner, the court shall at the petitioner's request state on the record why for good cause shown it is not directing the tenant to pay or post all sums demanded pursuant to a lease or rental agreement in the proceeding as rent and use and occupancy. (c) The provisions of this subdivision shall not apply if the housing accommodation in question or the public areas pertaining thereto are charged with immediately hazardous violations of record as defined by the New York city housing maintenance code. (d) The court may dismiss any summary proceeding without prejudice and with costs to the respondent by reason of excessive adjournments requested by the petitioner. (e) The provisions of this subdivision shall not be construed as to deprive a tenant of a trial of any summary proceeding.

Sec. 747. Judgment.

1. The court shall direct that a final judgment be entered determining the rights of the parties. The judgment shall award to the successful party the costs of the special proceeding.

2. The judgment shall not bar an action to recover the possession of real property. The judgment shall not bar an action, proceeding or counterclaim, commenced or interposed within sixty days of entry of the judgment, for affirmative equitable relief which was not sought by counterclaim in the proceeding because of the limited jurisdiction of the court.

3. If the proceeding is founded upon an allegation of forcible entry or forcible holding out the court may award to the successful party a fixed sum as costs, not exceeding fifty dollars, in addition to his disbursements.

4. The judgment, including such money as it may award for rent or otherwise, may be docketed in such books as the court maintains for recording the steps in a summary proceeding; unless a rule of the court, or the court by order in a given case, otherwise provides, such judgment need not be recorded or docketed in the books, if separately maintained, in which are docketed money judgments in an action.

Sec. 749. Warrant.

1. Upon rendering a final judgment for petitioner, the court shall issue a warrant directed to the sheriff of the county or to any constable or marshal of the city in which the property, or a portion thereof, is situated, or, if it is not situated in a city, to any constable of any town in the county, describing the property, and commanding the officer to remove all persons, and, except where the case is within section 715, to put the petitioner into full possession.

2. The officer to whom the warrant is directed and delivered shall give at least seventy-two hours notice, in writing and in the manner prescribed in this article for the service of a notice of petition, to the person or persons to be evicted or dispossessed and shall execute the warrant between the hours of sunrise and sunset.

3. The issuing of a warrant for the removal of a tenant cancels the agreement under which the person removed held the premises, and annuls the relation of landlord and tenant, but nothing contained herein shall deprive the court of the power to vacate such warrant for good cause shown prior to the execution thereof. Petitioner may recover by action any sum of money which was payable at the time when the special proceeding was commenced and the reasonable value of the use and occupation to the time when the warrant was issued, for any period of time with respect to which the agreement does not make any provision for payment of rent.

Sec. 751. Stay Upon Paying Rent or Giving Undertaking; Discretionary Stay Outside City of New York.

The respondent may, at any time before a warrant is issued, stay the issuing thereof and also stay an execution to collect the costs, as follows:

1. Where the lessee or tenant holds over after a default in the payment of rent, or of taxes or assessments, he may effect a stay by depositing the amount of the rent due or of such taxes or assessments, and interest and penalty, if any thereon due, and the costs of the special proceeding, with the clerk of the court, or where the office of clerk is not provided for, with the court, who shall thereupon, upon demand, pay the amount deposited to the petitioner or his duly authorized agent; or by delivering to the court or clerk his undertaking to the petitioner in such sum as the court approves to the effect that he will pay the rent, or such taxes or assessments, and interest and penalty and costs within ten days, at the expiration of which time a warrant may issue, unless he produces to the court satisfactory evidence of the payment.

2. Where the lessee or tenant has taken the benefit of an insolvency statute or has been adjudicated a bankrupt, he may effect a stay by paying the costs of the special proceeding and by delivering to the court or clerk his undertaking to the petitioner in such a sum as the court approves to the effect that he will pay the rent of the premises as it has become or thereafter becomes due.

3. Where he continues in possession of real property which has been sold by virtue of an execution against his property, he may effect a stay by paying the costs of the special proceeding, and delivering to the court

or clerk an affidavit that he claims the possession of the property by virtue of a right or title acquired after the sale or as guardian or trustee for another; together with his undertaking to the petitioner in such a sum as the court approves to the effect that he will pay any costs and damages which may be recovered against him in an action to recover the property brought against him by the petitioner within six months thereafter; and that he will not commit any waste upon or injury to the property during his occupation thereof.

4. (a) In a proceeding to recover the possession of premises outside the city of New York occupied for dwelling purposes, other than a room or rooms in an hotel, lodging house or rooming house, upon the ground that the occupant is holding over and continuing in possession of the premises after the expiration of his term and without the permission of the landlord, or, in a case where a new lessee is entitled to possession, without the permission of the new lessee, the court, on application of the occupant, may stay the issuance of a warrant and also stay any execution to collect the costs of the proceeding for a period of not more than four months, if it appears that the premises described in the petition are used for dwelling purposes; that the application is made in good faith; that the applicant cannot within the neighborhood secure suitable premises similar to those occupied by him and that he made due and reasonable efforts to secure such other premises, or that by reason of other facts it would occasion extreme hardship to him or his family if the stay were not granted.

(b) Such stay shall be granted and continue effective only upon the condition that the person against whom the judgment is entered shall make a deposit in court of the entire amount, or such installments thereof from time to time, as the court may direct, for the occupation of the premises for the period of the stay, at the rate for which he was liable as rent for the month immediately prior to the expiration of his term or tenancy, plus such additional amount, if any, as the court may determine to be the difference between such rent and the reasonable rent or value of the use and occupation of the premises; such deposit shall also include all rent unpaid by the occupant prior to the stay.

The amount of such deposit shall be determined by the court upon the application for the stay and such determination shall be final and conclusive in respect to the amount of such deposit, and the amount thereof shall be paid into court, in such manner and in such installments, if any, as the court may direct. A separate account shall be kept of the amount to the credit of each proceeding, and all such payments shall be deposited in a bank or trust company and shall be subject to the check of the clerk of the court, if there be one, or otherwise of the court. The clerk of the court, if there be one, and otherwise the court

shall pay to the landlord or his duly authorized agent, the amount of such deposit in accordance with the terms of the stay or the further order of the court. (c) The provisions of this subdivision shall not apply to a proceeding where the petitioner shows to the satisfaction of the court that he desires in good faith to recover the premises for the purposes of demolishing same with the intention of constructing a new building, plans for which new building shall have been duly filed and approved by the proper authority; nor shall it apply to a proceeding to recover possession upon the ground that an occupant is holding over and is objectionable if the landlord shall establish to the satisfaction of the court that such occupant is objectionable. (d) Any provision of a lease or other agreement whereby a lessee or tenant waives any provision of this subdivision shall be deemed against public policy and void. (e) The provisions of this subdivision shall continue in effect only until September first, nineteen hundred sixty-seven.

Sec. 753. Stay Where Tenants Holds Over in Premises Occupied for Dwelling Purposes in City of New York.

1. In a proceeding to recover the possession of premises in the city of New York occupied for dwelling purposes, other than a room or rooms in an hotel, lodging house, or rooming house, upon the ground that the occupant is holding over and continuing in possession of the premises after the expiration of his term and without the permission of the landlord, or, in a case where a new lessee is entitled to possession, without the permission of the new lessee, the court, on application of the occupant, may stay the issuance of a warrant and also stay any execution to collect the costs of the proceeding for a period of not more than six months, if it appears that the premises are used for dwelling purposes; that the application is made in good faith; that the applicant cannot within the neighborhood secure suitable premises similar to those occupied by him and that he made due and reasonable efforts to secure such other premises, or that by reason of other facts it would occasion extreme hardship to him or his family if the stay were not granted.

2. Such stay shall be granted and continue effective only upon the condition that the person against whom the judgment is entered shall make a deposit in court of the entire amount, or such installments thereof from time to time as the court may direct, for the occupation of the premises for the period of the stay, at the rate for which he was liable as rent for the month immediately prior to the expiration of his term or tenancy, plus such additional amount, if any, as the court may determine to be the difference between such rent and the reasonable rent or value of the use and occupation of the premises; such deposit shall also include all rent unpaid by the occupant prior to the period of the stay. The amount of such deposit shall be determined by the court upon

the application for the stay and such determination shall be final and conclusive in respect to the amount of such deposit, and the amount thereof shall be paid into court, in such manner and in such installments, if any, as the court may direct. A separate account shall be kept of the amount to the credit of each proceeding, and all such payments shall be deposited in a bank or trust company and shall be subject to the check of the clerk of the court, if there be one, or otherwise of the court. The clerk of the court, if there be one, and otherwise the court shall pay to the landlord or his duly authorized agent, the amount of such deposit in accordance with the terms of the stay or the further order of the court.

3. The provisions of this section shall not apply to a proceeding where the petitioner shows to the satisfaction of the court that he desires in good faith to recover the premises for the purpose of demolishing same with the intention of constructing a new building, plans for which new building shall have been duly filed and approved by the proper authority; nor shall it apply to a proceeding to recover possession upon the ground that an occupant is holding over and is objectionable if the landlord shall establish to the satisfaction of the court that such occupant is objectionable.

4. In the event that such proceeding is based upon a claim that the tenant or lessee has breached a provision of the lease, the court shall grant a ten day stay of issuance of the warrant, during which time the respondent may correct such breach.

5. Any provision of a lease or other agreement whereby a lessee or tenant waives any provision of this section shall be deemed against public policy and void.

Sec. 755. Stay of Proceeding or Action for Rent Upon Failure to Make Repairs.

1. (a) Upon proper proof that a notice or order to remove or cease a nuisance or a violation or to make necessary and proper repairs has been made by the municipal department charged with the enforcement of the multiple dwelling law, the multiple residence law, or any other applicable local housing code, or officer or officers thereof charged with the supervision of such matters, if the condition against which such notice or order is directed is, in the opinion of the court, such as to constructively evict the tenant from a portion of the premises occupied by him, or is, or is likely to become, dangerous to life, health, or safety, the court before which the case is pending may stay proceedings to dispossess the tenant for non-payment of rent or any action for rent or rental value. In any such proceeding, on the question of fact, as to the condition of the dwelling the landlord or petitioner shall have the burden of disproving the condition of the dwelling as such condition is described in the notice or order.

(b) Upon proper proof of the existence of a condition that is in the opinion of the court, such as to construc-

tively evict the tenant from a portion of the premises occupied by him, or is or is, likely to become, dangerous to life, health, or safety, the court before which the case is pending may stay proceedings to dispossess the tenant for non-payment of rent, or any action for rent or rental value.

(c) The court shall in no case grant a stay where it appears that the condition against which the notice or order is directed has been created by the willful or negligent act of the tenant or his agent. Such stay shall continue in force, until an order shall be made by the court vacating it, but no order vacating such stay shall be made, except upon three days' notice of hearing to the tenant, or respondent, or his attorney, and proof that such notice or order has been complied with.

2. The tenant or respondent shall not be entitled to the stay unless he shall deposit with the clerk of the court the rent then due, which shall, for the purposes of this section, be deemed the same as the tenant was liable for during the preceding month or such as is reserved as the monthly rent in the agreement under which he obtained possession of the premises. The stay may be vacated upon three days' notice upon failure to deposit with the clerk the rent within five days after it is due, during the pendency of the proceeding or action.

3. During the continuance of the stay, the court may direct, in its discretion, upon three days notice to all parties, the release to a contractor or materialman of all or such part of the moneys on deposit as shall be sufficient to pay bills properly presented by such contractor or materialman for the maintenance of and necessary repairs to the building (including but not limited to payments for fuel, electricity, gas, janitorial services and repairs necessary to remove violations), upon a showing by the tenant that the landlord is not meeting his legal obligations therefor or direct such release to a municipal department to pay bills and expenses for such maintenance and repairs upon a showing that the landlord did not meet his legal obligation to provide such maintenance or perform repairs and that the department incurred expenses therefor. Upon the entry of an order vacating the stay the remaining money deposited shall be paid to the plaintiff or landlord or his duly authorized agent.

4. Neither party shall be entitled to any costs in any proceeding or action wherein the stay shall be granted except that costs may be awarded against the tenant or defendant in the discretion of the court in the event the condition complained of shall be found to be due to the willful act of the tenant or defendant, such costs, however, not to exceed the sum of twenty-five dollars.

Sec. 756. Stay of Summary Proceedings or Actions for Rent Under Certain Conditions.

In the event that utilities are discontinued in any part of a multiple dwelling because of the failure of the landlord or other person having control of said multiple dwelling to pay for utilities for which he may have contracted, any proceeding to dispossess a tenant from said building or an action against any tenant of said building for rent shall be stayed until such time as the landlord or person having control of said multiple dwelling pays the amount owing for said utilities and until such time as the utilities are restored to working order.

Sec. 761. Redemption By Lessee.

Where the special proceeding is founded upon an allegation that a lessee holds over after a default in the payment of rent, and the unexpired term of the lease under which the premises are held exceeds five years at the time when the warrant is issued the lessee, his executor, administrator or assignee, at any time within one year after the execution of the warrant, unless by the terms of the lease such lessee shall have waived his right to redeem, or such lessee, executor, administrator or assignee shall have subsequently waived the right to redeem by a written instrument filed and recorded in the office in which the lease is recorded, or if not so recorded, in the office in which deeds are required to be recorded of the county in which the leased premises are located, may pay or tender to the petitioner, his heir, executor, administrator or assignee, or if, within five days before the expiration of the year he cannot be found with reasonable diligence within the city or town wherein the property or a portion thereof is situated, then to the court which issued the warrant, all rent in arrears at the time of the payment or tender with interest thereupon and the costs and charges incurred by the petitioner. Thereupon the person making the payment or tender shall be entitled to the possession of the demised premises under the lease and may hold and enjoy the same according to the terms of the original demise, except as otherwise prescribed in section 765.

Sec. 763. Redemption By Creditor of Lessee.

In a case specified in section 761, a judgment creditor of the lessee whose judgment was docketed in the county before the precept was issued, or a mortgagee of the lease whose mortgage was duly recorded in the county before the precept was issued, unless by the terms of the lease the lessee shall have waived his right to redeem, or such lessee, or his executor, administrator or assignee shall have subsequently waived the right to redeem by a written instrument filed and recorded in the office in which the lease is recorded, or if not so recorded, in the office in which deeds are required to be recorded of the county in which the leased premises are located, before such judgment was docketed or such mortgage recorded, or such judgment creditor or mortgagee himself shall have waived in writing his right to redeem, may at any time before the expiration of one year after the execution of the warrant, unless a redemption has been made as prescribed in section 761, file with the

court which issued the warrant a notice specifying his interest and the sum due to him, describing the premises, and stating that it is his intention to redeem as prescribed in this section. If a redemption is not made by the lessee, his executor, administrator or assignee within a year after the execution of the warrant, the person so filing a notice, or, if two or more persons have filed such notices the one who holds the first lien, at any time before two o'clock of the day, not a Sunday or a public holiday, next succeeding the last day of the year, may redeem for his own benefit in like manner as the lessee, his executor, administrator or assignee might have so redeemed. Where two or more judgment creditors or mortgagees have filed such notices, the holder of the second lien may so redeem at any time before two o'clock of the day, not a Sunday or a public holiday, next succeeding that in which the holder of the first lien might have redeemed; and the holder of the third and each subsequent lien may redeem in like manner at any time before two o'clock of the day, not a Sunday or a public holiday, next succeeding that in which his predecessor might have redeemed. But a second or subsequent redemption is not valid unless the person redeeming pays or tenders to each of his predecessors who has redeemed the sum paid by him to redeem and also the sum due upon his judgment or mortgage; or deposits those sums with the court for the benefit of his predecessor or predecessors.

Sec. 765. Effect of Redemption Upon Lease.

Where a redemption is made, as prescribed in this article, the rights of the person redeeming are subject to a lease, if any, executed by the petitioner since the warrant was issued, so far that the new lessee, his assigns, undertenants, or other representatives, upon complying with the terms of the lease, may hold the premises so leased until twelve o'clock, noon, of the first day of May next succeeding the redemption. And in all other respects, the person so redeeming, his assigns and representatives succeed to all the rights and liabilities of the petitioner under such a lease.

Sec. 767. Order of Redemption; Liability of Persons Redeeming.

The person redeeming, as prescribed in this article or the owner of the property so redeemed, may present to the court which issued the warrant a petition setting forth the facts of the redemption and praying for an order establishing the rights and liabilities of the parties upon the redemption, whereupon the court must make an order requiring the other party to the redemption to show cause at a time and place therein specified why the prayer of the petition should not be granted. The order to show cause must be made returnable not less than two nor more than ten days after it is granted; and it must be served at least two days before it is returnable. Upon the return thereof, the court must hear the allegations and proofs of the parties and must make such a judgment as justice requires. The costs and expenses must be paid by the petitioner. The judgment, or a certified copy thereof, may be recorded in like manner as a deed. A person, other than the lessee, who redeems as prescribed in this article succeeds to all the duties and liabilities of the lessee accruing after the redemption as if he was named as lessee in the lease.

Sec. 769. Jurisdiction; Court; Venue.
1. A special proceeding by tenants of a dwelling in the city of New York or the counties of Nassau, Suffolk, Rockland and Westchester for a judgment directing the deposit of rents into court and their use for the purpose of remedying conditions dangerous to life, health or safety may be maintained in the civil court of the city of New York, the district court of the counties of Suffolk and Nassau and the county courts or city courts in the counties of Rockland and Westchester.
2. The place of trial of the special proceeding shall be within the county in which the real property or a portion thereof from which the rents issue is situated.

REAL PROPERTY LAW (RPL)
ARTICLE 7
LANDLORD AND TENANT
220. Action for use and occupation.
221. Rent due on life leases recoverable.
222. When rent is apportionable.
223. Rights where property or lease is transferred.
223-a. Remedies of lessee when possession is not delivered.
223-b. Retaliation by landlord against tenant.
224. Attornment by tenant.
225. Notice of action adverse to possession of tenant.
226. Effect of renewal on sub-lease.
226-a. Effect of new lease on tenant's right to remove fixtures or improvements.
226-b. Right to sublease or assign.
227. When tenant may surrender premises.
227-a. Termination of residential lease by senior citizens entering certain health care facilities, adult care facilities or housing projects.
228. Termination of tenancies at will or by sufferance, by notice.
229. Liability of tenant holding over after giving notice of intention to quit.
230. Right of tenants to form, join or participate in tenants' groups.
231. Lease, when void; liability of landlord where premises are occupied for unlawful purpose.
232. Duration of certain agreements in New York.
232-a. Notice to terminate monthly tenancy or tenancy from month to month in the city of

New York.
232-b. Notification to terminate monthly tenancy or tenancy from month to month outside the city of New York.
232-c. Holding over by a tenant after expiration of a term longer than one month; effect of acceptance of rent.
233. Mobile home parks; duties, responsibilities.
234. Tenants' right to recover attorneys' fees in actions or summary proceedings arising out of leases of residential property.
235. Wilful violations.
235-a. Tenant right to offset payments and entitlement to damages in certain cases.
235-b. Warranty of habitability.
235-c. Unconscionable lease or clause.
235-d. Harassment.
235-e. Duty of landlord to provide written receipt.
235-f. Unlawful restrictions on occupancy.
236. Assignment of lease of a deceased tenant.
236. Discrimination against children in dwelling houses and mobile home parks.
237. Discrimination in leases with respect to bearing of children.
238. Agreements or contracts for privileges to deal with occupants of tenements, apartment houses or bungalow colonies.

Sec. 220. Action for use and occupation.
The landlord may recover a reasonable compensation for the use and occupation of real property, by any person, under an agreement, not made by deed; and a parol lease or other agreement may be used as evidence of the amount to which he is entitled.
Sec. 221. Rent due on life leases recoverable.
Rent due on a lease for life or lives is recoverable by action, as well after as before the death of the person on whose life the rent depends, and in the same manner as rent due on a lease for years.
Sec. 222. When rent is apportionable.
Where a tenant for life, who shall have demised the real property, dies before the first rent day, or between two rent days, his executor or administrator may recover the proportion of rent which accrued to him before his death.
Sec. 223. Rights where property or lease is transferred.
The grantee of leased real property, or of a reversion thereof, or of any rent, the devisee or assignee of the lessor of such a lease, or the heir or personal representative of either of them, has the same remedies, by entry, action or otherwise, for the nonperformance of any agreement contained in the assigned lease for the recovery of rent, for the doing of any waste, or for other cause of forfeiture as his grantor or lessor had, or would have had, if the reversion had remained in him. A lessee of real property, his assignee or

personal representative, has the same remedy against the lessor, his grantee or assignee, or the representative of either, for the breach of an agreement contained in the lease, that the lessee might have had against his immediate lessor, except a covenant against incumbrances or relating to the title or possession of the premises leased. This Section applies as well to a grant or lease in fee, reserving rent, as to a lease for life or for years; but not to a deed of conveyance in fee, made before the ninth day of April, eighteen hundred and five, or after the fourteenth day of April, eighteen hundred and sixty.

Sec. 223-a. Remedies of lessee when possession is not delivered.

In the absence of an express provision to the contrary, there shall be implied in every lease of real property a condition that the lessor will deliver possession at the beginning of the term. In the event of breach of such implied condition the lessee shall have the right to rescind the lease and to recover the consideration paid. Such right shall not be deemed inconsistent with any right of action he may have to recover damages.

Sec. 223-b. Retaliation by landlord against tenant.

1. No landlord of premises or units to which this section is applicable shall serve a notice to quit upon any tenant or commence any action to recover real property or summary proceeding to recover possession of real property in retaliation for:

a. A good faith complaint, by or in behalf of the tenant, to a governmental authority of the landlord's alleged violation of any health or safety law, regulation, code, or ordinance, or any law or regulation which has as its objective the regulation of premises used for dwelling purposes or which pertains to the offense of rent gouging in the third, second or first degree; or b. Actions taken in good faith, by or in behalf of the tenant, to secure or enforce any rights under the lease or rental agreement, under Section two hundred thirty-five-b of this chapter, or under any other law of the state of New York, or of its governmental subdivisions, or of the United States which has as its objective the regulation of premises used for dwelling purposes or which pertains to the offense of rent gouging in the third, second or first degree; or c. The tenant's participation in the activities of a tenant's organization.

2. No landlord or premises or units to which this section is applicable shall substantially alter the terms of the tenancy in retaliation for any actions set forth in paragraphs a, b, and c of subdivision one of this section. Substantial alteration shall include, but is not limited to, the refusal to continue a tenancy of the tenant or, upon expiration of the tenant's lease, to renew the lease or offer a new lease; provided, however, that a landlord shall not be required under this section to offer a new lease or a lease renewal for a term greater than one year and after such extension of a tenancy for one year shall not be required to further extend or continue such tenancy.

3. A landlord shall be subject to a civil action for damages and other appropriate relief, including injunctive and other equitable remedies, as may be determined by a court of competent jurisdiction in any case in which the landlord has violated the provisions of this section.

4. In any action to recover real property or summary proceeding to recover possession of real property, judgment shall be entered for the tenant if the court finds that the landlord is acting in retaliation for any action set forth in paragraphs a, b, and c of subdivision one of this section and further finds that the landlord would not otherwise have commenced such action or proceeding. Retaliation shall be asserted as an affirmative defense in such action or proceeding. The tenant shall not be relieved of the obligation to pay any rent for which he is otherwise liable.

5. In an action or proceeding instituted against a tenant of premises or a unit to which this section is applicable, a rebuttable presumption that the landlord is acting in retaliation shall be created if the tenant establishes that the landlord served a notice to quit, or instituted an action or proceeding to recover possession, or attempted to substantially alter the terms of the tenancy, within six months after:

a. A good faith complaint was made, by or in behalf of the tenant, to a governmental authority of the landlord's violation of any health or safety law, regulation, code, or ordinance, or any law or regulation which has as its objective the regulation of premises used for dwelling purposes or which pertains to the offense of rent gouging in the third, second or first degree; or b. The tenant in good faith commenced an action or proceeding in a court or administrative body of competent jurisdiction to secure or enforce against the landlord or his agents any rights under the lease or rental agreement, under section two hundred thirty-five-b of this chapter, or under any other law of the state of New York, or of its governmental subdivisions, or of the United States which has as its objective the regulation of premises used for dwelling purposes or which pertains to the offense of rent gouging in the third, second or first degree. c. Judgment under subdivision three or four of this section was entered for the tenant in a previous action between the parties; or an inspection was made, an order was entered, or other action was taken as a result of a complaint or act described in paragraph a or b of this subdivision.

But the presumption shall not apply in an action or proceeding based on the violation by the tenant of the terms and conditions of the lease or rental agreement, including nonpayment of the agreed-upon rent. The effect of the presumption shall be to require the landlord to provide a credible explanation of a non- retaliatory motive for his acts. Such an explanation shall overcome and remove the presumption unless the tenant disproves it by a preponderance of the evidence.

6. This section shall apply to all rental residential premises except owner-occupied dwellings with less than four units. However, its provisions shall not be given effect in any case in which it is established that the condition from which the complaint or action arose was caused by the tenant, a member of the tenant's household, or a guest of the tenant. Nor shall it apply in a case where a tenancy was terminated pursuant to the terms of a lease as a result of a bona fide transfer of ownership.

Sec. 224. Attornment by tenant.

The attornment of a tenant to a stranger is absolutely void and does not in any way affect the possession of the landlord unless made either:

1. With the consent of the landlord; or,

2. Pursuant to or in consequence of a judgment, order, or decree of a court of competent jurisdiction; or

3. To a purchaser at foreclosure sale.

Sec. 225. Notice of action adverse to possession of tenant.

Where a process or summons in an action to recover the real property occupied by him, or the possession thereof, is served upon a tenant, he must forthwith give notice thereof to his landlord; otherwise he forfeits the value of three years' rent of such property, to the landlord or other person of whom he holds.

Sec. 226. Effect of renewal on sub-lease.

The surrender of an under-lease is not requisite to the validity of the surrender of the original lease, where a new lease is given by the chief landlord. Such a surrender and renewal do not impair any right or interest of the chief landlord, his lessee or the holder of an under-lease, under the original lease; including the chief landlord's remedy by entry, for the rent or duties secured by the new lease, not exceeding the rent and duties reserved in the original lease surrendered.

Sec. 226-a. Effect of new lease on tenant's right to remove fixtures or improvements.

Unless otherwise expressly agreed, where a tenant has a right to remove fixtures or improvements, such right shall not be lost or impaired by reason of his acceptance of a new lease of the same premises without any surrender of possession between terms.

Sec. 226-b. Right to sublease or assign.

1. Unless a greater right to assign is conferred by the lease, a tenant renting a residence may not assign his lease without the written consent of the owner, which consent may be unconditionally withheld without cause provided that the owner shall release the tenant from the lease upon request of the tenant upon thirty days notice if the owner unreasonably withholds consent which release shall be the sole remedy of the tenant. If the owner reasonably withholds consent, there shall be no assignment and the tenant shall not be released from the lease.

2. (a) A tenant renting a residence pursuant to an existing lease in a dwelling having four or more residential units shall have the right to sublease his premises subject to the written consent of the landlord in advance of the subletting. Such consent shall not be unreasonably withheld.

(b) The tenant shall inform the landlord of his intent to sublease by mailing a notice of such intent by certified mail, return receipt requested. Such request shall be accompanied by the following information: (i) the term of the sublease, (ii) the name of the proposed sublessee, (iii) the business and permanent home address of the proposed sublessee, (iv) the tenant's reason for subletting, (v) the tenant's address for the term of the sublease, (vi) the written consent of any co-tenant or guarantor of the lease, and (vii) a copy of the proposed sublease, to which a copy of the tenant's lease shall be attached if available, acknowledged by the tenant and proposed subtenant as being a true copy of such sublease.

(c) Within ten days after the mailing of such request, the landlord may ask the tenant for additional information as will enable the landlord to determine if rejection of such request shall be unreasonable. Any such request for additional information shall not be unduly burdensome. Within thirty days after the mailing of the request for consent, or of the additional information reasonably asked for by the landlord, whichever is later, the landlord shall send a notice to the tenant of his consent or, if he does not consent, his reasons therefor. Landlord's failure to send such a notice shall be deemed to be a consent to the proposed subletting. If the landlord consents, the premises may be sublet in accordance with the request, but the tenant thereunder, shall nevertheless remain liable for the performance of tenant's obligations under said lease. If the landlord reasonably withholds consent, there shall be no subletting and the tenant shall not be released from the lease. If the landlord unreasonably withholds consent, the tenant may sublet in accordance with the request and may recover the costs of the proceeding and attorneys fees if it is found that the owner acted in bad faith by withholding consent.

3. The provisions of this section shall apply to leases entered into or renewed before or after the effective date of this section, however they shall not apply to public housing and other units for which there are constitutional or statutory criteria covering admission thereto nor to a proprietary lease, viz.: a lease to, or held by, a tenant entitled thereto by reason of ownership of stock in a corporate owner of premises which operates the same on a cooperative basis.

4. With respect to units covered by the emergency tenant protection act of nineteen seventy-four or the rent stabilization law of nineteen hundred sixty-nine the exercise of the rights granted by this section shall be subject to the applicable provisions of such laws. Nothing contained in this section two hundred

twenty-six-b shall be deemed to affect the rights, if any, of any tenant subject to title Y of chapter 51 of the administrative code of the city of New York or the emergency housing rent control law.

5. Any sublet or assignment which does not comply with the provisions of this section shall constitute a substantial breach of lease or tenancy.

6. Any provision of a lease or rental agreement purporting to waive a provision of this section is null and void.

7. The provisions of this section except for items in paragraph (b) of subdivision two of this section not previously required, shall apply to all actions and proceedings pending on the effective date of this section.

8. Nothing contained in this section shall be deemed to prevent or limit the right of a tenant to sell improvements to a unit pursuant to article seven-C of the multiple dwelling law.

Sec. 227. When tenant may surrender premises. Where any building, which is leased or occupied, is destroyed or so injured by the elements, or any other cause as to be untenantable, and unfit for occupancy, and no express agreement to the contrary has been made in writing, the lessee or occupant may, if the destruction or injury occurred without his or her fault or neglect, quit and surrender possession of the leasehold premises, and of the land so leased or occupied; and he or she is not liable to pay to the lessor or owner, rent for the time subsequent to the surrender. Any rent paid in advance or which may have accrued by the terms of a lease or any other hiring shall be adjusted to the date of such surrender.

Sec. 227-a. Termination of residential lease by senior citizens entering certain health care facilities, adult care facilities or housing projects.

1. In any lease or rental agreement covering premises occupied for dwelling purposes in which a lessee or tenant has attained the age of sixty-two years or older, or will attain such age during the term of such lease or rental agreement or a husband or wife of such a person residing with him or her, there shall be implied a covenant by the lessor or owner to permit such lessee or tenant who is notified of his or her opportunity to commence occupancy in an adult care facility (as defined in subdivision twenty-one of section two of the social services law) except for a shelter for adults (as defined in subdivision twenty-three of section two of such law), a residential health care facility (as defined in section two thousand eight hundred one of the public health law), or a housing unit which receives substantial assistance of grants, loans or subsidies from any federal, state or local agency or instrumentality, or any not-for-profit philanthropic organization one of whose primary purposes is providing low or moderate income housing, or in less expensive premises in a housing project or complex erected for the specific purpose of housing senior citizens, to terminate such lease or rental agreement and quit and surrender possession of the leasehold premises, and of the land so leased or occupied; and to release the lessee or tenant from any liability to pay to the lessor or owner, rent or other payments in lieu of rent for the time subsequent to the date of termination of such lease in accordance with subdivision two of this section; and to adjust to the date of surrender any rent or other payments made in advance or which have accrued by the terms of such lease or rental agreement.

2. Any lease or rental agreement covered by subdivision one of this Section may be terminated by notice in writing delivered to the lessor or owner or to the lessor's or owner's agent by a lessee or tenant. Such termination shall be effective no earlier than thirty days after the date on which the next rental payment subsequent to the date when such notice is delivered is due and payable. Such notice shall be accompanied by a documentation of admission or pending admission to a facility set forth in subdivision one of this section. Such notice shall be deemed delivered five days after mailing.

3. Any person who shall knowingly seize, hold, or detain the personal effects, clothing, furniture or other property of any person who has lawfully terminated a lease or rental agreement covered by this section or the spouse or dependent of any such person, or in any manner interferes with the removal of such property from the premises covered by such lease or rental agreement, for the purpose of subjecting or attempting to subject any of such property to a purported claim for rent accruing subsequent to the date of termination of such lease or rental agreement, or attempts so to do, shall be guilty of a misdemeanor and shall be punished by imprisonment not to exceed one year or by fine not to exceed one thousand dollars, or by both such fine and imprisonment.

3-a. Each owner or lessor of a facility or unit into which a lessee or tenant is entitled to move after quitting and surrendering as provided for herein shall in writing, upon an application, notify prospective tenants of the provision of this section. Such notice shall include, in plain and simple English, in conspicuous print of at least eighteen point type, an explanation of a tenants right to terminate the existing lease and all other applicable requirements and duties relating thereto. Such notice shall read as follows:

NOTICE TO SENIOR CITIZENS: RESIDENTIAL LEASE TERMINATION SECTION 227-a OF THE REAL PROPERTY LAW OF THE STATE OF NEW YORK ALLOWS FOR THE TERMINATION OF A RESIDENTIAL LEASE BY SENIOR CITIZENS ENTERING CERTAIN HEALTH CARE FACILITIES, ADULT CARE FACILITIES OR HOUSING PROJECTS.

Who is eligible? Any lessee or tenant who is age sixty-two years or older, or who will attain such age during the term of the lease or rental agreement, or a spouse of such person residing with him or her. What kind of facilities does this law apply to? This law will apply if the senior citizen is relocating to: A. An adult care facility; B. A residential health care facility; C. Subsidized low income housing; or D. Senior citizen housing. What are the responsibilities of the rental property owner? When the tenant gives notice of his or her opportunity to move into one of the above facilities the landlord must allow: A. for the termination of the lease or rental agreement, and B. the release of the tenant from any liability to pay rent or other payments in lieu of rent from the termination of the lease in accordance with section 227-a of the real property law, to the time of the original termination date, and C. to adjust any payments made in advance or payments which have accrued by the terms of such lease or rental agreement. How do you terminate the lease? If the tenant can move into one of the specified facilities, he or she must terminate the lease or agreement in writing no earlier than thirty days after the date on which the next rental payment (after the notice is delivered) is due and payable. The notice is deemed delivered five days after being mailed. The written notice must include documentation of admission or pending admission to one of the above mentioned facilities. For example: Mail the notice: May 5th Notice received: May 10th Next rental payment due: June 1st Termination effective: July 1st Will the landlord face penalties if he or she does not comply? Yes, according to section 227-a of the real property law, if anyone interferes with the removal of your property from the premises they will be guilty of a misdemeanor and will be either imprisoned for up to one year or fined up to $1000.00 or both. 4. Any agreement by a lessee or tenant of premises occupied for dwelling purposes waiving or modifying his or her rights as set forth in this section shall be void as contrary to public policy.

Sec. 228. Termination of tenancies at will or by sufferance, by notice.

A tenancy at will or by sufferance, however created, may be terminated by a written notice of not less than thirty days given in behalf of the landlord, to the tenant, requiring him to remove from the premises; which notice must be served, either by delivering to the tenant or to a person of suitable age and discretion, residing upon the premises, or if neither the tenant nor such a person can be found, by affixing it upon a conspicuous part of the premises, where it may be conveniently read. At the expiration of thirty days after the service of such notice, the landlord may re-enter, maintain an action to recover possession, or proceed, in the manner prescribed by law, to remove the tenant, without further or other notice to quit.

Sec. 229. Liability of tenant holding over after giving notice of intention to quit.

If a tenant gives notice of his intention to quit the premises held by him, and does not accordingly deliver up the possession thereof, at the time specified in such notice, he or his personal representatives must, so long as he continue in possession, pay to the landlord, his heirs or assigns, double the rent which he should otherwise have paid, to be recovered at the same time, and in the same manner, as the single rent.

Sec. 230. Right of tenants to form, join or participate in tenants' groups.

1. No landlord shall interfere with the right of a tenant to form, join or participate in the lawful activities of any group, committee or other organization formed to protect the rights of tenants; nor shall any landlord harass, punish, penalize, diminish, or withhold any right, benefit or privilege of a tenant under his tenancy for exercising such right.
2. Tenants' groups, committees or other tenants' organizations shall have the right to meet in any location on the premises which is devoted to the common use of all tenants in a peaceful manner, at reasonable hours and without obstructing access to the premises or facilities. No landlord shall deny such right.

Sec. 231. Lease, when void; liability of landlord where premises are occupied for unlawful purpose.

1. Whenever the lessee or occupant other than the owner of any building or premises, shall use or occupy the same, or any part thereof, for any illegal trade, manufacture or other business, the lease or agreement for the letting or occupancy of such building or premises, or any part thereof shall thereupon become void, and the landlord of such lessee or occupant may enter upon the premises so let or occupied.
2. The owner of real property, knowingly leasing or giving possession of the same to be used or occupied, wholly or partly, for any unlawful trade, manufacture or business, or knowingly permitting the same to be so used, is liable severally, and also jointly with one or more of the tenants or occupants thereof, for any damage resulting from such unlawful use, occupancy, trade, manufacture or business.
3. For the purposes of this section, two or more convictions of any person or persons had, within a period of one year, for any of the offenses described in section 230.00, 230.05, 230.20, 230.25, 230.30, or 230.40 of the penal law arising out of conduct engaged in at the same premises consisting of a dwelling as that term is defined in subdivision four of section four of the multiple dwelling law shall be presumptive evidence of unlawful use of such premises and of the owners knowledge of the same.
4. Any lease or agreement hereafter executed for the letting or occupancy of real property or any portion thereof, to be used by the lessee as a residence, which

contains therein a provision pledging personal property exempt by law from levy and sale by virtue of an execution, as security for the payment of rent due or to become due thereunder, is void as to such provision.

5. For the purposes of this section, two or more convictions of any person or persons had, within a period of one year, for any of the offenses described in section 225.00, 225.05, 225.10, 225.15, 225.20, 225.30, 225.32, 225.35 or 225.40 of the penal law, arising out of conduct engaged in at the same premises consisting of a dwelling as that term is defined in subdivision four of section four of the multiple dwelling law shall be presumptive evidence of unlawful use of such premises and of the owner's knowledge of the same.

5. The attorney general may commence an action or proceeding in the supreme court to enjoin the continued unlawful trade, manufacture or business in such premises.

6. Any owner or tenant, including a tenant of one or more rooms of an apartment house, tenement house or multiple dwelling of any premises within two hundred feet of the demised real property, may commence an action or proceeding in supreme court to enjoin the continued unlawful trade, manufacture or other business in such premises.

Sec. 232. Duration of certain agreements in New York.

An agreement for the occupation of real estate in the city of New York, which shall not particularly specify the duration of the occupation, shall be deemed to continue until the first day of October next after the possession commences under the agreement.

Sec. 232-a. Notice to terminate monthly tenancy or tenancy from month to month in the city of New York.

No monthly tenant, or tenant from month to month, shall hereafter be removed from any lands or buildings in the city of New York on the grounds of holding over his term unless at least thirty days before the expiration of the term the landlord or his agent serve upon the tenant, in the same manner in which a notice of petition in summary proceedings is now allowed to be served by law, a notice in writing to the effect that the landlord elects to terminate the tenancy and that unless the tenant removes from such premises on the day on which his term expires the landlord will commence summary proceedings under the statute to remove such tenant therefrom.

Sec. 232-b. Notification to terminate monthly tenancy or tenancy from month to month outside the city of New York.

A monthly tenancy or tenancy from month to month of any lands or buildings located outside of the city of New York may be terminated by the landlord or the tenant upon his notifying the other at least one month before the expiration of the term of his election to terminate; provided, however, that no notifica-

tion shall be necessary to terminate a tenancy for a definite term.

Sec. 232-c. Holding over by a tenant after expiration of a term longer than one month; effect of acceptance of rent.

Where a tenant whose term is longer than one month holds over after the expiration of such term, such holding over shall not give to the landlord the option to hold the tenant for a new term solely by virtue of the tenant's holding over. In the case of such a holding over by the tenant, the landlord may proceed, in any manner permitted by law, to remove the tenant, or, if the landlord shall accept rent for any period subsequent to the expiration of such term, then, unless an agreement either express or implied is made providing otherwise, the tenancy created by the acceptance of such rent shall be a tenancy from month to month commencing on the first day after the expiration of such term.

Sec. 233. Mobile home parks; duties, responsibilities.

a. Wherever used in this section:

1. The term "mobile home tenant" means one who rents space in a mobile home park from a mobile home park owner or operator for the purpose of parking his mobile home or one who rents a mobile home in a mobile home park from a mobile home park owner or operator. 2. The term "mobile home owner" means one who holds title to a mobile home. 3. The term "mobile home park" means a contiguous parcel of privately owned land which is used for the accommodation of three or more mobile homes occupied for year-round living.

b. A mobile home park owner or operator may not evict a mobile home tenant other than for the following reasons:

1. The mobile home tenant continues in possession of any portion of the premises after the expiration of his term without the permission of the mobile home park owner or operator.

2. The mobile home tenant has defaulted in the payment of rent, pursuant to the agreement under which the premises are held, and a demand of the rent with at least thirty days' notice in writing has been served upon him as prescribed in section seven hundred thirty-five of the real property actions and proceedings law. Upon the acceptance of such delinquent rent together with allowable costs, an action instituted for nonpayment of rent shall be terminated. Any person succeeding to the mobile home park owner or operator's interest in the premises may proceed under this subdivision for rent due his predecessor in interest if he has a right thereto. 3. The premises, or any part thereof, are used or occupied as a bawdy-house, or house or place of assignation for lewd purposes or for purposes of prostitution, or for any illegal trade or business. 4. The mobile home tenant is in violation of some federal, state or local law or ordinance which may be deemed detri-

mental to the safety and welfare of the other persons residing in the mobile home park. 5. The mobile home tenant or anyone occupying the mobile home is in violation of any lease term or rule or regulation established by the mobile home park owner or operator pursuant to this section, and has continued in violation for more than ten days after the mobile home park owner or operator has given written notice of such violation to the mobile home tenant setting forth the lease term or rule or regulation violated and directing that the mobile home tenant correct or cease violation of such lease term or rule or regulation within ten days from the receipt of said notice. Upon the expiration of such period should the violation continue or should the mobile home tenant or anyone occupying the mobile home be deemed a persistent violator of the lease term or rules and regulations, the park owner or operator may serve written notice upon the mobile home tenant directing that he vacate the premises within thirty days of the receipt of said notice.

6. The mobile home park owner or operator proposes a change in the use of the land comprising the mobile home park, or a portion thereof, on which the mobile home is located, from mobile home lot rentals to some other use, provided the mobile home owner is given written notice of the proposed change of use and the mobile home owner's need to secure other accommodations. Whenever a mobile home park owner or operator gives a notice of proposed change of use to any mobile home owner, the mobile home park owner or operator shall, at the same time, give notice of the proposed change of use to all other mobile home owners in the mobile home park who will be required to secure other accommodations as a result of such proposed change of use. Eviction proceedings based on a change in use shall not be commenced prior to six months from the service of notice of proposed change in use or the end of the lease term, whichever is later. Such notice shall be served in the manner prescribed in section seven hundred thirty-five of the real property actions and proceedings law or by certified mail, return receipt requested.

c. If the mobile home park owner or operator does not have one of the above grounds available, the mobile home tenant may raise the same by affirmative defense to an action for eviction.

d. The proceedings to evict shall be governed by the procedures set forth in article seven of the real property actions and proceedings law, except for the provisions of subdivision two of section seven hundred forty-nine of the real property actions and proceedings law which shall be superseded by the provisions of this subdivision.

1. The officer to whom the warrant is directed and delivered shall give at least ninety days notice, in writing and in the manner prescribed in article seven of the real property actions and proceedings law for the service of notice of petition, to the person or persons to be evicted or dispossessed and shall execute the warrant between the hours of sunrise and sunset. 2. The court may order that such warrant be directed and delivered with only thirty days written notice to the person or persons to be evicted or dispossessed if the conditions upon which the eviction is founded pose an imminent threat to the health, safety, or welfare of the other mobile home tenants in the mobile home park. 3. The court shall order that such warrant be directed and delivered with thirty days written notice to the person or persons to be evicted or dispossessed if the condition upon which the eviction is founded is that such person is in default in the payment of rent.

4. Notwithstanding the provisions of paragraphs one and two of this subdivision, nor of any other general, special or local law, rule or regulation to the contrary, the officer to whom the warrant is directed and delivered shall give seventy-two hours written notice to the person or persons to be evicted or dispossessed, if such person or persons rents a mobile home in a mobile home park from a mobile home park owner or operator and such officer shall execute such warrant between the hours of sunrise and sunset.

e. Leases.

1. The mobile home park owner or operator shall offer every mobile home tenant prior to occupancy, the opportunity to sign a lease for a minimum of one year, which offer shall be made in writing.

2. (i) On or before, as appropriate, (a) the first day of October of each calendar year with respect to a mobile home owner then in good standing who is not currently a party to a written lease with a mobile home park owner or operator or (b) the ninetieth day next preceding the expiration date of any existing written lease between a mobile home owner then in good standing and a mobile home park owner or operator, the mobile home park owner or operator shall submit to each such mobile home owner a written offer to lease for a term of at least twelve months from the commencement date thereof unless the mobile home park owner or operator has previously furnished the mobile home owner with written notification of a proposed change of use pursuant to paragraph six of subdivision b of this section. Any such offer shall include a copy of the proposed lease containing such terms and conditions, including provisions for rent and other charges, as the mobile home park owner shall deem appropriate; provided such terms and conditions are consistent with all rules and regulations promulgated by the mobile home park operator prior to the date of the offer and are not otherwise prohibited or limited by applicable law. Such offer shall also contain a statement advising the mobile home owner that if he or she fails to execute and return the lease to the mobile home park owner or operator within thirty days after submission of such lease, the mobile home owner shall be deemed to have declined the offer of a lease

and shall not have any right to a lease from the mobile home park owner or operator for the next succeeding twelve months.

(ii) For purposes of this paragraph, a mobile home owner shall be deemed in good standing if he or she is not in default in the payment of more than one month's rent to the mobile home park owner, and is not in violation of paragraph three, four or five of subdivision b of this Section. No mobile home park owner or operator shall refuse to provide a written offer to lease based on a default of rent payments or a violation of paragraph three, four or five of subdivision b of this Section unless, at least thirty days prior to the last date on which the owner or operator would otherwise be required to provide such written offer to lease, the owner or operator notifies the mobile home owner, in writing, of the default in rent or the specific grounds constituting the violation and such grounds continues up and until the fifth calendar day immediately preceding the last date on which the written offer would otherwise be required to be made.

(iii) For purposes of this paragraph, the commencement date of any lease offered by the mobile home park owner to the mobile home owner shall be the ninetieth day after the date upon which the mobile home park owner shall have provided the offer required pursuant to this paragraph; provided, however, that no such lease shall be effective if, on such commencement date, the mobile home owner is in default of more than one month's rent. In the event the mobile home owner shall have failed to execute and return said lease to the mobile home park owner or operator within thirty days after it is submitted to the mobile home owner as required by subparagraph (i) of this paragraph the mobile home owner shall be deemed to have declined to enter said lease.

3. No lease provision shall be inconsistent with any rule or regulation in effect at the commencement of the lease.

f. Rules and regulations.

1. A mobile home park owner or operator may promulgate rules and regulations governing the rental or occupancy of a mobile home lot provided such rules and regulations shall not be unreasonable, arbitrary or capricious. A copy of all rules and regulations shall be delivered by the mobile home park owner or operator to all mobile home tenants at the commencement of occupancy. A copy of the rules and regulations shall be posted in a conspicuous place upon the mobile home park grounds.

2. If a rule or regulation is not applied uniformly to all mobile home tenants of the mobile home park there shall be a rebuttable presumption that such rule or regulation is unreasonable, arbitrary and capricious, provided, however, that an inconsistency between a rule or regulation and a lease term contained in a lease signed before the date the rule or regulation is effective shall not raise a rebuttable presumption that such rule is unreasonable, arbi-

trary or capricious.

3. Any rule or regulation which does not conform to the requirements of this section or which has not been supplied or posted as required by paragraph one of this subdivision shall be unenforceable and may be raised by the mobile home tenant as an affirmative defense in any action to evict on the basis of a violation of such rule or regulation. 4. No rules or regulations may be changed by the mobile home park owner or operator without specifying the date of implementation of said changed rules and regulations, which date shall be no fewer than thirty days after written notice to all tenants.

g. 1. No tenant shall be charged a fee for other than rent, utilities and charges for facilities and services available to the tenant. All fees, charges or assessments must be reasonably related to services actually rendered.

2. A mobile home park owner or operator shall be required to fully disclose in writing all fees, charges, assessments, including rental fees, rules and regulations prior to a mobile home tenant assuming occupancy in the mobile home park.

3. No fees, charges, assessments or rental fees may be increased by mobile home park owner or operator without specifying the date of implementation of said fees, charges, assessments or rental fees which date shall be no less than ninety days after written notice to all mobile home tenants. Failure on the part of the mobile home park owner or operator to fully disclose all fees, charges or assessments shall prevent the mobile home park owner or operator from collecting said fees, charges or assessments, and refusal by the mobile home tenant to pay any undisclosed charges shall not be used by the mobile home park owner or operator as a cause for eviction in any court of law. 4.

(a) Whenever money shall be deposited or advanced on a contract or license agreement for the use or rental of premises and the mobile home, if rented, in a mobile home park as security for performance of the contract or agreement or to be applied to payments upon such contract or agreement when due, such money with interest accruing thereon, if any, until repaid or so applied, shall continue to be the money of the person making such deposit or advance and shall be a trust fund in the possession of the person with whom such deposit or advance shall be made and shall not be mingled with other funds or become an asset of the park owner, operator or his agent.

(b) Whenever the person receiving money so deposited or advanced shall deposit such money in a banking organization, such person shall thereupon notify in writing each of the persons making such security deposit or advance, giving the name and address of the banking organization in which the deposit of security money is made, and the amount of such deposit. Deposits in a banking organization pursuant to the provisions of this subdivision shall be made in a banking organization having a place of business within the state. If the person depositing such security money in a banking organization shall deposit same in an interest bearing account, he shall be entitled to receive, as administration expenses, a sum equivalent to one percent per annum upon the security money so deposited, which shall be in lieu of all other administrative and custodial expenses. The balances of the interest paid by the banking organization shall be the money of the person making the deposit or advance and shall either be held in trust by the person with whom such deposit or advance shall be made, until repaid or applied for the use or rental of the leased premises, or annually paid to the person making the deposit of security money.

(c) Whenever the money so deposited or advanced is for the rental of a mobile home park lot on property on which are located six or more mobile home park lots, the person receiving such money shall, subject to the provisions of this section, deposit it in an interest bearing account in a banking organization within the state which account shall earn interest at a rate which shall be the prevailing rate earned by other such deposits made with the banking organizations in such area. (d) In the event that a lease terminates other than at the time that a banking organization in such area regularly pays interest, the person depositing such security money shall pay over to his mobile home tenant such interest as he is able to collect at the date of such lease termination.

(e) Any provision of such a contract or agreement whereby a person who so deposits or advances money waives any provision of this subdivision is void.

h. No mobile home park owner shall:

"3. Require, by contract, rule, regulation or otherwise, a mobile home dweller to purchase from the mobile home park owner or any person acting directly or indirectly on behalf of the park owner, commodities or services incidental to placement or rental within such park; nor shall the park owner restrict access to the mobile home park to any person employed, retained or requested by the mobile home dweller to provide such commodity or service, unless the mobile home park owner establishes that such requirement or restriction is necessary to protect the property of such park owner from substantial harm or impairment. 4. Require a mobile home owner or a prospective mobile home owner to purchase his or her mobile home from the mobile home park owner or operator, or from any person or persons designated by the mobile home park owner or operator. Nothing herein shall be construed to prevent a mobile home park owner or operator from requiring that any new mobile home to be installed in his or her mobile home park comply with the rules and regulations of said mobile home park or conform to the physical facilities then existing for installation of a mobile home in said mobile home park.

i. 1. No mobile home park owner or operator shall deny any mobile home tenant the right to sell his mobile home within the mobile home park provided the mobile home tenant shall give to the mobile home park owner or operator twenty days' written notice of his intention to sell, or require the mobile home owner or subsequent purchaser to remove the mobile home from the mobile home park solely on the basis of the sale thereof. The mobile home park owner or operator may reserve the right to approve the purchaser of said mobile home as a mobile home tenant for the remainder of the seller's term but such permission may not be unreasonably withheld. If the mobile home park owner or operator unreasonably withholds his permission, the mobile home tenant may recover the costs of the proceedings and attorneys' fees if it is found that the mobile home park owner or operator acted in bad faith by withholding permission.

2. The mobile home park owner or operator shall not exact a commission or fee with respect to the price realized by the seller unless the mobile home park owner or operator has acted as agent for the mobile home owner in the sale pursuant to a written contract. 3. If the ownership or management rejects a purchaser as a prospective tenant, the selling tenant must be informed in writing of the reasons therefor.

j. The owner or operator of a mobile home park may enter a mobile home owner's mobile home without the prior consent of the occupant only in case of emergency. The owner or operator of a mobile home park may enter a mobile home tenant's mobile home during reasonable hours on reasonable notice.

k. The owner or operator shall provide reasonable notice where practicable to all mobile home tenants who would be affected by any planned disruption of necessary services caused by the owner, operator or his agent.

l. The park owner shall designate an agent on the premises or in close proximity to the mobile home park to insure the availability of emergency response actions in matters affecting the health, safety, well-being and welfare of mobile home tenants in the park. The designated agent's name, address and telephone number shall be posted in a conspicuous location in the park, given in writing to each tenant and registered with appropriate county law enforcement and health officials and local fire officials.

m. Warranty of habitability, maintenance, disruption of services. In every written or oral lease or rental agreement entered into by a mobile home tenant, the mobile home park owner or operator shall be deemed to covenant and warrant that the premises so leased or rented and the mobile home if rented and all areas used in connection therewith in common with other mobile home tenants or residents including all roads within the mobile home park are fit for human habitation and for the uses reasonably intended by the parties and that the occupants of such premises and such mobile homes if rented shall not be subjected to any conditions which would be dangerous, hazardous or detrimental to their life, health or safety. When any such condition has been caused by the misconduct of the mobile home tenant or lessee or persons under his direction or control, it shall not constitute a breach of such covenants and warranties. The rights and obligations of the mobile home park owner or operator and the mobile home tenant shall be governed by the provisions of this subdivision and subdivisions two and three of section two hundred thirty- five-b of this article.

n. 1. No mobile home park owner or operator shall serve a notice to quit upon any mobile home tenant or commence any action to recover real property or summary proceeding to recover possession of real property in retaliation for:

(a) A good faith complaint, by or in behalf of the tenant, to a governmental authority of the mobile home park owner's or operator's alleged violation of any health or safety law, regulation, code, or ordinance, or any law or regulation which has as its objective the regulation of premises used for dwelling purposes; or (b) Actions taken in good faith, by or in behalf of the mobile home tenant, to secure or enforce any rights under the lease or rental agreement, under subdivision m of this section and subdivisions two and three of section two hundred thirty-five-b of this article, or under any other local law, law of the state of New York, or of its governmental subdivisions, or of the United States which has as its objective the regulation of premises used for dwelling purposes; or

(c) The mobile home tenant's participation in the activities of a tenant's organization.

2. No mobile home park owner or operator shall substantially alter the terms of the tenancy in retaliation for any actions set forth in subparagraphs (a), (b), and (c) of paragraph one of this subdivision. Substantial alteration shall include, but is not limited to, the refusal to continue a tenancy of the mobile home tenant or, upon expiration of the mobile home owner's lease, to renew the lease or offer a new lease; provided, however, that a mobile home park owner or operator shall not be required under this subdivision to offer a mobile home owner a new lease or a lease renewal for a term greater than one year.

3. This subdivision shall apply to all mobile home parks with four or more mobile homes. However, its provisions shall not be given effect in any case in which it is established that the condition from which the complaint or action arose was caused by the mobile home tenant, a member of the mobile home tenant's household, or a guest of the mobile home tenant. Nor shall it apply in a case where a tenancy was terminated pursuant to the terms of a lease as a result of a bona fide transfer of ownership. The rights and obligations of the mobile home park owner or operator and the mobile home tenant shall be governed by the provisions of this subdivision and subdivisions three, four and five of section two hundred twenty-three-b of this article.

o. Whenever a lease shall provide that in any action or summary proceeding the mobile home park owner or operator may recover attorney's fees and/or expenses incurred as the result of the failure of the tenant to perform any covenant or agreement contained in such lease, or that amounts paid by the mobile home park owner or operator therefor shall be paid by the tenant as additional rent, there shall be implied in such lease a covenant by the mobile home park owner or operator, to pay to the tenant the reasonable attorney's fees and/or expenses incurred by the tenant to the same extent as is provided in section two hundred thirty- four of this article which section shall apply in its entirety.

p. Any mobile home park owner or operator who has agreed to provide hot or cold water, heat, light, power, or any other service or facility to any occupant of the mobile home park who willfully or intentionally without just cause fails to furnish such water, heat, light, power, or other service or facility, or who interferes with the quiet enjoyment of the leased premises, is guilty of a violation.

q. Upon receipt of rent, fees, charges or other assessments, in the form of cash or any instrument other than the personal check of the tenant, it shall be the duty of the mobile home park owner or operator to provide the payor with a written receipt containing the following:

1. the date; 2. the amount; 3. the identity of the premises and the period for which paid; 4. the signature and title of the person receiving rent.

r. Limitation on late charges. A late charge on any rental payment by a mobile home owner which has become due and remains unpaid shall not exceed and shall be enforced to the extent of five percent of such delinquent payment; provided, however, that no charge shall be imposed on any rental payment by a mobile home owner received within ten days after the due date. In the absence of a specific provision in the lease or the mobile home park's rules and regulations, no late charge on any delinquent rental payment shall be assessed or collected.

s. It shall be a violation for a mobile home park owner, operator or his agent to restrict occupancy of a mobile home or mobile home park lot intended for residential purposes by express lease terms or otherwise, to a mobile home tenant or tenants or to such tenants and immediate family. Any such restriction in a lease or rental agreement entered into or renewed before or after the effective date of this subdivision shall be unenforceable as against public policy. The rights and obligations of a mobile home park owner or operator and the mobile home tenant shall be governed by the provisions of this subdivision and subdivisions one, three, four, five, six, seven, eight and nine of section two hundred thirty-five-f of this article.

t. 1. Unless a greater right to assign is conferred by the lease, a mobile home tenant may not assign his lease without the written consent of the mobile home park owner or operator, which consent may be unconditionally withheld without cause provided that the mobile home park owner or operator shall release the mobile home tenant from the lease upon request of the mobile home tenant upon thirty days notice if the mobile home park owner or operator unreasonably withholds consent which release shall be the sole remedy of the tenant. If the owner reasonably withholds consent, there shall be no assignment and the mobile home tenant shall not be released from the lease.

2. (a) A mobile home tenant renting space or a mobile home in a mobile home park with four or more mobile homes pursuant to an existing lease shall have a right to sublease his premises subject to the written consent of the park owner in advance of the subletting. Such consent shall not be unreasonably withheld.

(b) The mobile home tenant shall inform the mobile home park owner or operator of his intent to sublease by mailing a notice of such intent by certified mail, return receipt requested. Such request shall be accompanied by the following information: (i) the term of the sublease, (ii) the name of the proposed sublessee, (iii) the business and permanent home address of the proposed sublessee, (iv) the tenant's reason for subletting, (v) the tenant's address for the term of the sublease, (vi) the written consent of any co-tenant or guarantor of the lease, and (vii) a copy of the proposed sublease, to which a copy of the mobile home tenant's lease shall be attached if available, acknowledged by the mobile home tenant and proposed subtenant as being a true copy of such sublease.

(c) Within ten days after the mailing of such request, the mobile home park owner or operator may ask the mobile home tenant for additional information as will enable the mobile home park owner or operator to determine if rejection of such request shall be unreasonable. Any such request for additional information shall not be unduly burdensome. Within thirty days after the mailing of the request for consent, or of the additional information reasonably asked for by the mobile home park owner or operator, whichever is later, the mobile home park owner or operator shall send a notice to the mobile home tenant of his consent or, if he does not consent, his reasons therefor. Mobile home park owner's or operator's failure to send such a notice shall be deemed to be a consent to the proposed subletting. If the mobile home park owner or operator consents, the premises may be sublet in accordance with the request, but the mobile home tenant thereunder, shall nevertheless remain liable for the performance of mobile home tenant's obligations under said lease. If the mobile home park owner or operator reasonably withholds

consent, there shall be no subletting and the mobile home tenant shall not be released from the lease. If the mobile home park owner or operator unreasonably withholds consent, the mobile home tenant may sublet in accordance with the request and may recover the costs of the proceeding and attorneys fees if it is found that the mobile home park owner or operator acted in bad faith by withholding consent. The rights and obligations of the mobile home park owner or operator and the mobile home tenant shall be governed by the provisions of this subdivision and subdivisions three, five, six, seven and eight of section two hundred twenty-six-b of this article.

u. In the event of a breach by a mobile home park owner or operator of any of the requirements of this section, the mobile home tenant may commence an action for damages actually incurred as a result of such breach, or in an action or summary proceeding commenced by such mobile home park owner or operator, may counterclaim for damages occasioned by such breach.

v. On and after April first, nineteen hundred eighty-nine, the commissioner of housing and community renewal shall have the power and duty to enforce and ensure compliance with the provisions of this Section. However, the commissioner shall not have the power or duty to enforce mobile home park rules and regulations established under subdivision f of this section. On or before January first, nineteen hundred eighty- nine, each mobile home park owner or operator shall file a registration statement with the commissioner and shall thereafter file an annual registration statement on or before January first of each succeeding year. The commissioner, by regulation, shall provide that such registration statement shall include only the names of all persons owning an interest in the park, the names of all tenants of the park, all services provided by the park owner to the tenants and a copy of all current mobile home park rules and regulations. Whenever there shall be a violation of this section, an application may be made by the commissioner of housing and community renewal in the name of the people of the state of New York to a court or justice having jurisdiction by a special proceeding to issue an injunction, and upon notice to the defendant of not less than five days, to enjoin and restrain the continuance of such violation; and if it shall appear to the satisfaction of the court or justice that the defendant has, in fact, violated this section, an injunction may be issued by such court or justice, enjoining and restraining any further violation and with respect to this subdivision, directing the filing of a registration statement. In any such proceeding, the court may make allowances to the commissioner of housing and community renewal of a sum not exceeding two thousand dollars against each defendant, and direct restitution. Whenever the court shall determine that a violation of this section has occurred, the court may impose a civil penalty of not more than one thousand five hundred dollars for each violation. Such penalty shall be deposited in the mobile home cooperative fund, created pursuant to Section fifty-nine-h of the private housing finance law. In connection with any such proposed application, the commissioner of housing and community renewal is authorized to take proof and make a determination of the relevant facts and to issue subpoenas in accordance with the civil practice law and rules. The provisions of this subdivision shall not impair the rights granted under subdivision u of this section.

Sec. 234. Tenants' right to recover attorneys' fees in actions or summary proceedings arising out of leases of residential property.

Whenever a lease of residential property shall provide that in any action or summary proceeding the landlord may recover attorneys' fees and/or expenses incurred as the result of the failure of the tenant to perform any covenant or agreement contained in such lease, or that amounts paid by the landlord therefor shall be paid by the tenant as additional rent, there shall be implied in such lease a covenant by the landlord to pay to the tenant the reasonable attorneys' fees and/or expenses incurred by the tenant as the result of the failure of the landlord to perform any covenant or agreement on its part to be performed under the lease or in the successful defense of any action or summary proceeding commenced by the landlord against the tenant arising out of the lease, and an agreement that such fees and expenses may be recovered as provided by law in an action commenced against the landlord or by way of counterclaim in any action or summary proceeding commenced by the landlord against the tenant. Any waiver of this section shall be void as against public policy.

Sec. 235. Wilful violations.

1. Any lessor, agent, manager, superintendent or janitor of any building, or part thereof, the lease or rental agreement whereof by its terms, expressed or implied, requires the furnishing of hot or cold water, heat, light, power, elevator service, telephone service or any other service or facility to any occupant of said building, who wilfully or intentionally fails to furnish such water, heat, light, power, elevator service, telephone service or other service or facility at any time when the same are necessary to the proper or customary use of such building, or part thereof, or any lessor, agent, manager, superintendent or janitor who wilfully and intentionally interferes with the quiet enjoyment of the leased premises by such occupant, is guilty of a violation.

2. Any lessor, agent, manager, superintendent or janitor of any building, or part thereof, who wilfully or intentionally acts to prevent or obstruct the delivery of fuel oil ordered in compliance with either section three hundred two-c of the multiple dwelling law or section three hundred five-c of the multiple residence law or the refiring of an oil burner after such a delivery shall be guilty of a violation.

Sec. 235-a. Tenant right to offset payments and entitlement to damages in certain cases.

1. In any case in which a tenant shall lawfully make a payment to a utility company pursuant to the provisions of sections thirty-three, thirty-four and one hundred sixteen of the public service law, such payment shall be deductible from any future payment of rent.

2. Any owner (as defined in the multiple dwelling law or multiple residence law) of a multiple dwelling responsible for the payment of charges for gas, electric, steam or water service who causes the discontinuance of that service by failure or refusal to pay the charges for past service shall be liable for compensatory and punitive damages to any tenant whose utility service is so discontinued.

*3. Nothing contained in this section and no payment made pursuant to this section shall be deemed to discharge the liability of a renter with an interest in real property pursuant to subdivision two of section three hundred four of the real property tax law from taxes levied on such interest.

*NB (Effective pending ruling by Commissioner of Internal Revenue)

Sec. 235-b. Warranty of habitability.

1. In every written or oral lease or rental agreement for residential premises the landlord or lessor shall be deemed to covenant and warrant that the premises so leased or rented and all areas used in connection therewith in common with other tenants or residents are fit for human habitation and for the uses reasonably intended by the parties and that the occupants of such premises shall not be subjected to any conditions which would be dangerous, hazardous or detrimental to their life, health or safety. When any such condition has been caused by the misconduct of the tenant or lessee or persons under his direction or control, it shall not constitute a breach of such covenants and warranties.

2. Any agreement by a lessee or tenant of a dwelling waiving or modifying his rights as set forth in this section shall be void as contrary to public policy.

3. In determining the amount of damages sustained by a tenant as a result of a breach of the warranty set forth in the section, the court;

(a) need not require any expert testimony; and (b) shall, to the extent the warranty is breached or cannot be cured by reason of a strike or other labor dispute which is not caused primarily by the individual landlord or lessor and such damages are attributable to such strike, exclude recovery to such extent, except to the extent of the net savings, if any, to the landlord or lessor by reason of such strike or labor dispute allocable to the tenant's premises, provided, however, that the landlord or lesser has made a good faith attempt, where practicable, to cure the breach.

Sec. 235-c. Unconscionable lease or clause.

1. If the court as a matter of law finds a lease or any clause of the lease to have been unconscionable at the time it was made the court may refuse to enforce the lease, or it may enforce the remainder of the lease without the unconscionable clause, or it may so limit the application of any unconscionable clause as to avoid any unconscionable result.

2. When it is claimed or appears to the court that a lease or any clause thereof may be unconscionable the parties shall be afforded a reasonable opportunity to present evidence as to its setting, purpose and effect to aid the court in making the determination.

Sec. 235-d. Harassment.

1. Notwithstanding any other provision of law, within a city having a population of one million or more, it shall be unlawful and shall constitute harassment for any landlord of a building which at any time was occupied for manufacturing or warehouse purposes, or other person acting on his behalf, to engage in any course of conduct, including, but not limited to intentional interruption or discontinuance or willful failure to restore services customarily provided or required by written lease or other rental agreement, which interferes with or disturbs the comfort, repose, peace or quiet of a tenant in the tenant's use or occupancy of rental space if such conduct is intended to cause the tenant (i) to vacate a building or part thereof; or (ii) to surrender or waive any rights of such tenant under the tenant's written lease or other rental agreement.

2. The lawful termination of a tenancy or lawful refusal to renew or extend a written lease or other rental agreement shall not constitute harassment for purposes of this section.

3. As used in this section the term "tenant" means only a person or business occupying or residing at the premises pursuant to a written lease or other rental agreement, if such premises are located in a building which at any time was occupied for manufacturing or warehouse purposes and a certificate of occupancy for residential use of such building is not in effect at the time of the last alleged acts or incidents upon which the harassment claim is based.

4. A tenant may apply to the supreme court for an order enjoining acts or practices which constitute harassment under subdivision one of this section; and upon sufficient showing, the supreme court may issue a temporary or permanent injunction, restraining order or other order, all of which may, as the court determines in the exercise of its sound discretion, be granted without bond. In the event the court issues a preliminary injunction it shall make provision for an expeditious trial of the underlying action.

5. The powers and remedies set forth in this section shall be in addition to all other powers and remedies in relation to harassment including the award of damages. Nothing contained herein shall be construed to amend, repeal, modify or affect any existing local law or ordinance, or provision of the charter or administrative code of the city of New York, or to limit or restrict the power of the city to amend or modify any existing local law, ordinance or provision of the charter or administrative code, or to restrict or limit any power otherwise conferred by law with respect to harassment.

6. Any agreement by a tenant in a written lease or other rental agreement waiving or modifying his rights as set forth in this section shall be void as contrary to public policy.

Sec. 235-e. Duty of landlord to provide written receipt.

(a) Upon the receipt of rent for residential premises in the form of cash or any instrument other than the personal check of the tenant, it shall be the duty of the landlord to provide the payor with a written receipt containing the following:

1. The date; 2. The amount;

3. The identity of the premises and period for which paid; and

4. The signature and title of the person receiving the rent. (b) Where a tenant, in writing, requests that a landlord provide a receipt for rent paid by personal check, it shall be the duty of the landlord to provide the payor with the receipt described in subdivision (a) of this Section for each such request made in writing.

Sec. 235-f. Unlawful restrictions on occupancy.

1. As used in this Section, the terms:

(a) "Tenant" means a person occupying or entitled to occupy a residential rental premises who is either a party to the lease or rental agreement for such premises or is a statutory tenant pursuant to the emergency housing rent control law or the city rent and rehabilitation law or article seven-c of the multiple dwelling law. (b) "Occupant" means a person, other than a tenant or a member of a tenant's immediate family, occupying a premises with the consent of the tenant or tenants.

2. It shall be unlawful for a landlord to restrict occupancy of residential premises, by express lease terms or otherwise, to a tenant or tenants or to such tenants and immediate family. Any such restriction in a lease or rental agreement entered into or renewed before or after the effective date of this section shall be unenforceable as against public policy.

3. Any lease or rental agreement for residential premises entered into by one tenant shall be construed to permit occupancy by the tenant, immediate family of the tenant, one additional occupant, and dependent children of the occupant provided that the tenant or the tenant's spouse occupies the premises as his primary residence.

4. Any lease or rental agreement for residential premises entered into by two or more tenants shall be construed to permit occupancy by tenants, imme-

diate family of tenants, occupants and dependent children of occupants; provided that the total number of tenants and occupants, excluding occupants' dependent children, does not exceed the number of tenants specified in the current lease or rental agreement, and that at least one tenant or a tenants' spouse occupies the premises as his primary residence.

5. The tenant shall inform the landlord of the name of any occupant within thirty days following the commencement of occupancy by such person or within thirty days following a request by the landlord.

6. No occupant nor occupant's dependent child shall, without express written permission of the landlord, acquire any right to continued occupancy in the event that the tenant vacates the premises or acquire any other rights of tenancy; provided that nothing in this section shall be construed to reduce or impair any right or remedy otherwise available to any person residing in any housing accommodation on the effective date of this section which accrued prior to such date.

7. Any provision of a lease or rental agreement purporting to waive a provision of this section is null and void.

8. Nothing in this section shall be construed as invalidating or impairing the operation of, or the right of a landlord to restrict occupancy in order to comply with federal, state or local laws, regulations, ordinances or codes.

9. Any person aggrieved by a violation of this section may maintain an action in any court of competent jurisdiction for:

(a) an injunction to enjoin and restrain such unlawful practice; (b) actual damages sustained as a result of such unlawful practice; and (c) court costs.

Sec. 236. Assignment of lease of a deceased tenant.

Notwithstanding any contrary provision contained in any lease hereafter made which affects premises demised for residential use, or partly for residential and partly for professional use, the executor, administrator or legal representative of a deceased tenant under such a lease, may request the landlord thereunder to consent to the assignment of such a lease, or to the subletting of the premises demised thereby. Such request shall be accompanied by the written consent thereto of any co-tenant or guarantor of such lease and a statement of the name, business and home addresses of the proposed assignee or sublessee. Within ten days after the mailing of such request, the landlord may ask the sender thereof for additional information as will enable the landlord to determine if rejection of such request shall be unreasonable. Within thirty days after the mailing of the request for consent, or of the additional information reasonably asked for by the landlord, whichever is later, the landlord shall send a notice to the sender

thereof of his election to terminate said lease or to grant or refuse his consent. Landlord's failure to send such a notice shall be deemed to be a consent to the proposed assignment or subletting. If the landlord consents, said lease may be assigned in accordance with the request provided a written agreement by the assignee assuming the performance of the tenant's obligations under the lease is delivered to the landlord in form reasonably satisfactory to the landlord, or the premises may be sublet in accordance with the request, as the case may be, but the estate of the deceased tenant, and any other tenant thereunder, shall nevertheless remain liable for the performance of tenant's obligations under said lease. If the landlord terminates said lease or unreasonably refuses his consent, said lease shall be deemed terminated, and the estate of the deceased tenant and any other tenant thereunder shall be discharged from further liability thereunder as of the last day of the calendar month during which the landlord was required hereunder to exercise his option. If the landlord reasonably refuses his consent, said lease shall continue in full force and effect, subject to the right to make further requests for consent hereunder. Any request, notice or communication required or authorized to be given hereunder shall be sent by registered or certified mail, return receipt requested. This act shall not apply to a proprietary lease, viz.: a lease to, or held by, a tenant entitled thereto by reason of ownership of stock in a corporate owner of premises which operates the same on a cooperative basis. Any waiver of any part of this section shall be void as against public policy.

Sec. 236*. Discrimination against children in dwelling houses and mobile home parks.

a. Any person, firm or corporation owning or having in charge any apartment house, tenement house or other building or mobile home park used for dwelling purposes who shall refuse to rent any or part of any such building of mobile home park to any person or family, or who discriminates in the terms, conditions, or privileges of any such rental, solely on the ground that such person or family has or have a child or children shall be guilty of a misdemeanor and on conviction thereof shall be punished by a fine of not less than fifty nor more than one hundred dollars for each offense; provided, however, the prohibition against discrimination against children in dwelling houses and mobile home parks contained in this section shall not apply to:

(1) housing units for senior citizens subsidized, insured, or guaranteed by the federal government; or
(2) one or two family owner occupied dwelling houses or mobile homes; or
(3) mobile home parks exclusively for persons fifty-five years of age or over.

b. Civil liability:
(1) where discriminatory conduct prohibited by this section has occurred, an aggrieved individual shall

have a cause of action in any court of appropriate jurisdiction for damages, declaratory and injunctive relief; (2) in all actions brought under this section, reasonable attorney's fees as determined by the court may be awarded to a prevailing plaintiff.

Sec. 237. Discrimination in leases with respect to bearing of children.

Any person, firm or corporation owning or having in charge any apartment house, tenement house or other building or mobile home park used for dwelling purposes who shall, in any lease of any or part of any such building or mobile home park, have a clause therein providing that during the term thereof the tenants shall remain childless or shall not bear children, shall be guilty of a violation.

Sec. 238. Agreements or contracts for privileges to deal with occupants of tenements, apartment houses or bungalow colonies.

1. A contract, agreement or arrangement entered into or executed by and between the owner or prospective owner of an apartment house, tenement or what is commonly known as a bungalow colony connected with common or joint means of ingress and egress, whether such apartment house, tenement or bungalow colony is in existence or in process of construction or to be constructed in the future, or any person in possession or claiming possession of such apartment house, tenement or bungalow colony, or any part thereof, including the common or joint means of ingress or egress, or any of the agents, employees or servants of such an owner or possessors thereof and a dealer in or seller of fuel, ice or food, or his agents, employees or representatives for the purpose of giving to such dealer or seller the privilege of selling or delivering fuel, ice or food, to the persons occupying or to occupy such apartment house, tenement or bungalow colony, or any part thereof, is against public policy and void.

2. Any person who shall, directly or indirectly, either as the owner or prospective owner of such apartment house, tenement or bungalow colony, or any part thereof, including the common or joint means of ingress or egress, or as an agent, employee or servant of such an owner, or any person in possession or claiming possession of such apartment house, tenement or bungalow colony, or any part thereof, including the common or joint means of ingress or egress, accept any money, property or thing of value for permitting or giving to any person, or his agents, employees or representatives, the privilege of selling or delivering fuel, ice or food, to the persons occupying or to occupy such apartment house, tenement or bungalow colony, or any part thereof, and any person who shall, directly or indirectly, either as a seller of, or dealer in, fuel, ice or food, as an agent, employee, or representative of such seller or dealer, pay or give any money, property or thing of value, for such privilege shall be guilty of a misdemeanor. If a corporation is convicted of a violation of this section, it shall be punished by a fine of not less than fifty nor more than one thousand dollars.

3. A person occupying an apartment house, tenement or bungalow colony, or any part thereof, to whom fuel, ice or food, shall be sold or delivered by a seller or dealer who has paid or given any money, property or thing of value for the privilege of selling or delivering fuel, ice or food, to the persons occupying or to occupy such apartment house, tenement or bungalow colony, or any part thereof, may recover of such seller or dealer for his benefit a penalty, in the sum of two hundred and fifty dollars, in a civil action brought in a court of competent jurisdiction.

Eviction Flowcharts and Legal Holidays

On the next two pages are flowcharts that show each step in the eviction process. The first one is for an eviction for nonpayment of rent, and the second one is for evictions based on holdover proceedings.

On the final page of this appendix is a list of the legal holidays in New York. Keep these in mind when calculating time limits for notices.

EVICTION FLOWCHART - NONPAYMENT OF RENT

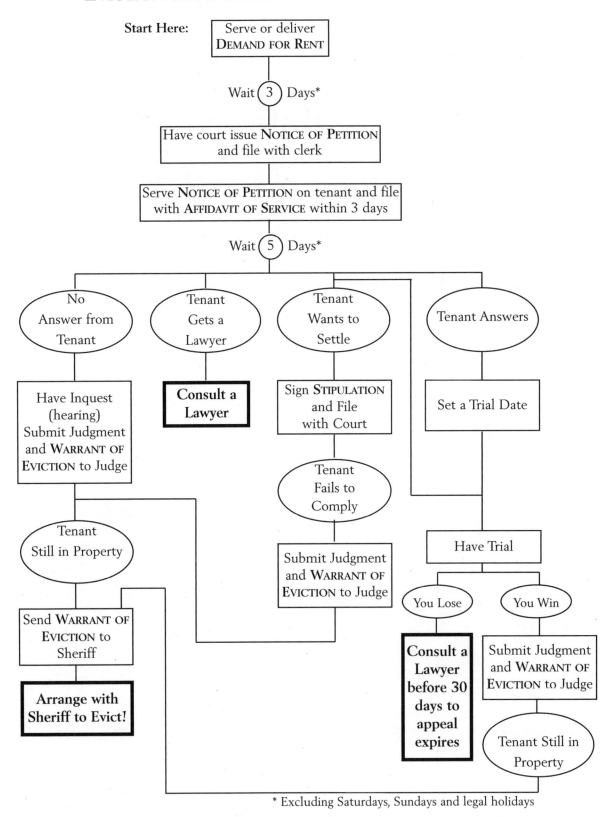

Start Here: Serve or deliver DEMAND FOR RENT

Wait ③ Days*

Have court issue NOTICE OF PETITION and file with clerk

Serve NOTICE OF PETITION on tenant and file with AFFIDAVIT OF SERVICE within 3 days

Wait ⑤ Days*

No Answer from Tenant

Tenant Gets a Lawyer

Tenant Wants to Settle

Tenant Answers

Have Inquest (hearing) Submit Judgment and WARRANT OF EVICTION to Judge

Consult a Lawyer

Sign STIPULATION and File with Court

Set a Trial Date

Tenant Still in Property

Tenant Fails to Comply

Send WARRANT OF EVICTION to Sheriff

Submit Judgment and WARRANT OF EVICTION to Judge

Have Trial

You Lose

You Win

Arrange with Sheriff to Evict!

Consult a Lawyer before 30 days to appeal expires

Submit Judgment and WARRANT OF EVICTION to Judge

Tenant Still in Property

* Excluding Saturdays, Sundays and legal holidays

EVICTION FLOWCHART - BREACH OF LEASE

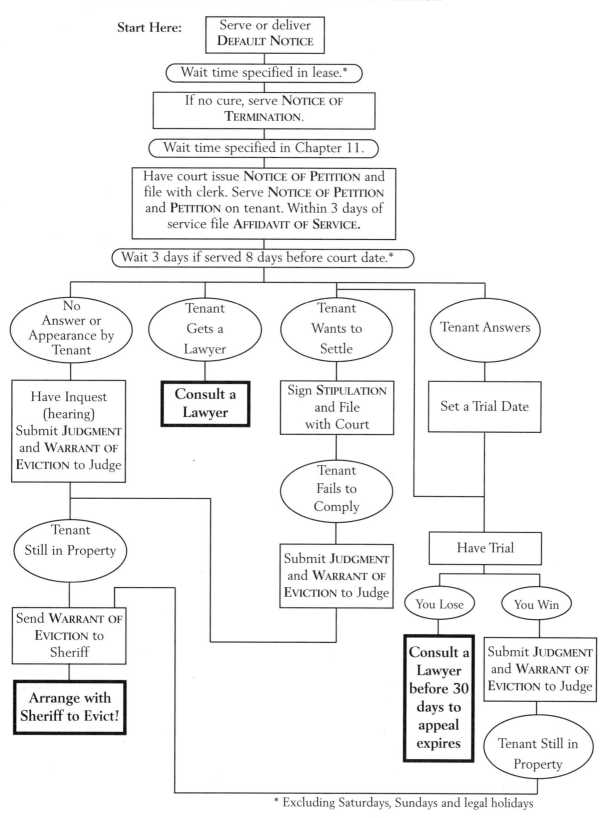

* Excluding Saturdays, Sundays and legal holidays

LEGAL HOLIDAYS IN NEW YORK

Every Sunday

New Year's Day   Jan. 1

Martin Luther King, Jr.'s Birthday   Third Mon. in Jan.

Presidents' Day   Third Mon. in Feb.

Good Friday   (varies)

Memorial Day   Last Mon. in May

Independence Day   July 4

Labor Day   First Mon. In Sept

Columbus Day   Second Mon. in Oct.

General Election Day   (varies)

Veterans' Day   Nov. 11

Thanksgiving Day   Fourth Thurs. in Nov.

Christmas Day   Dec. 25

Blank Forms

Use of the following forms is described in the text or should be self-explanatory. If you do not understand any aspect of a form, you should seek advice from an attorney.

Although the forms in this appendix may be grouped according to the type of form, the forms are not necessarily in any particular order. Be sure to read this book to determine which forms you will need in a particular situation. Also, be sure to look at the form's name and form number to be sure you are using the correct form.

Also know that some local courts will require you to use their own particular forms. Always check first with the clerk of the court where you will be filing if any special or particular form will be needed or must be used.

License: Although this book is copyrighted, purchasers of the book are granted a license to copy the forms created by the authors for their own personal use or for use in their law practices.

Table of Forms

TENANT APPLICATION

Name _____ Date of Birth _____

Name _____ Date of Birth _____

Soc. Sec. Nos. _____

Drivers' License Nos. _____

Children & Ages _____

Present Landlord _____ Phone _____

Address _____ How Long? _____

Previous Landlord _____ Phone _____

Address _____

Second Previous Landlord _____ Phone _____

Address _____

Nearest Relative _____ Phone _____

Address _____

Employer _____ Phone _____

Address _____

Second Applicant's Employer _____ Phone _____

Address _____

Pets _____

Other persons who will stay at premises for more than one week _____

_____

Bank Name _____ Acct. # _____

Bank Name _____ Acct. # _____

Have you ever been evicted? _____

Have you ever been in litigation with a landlord? _____

The undersigned hereby attest that the above information is true.

Date: _____   _____

                                     _____

This page intentionally left blank.

INSPECTION REPORT

Date: _____

Unit: _____

AREA   CONDITION

	Move-In		Move-out	
	Good	Poor	Good	Poor
Yard/garden				
Driveway				
Patio/porch				
Exterior				
Entry light/bell				
Living room/Dining room/Halls:				
Floors/carpets				
Walls/ceiling				
Doors/locks				
Fixtures/lights				
Outlets/switches				
Other				
Bedrooms:				
Floors/carpets				
Walls/ceiling				
Doors/locks				
Fixtures/lights				
Outlets/switches				
Other				
Bathrooms:				
Faucets				
Toilet				
Sink/tub				
Floors/carpet				
Walls/ceiling				
Doors/locks				
Fixtures/lights				
Outlets/switches				
Other				
Kitchen:				
Refrigerator				
Range				
Oven				
Dishwasher				
Sink/disposal				
Cabinets/counters				
Floors/carpets				
Walls/ceiling				
Doors/locks				
Fixtures/lights				
Outlets/switches				
Other				
Misc.				
Closets/pantry				
Garage				
Keys				
Other				

_____   _____
Tenant   Landlord

This page intentionally left blank.

PET AGREEMENT

THIS AGREEMENT is made pursuant to the Lease dated _____,
between _____ as
Landlord and _____ as Tenant.

In consideration of $_____ as non-refundable cleaning payment and $_____ as
additional security deposit paid by Tenant to Landlord, Tenant is allowed to keep the
following pet(s): _____
on the premises _____
under the following conditions:

1. In the event the pet produces a litter, Tenant may keep them at the premises no
    longer than one month past weaning.

2. Tenant shall not engage in any commercial pet-raising activities.

3. No pets other than those listed above shall be kept on the premises without the
    further written permission of the Landlord.

4. Tenant agrees at all times to keep the pet from becoming a nuisance to neighbors
    and/or other tenants. This includes controlling the barking of the pet, if necessary,
    and cleaning any animal waste on and about the premises.

5. In the event the pet causes destruction of the property, becomes a nuisance, or
    Tenant otherwise violates this agreement, Landlord may terminate the Lease
    according to New York law.

Date: _____

Landlord: Tenant:

_____   _____

_____   _____

This page intentionally left blank.

HOUSE OR DUPLEX LEASE

LANDLORD: _____   TENANT: _____

_____   _____

PROPERTY:_____

IN CONSIDERATION of the mutual covenants and agreements herein contained, Landlord hereby leases to Tenant and Tenant hereby leases from Landlord the above-described property under the following terms:

1. TERM. This lease shall be for a term of _____, beginning _____, _____ and ending _____, _____.

2. RENT. The rent shall be $_____ per _____ and shall be due on or before the _____ day of each _____. In the event the rent is received more than three (3) days late, a late charge of $_____ shall be due. In the event a check bounces or an eviction notice must be posted, Tenant agrees to pay a $15.00 charge.

3. PAYMENT. Payment must be received by Landlord on or before the due date at the following address: _____ or such place as designated by Landlord in writing. Tenant understands that this may require early mailing. In the event a check bounces, Landlord may require cash or certified funds.

4. DEFAULT. In the event Tenant defaults under any terms of this lease, Landlord may recover possession as provided by Law and seek monetary damages.

5. SECURITY. Landlord acknowledges receipt of the sum of $_____ as the last month's rent under this lease, plus $_____ as security deposit. In the event Tenant terminates the lease prior to its expiration date, said amounts are non-refundable as a charge for Landlord's trouble in securing a new tenant, but Landlord reserves the right to seek additional damages if they exceed the above amounts.

6. UTILITIES. Tenant agrees to pay all utility charges on the property except: _____ _____.

7. MAINTENANCE. Tenant has examined the property, acknowledges it to be in good repair, and in consideration of the reduced rental rate, Tenant agrees to keep the premises in good repair and to do all minor maintenance promptly (under $_____ excluding labor) and provide extermination service.

8. LOCKS. If Tenant adds or changes locks on the premises, Landlord shall be given copies of the keys. Landlord shall at all times have keys for access to the premises in case of emergencies.

9. ASSIGNMENT. This lease may not be assigned by Tenant without the written consent of the Landlord.

10. USE. Tenant shall not use the premises for any illegal purpose or any purpose which will

increase the rate of insurance and shall not cause a nuisance for Landlord or neighbors. Tenant shall not create any environmental hazards on the premises.

11. LAWN. Tenant agrees to maintain the lawn and shrubbery on the premises at Tenant's expense.

12. LIABILITY. Tenant shall be responsible for insurance on his own property and agrees not to hold Landlord liable for any damages to Tenant's property on the premises.

13. ACCESS. Landlord reserves the right to enter the premises for the purposes of inspection and to show to prospective purchasers.

14. PETS. No pets shall be allowed on the premises except: _____ and there shall be a $_____ non-refundable pet deposit.

15. OCCUPANCY. The premises shall not be occupied by more than _____ adults and _____ children.

16. TENANT'S APPLIANCES. Tenant agrees not to use any heaters, fixtures, or appliances drawing excessive current without consent of the Landlord.

17. PARKING. Tenant agrees that no parking is allowed on the premises except: _____. No boats, recreation vehicles, or disassembled automobiles may be stored on the premises.

18. FURNISHINGS. Any articles provided to Tenant and listed on attached schedule are to be returned in good condition at the termination of this lease.

19. ALTERATIONS AND IMPROVEMENTS. Tenant shall make no alterations to the property without the written consent of the Landlord and any such alterations or improvements shall become the property of the Landlord.

20. ENTIRE AGREEMENT. This lease constitutes the entire agreement between the parties and may not be modified except in writing signed by both parties.

21. HARASSMENT. Tenant shall not do any acts to intentionally harass the Landlord or other tenants.

22. ATTORNEY'S FEES. In the event it becomes necessary to enforce this Agreement through the services of an attorney, Tenant shall be required to pay Landlord's attorney's fees.

23. SEVERABILITY. In the event any section of this Agreement shall be held to be invalid, all remaining provisions shall remain in full force and effect.

24. RECORDING. This lease shall not be recorded in any public records.

25. WAIVER. Any failure by Landlord to exercise any rights under this Agreement shall not constitute a waiver of Landlord's rights.

26. ABANDONMENT. In the event Tenant abandons the property prior to the expiration of the lease, Landlord may relet the premises and hold Tenant liable for any costs, lost rent, or damage to the premises. Lessor may dispose of any property abandoned by Tenant.

27. SUBORDINATION. Tenant's interest in the premises shall be subordinate to any encumbrances now or hereafter placed on the premises, to any advances made under such encumbrances, and to any extensions or renewals thereof. Tenant agrees to sign any documents indicating such subordination that may be required by lenders.

28. SURRENDER OF PREMISES. At the expiration of the term of this lease, Tenant shall immediately surrender the premises in as good condition as at the start of this lease.

29. LIENS. The estate of Landlord shall not be subject to any liens for improvements contracted by Tenant.

30. SMOKE DETECTORS. Tenant shall be responsible for supplying smoke detectors, for keeping them operational, and for changing the battery when needed.

31. ABANDONED PROPERTY. By signing this Agreement the Tenant agrees that upon surrender or abandonment, the Landlord shall not be liable or responsible for storage or disposition of the Tenant's personal property.

32. MISCELLANEOUS PROVISIONS. _____
_____
_____.

WITNESS the hands and seals of the parties hereto as of this _____ day of _____, ____.

LANDLORD: TENANT:

_____   _____

_____   _____

This page intentionally left blank.

APARTMENT LEASE

LANDLORD: _____   TENANT: _____

_____   _____

PROPERTY:_____

IN CONSIDERATION of the mutual covenants and agreements herein contained, Landlord hereby leases to Tenant and Tenant hereby leases from Landlord the above-described property under the following terms:

1. TERM. This lease shall be for a term of _____ beginning _____, _____ and ending _____, _____.

2. RENT. The rent shall be $_____ per _____ and shall be due on or before the _____ day of each _____. In the event the rent is received more than three (3) days late, a late charge of $_____ shall be due. In the event a check bounces or an eviction notice must be posted, Tenant agrees to pay a $15.00 charge.

3. PAYMENT. Payment must be received by Landlord on or before the due date at the following address: _____ or such place as designated by Landlord in writing. Tenant understands that this may require early mailing. In the event a check bounces, Landlord may require cash or certified funds.

4. DEFAULT. In the event Tenant defaults under any terms of this lease, Landlord may recover possession as provided by Law and seek monetary damages.

5. SECURITY. Landlord acknowledges receipt of the sum of $_____ as the last month's rent under this lease, plus $_____ as security deposit. In the event Tenant terminates the lease prior to its expiration date, said amounts are non-refundable as a charge for Landlord's trouble in securing a new tenant, but Landlord reserves the right to seek additional damages if they exceed the above amounts.

6. UTILITIES. Tenant agrees to pay all utility charges on the property except: _____ _____.

7. MAINTENANCE. Tenant has examined the property and acknowledges it to be in good repair. Tenant shall immediately repay any and all damage to the premises caused by Tenant or Tenant's guests. In the event of maintenance problems not caused by Tenant, they shall be immediately reported to Landlord or Landlord's agent.

8. LOCKS. If Tenant adds or changes locks on the premises, Landlord shall be given copies of the keys. Landlord shall at all times have keys for access to the premises in case of emergencies.

9. ASSIGNMENT. This lease may not be assigned by Tenant without the written consent of the Landlord.

10. USE. Tenant shall not use the premises for any illegal purpose or any purpose which will increase the rate of insurance and shall not cause a nuisance for Landlord or neighbors. Tenant shall not create any environmental hazards on the premises.

11. CONDOMINIUM. In the event the premises are a condominium unit, Tenant agrees to abide by all rules, regulations, and the declaration of condominium. Maintenance and recreation fees are to be paid by _____. This lease is subject to approval by the condominium association and Tenant agrees to pay any fees necessary for such approval.

12. LIABILITY. Tenant shall be responsible for insurance on his own property and agrees not to hold Landlord liable for any damages to Tenant's property on the premises.

13. ACCESS. Landlord reserves the right to enter the premises for the purposes of inspection and to show to prospective purchasers.

14. PETS. No pets shall be allowed on the premises except: _____ and there shall be a $_____ non-refundable pet deposit.

15. OCCUPANCY. The premises shall not be occupied by more than _____ adults and _____ children.

16. TENANT'S APPLIANCES. Tenant agrees not to use any heaters, fixtures, or appliances drawing excessive current without consent of the Landlord.

17. PARKING. Tenant agrees that no parking is allowed on the premises except: _____. No boats, recreation vehicles, or disassembled automobiles may be stored on the premises.

18. FURNISHINGS. Any articles provided to Tenant and listed on attached schedule are to be returned in good condition at the termination of this lease.

19. ALTERATIONS AND IMPROVEMENTS. Tenant shall make no alterations to the property without the written consent of the Landlord and any such alterations or improvements shall become the property of the Landlord.

20. ENTIRE AGREEMENT. This lease constitutes the entire agreement between the parties and may not be modified except in writing signed by both parties.

21. HARASSMENT. Tenant shall not do any acts to intentionally harass the Landlord or other tenants.

22. ATTORNEY'S FEES. In the event it becomes necessary to enforce this Agreement through the services of an attorney, Tenant shall be required to pay Landlord's attorney's fees.

23. SEVERABILITY. In the event any section of this Agreement shall be held to be invalid, all remaining provisions shall remain in full force and effect.

24. RECORDING. This lease shall not be recorded in any public records.

25. WAIVER. Any failure by Landlord to exercise any rights under this Agreement shall not constitute a waiver of Landlord's rights.

26. ABANDONMENT. In the event Tenant abandons the property prior to the expiration of the lease, Landlord may relet the premises and hold Tenant liable for any costs, lost rent or damage to the premises. Lessor may dispose of any property abandoned by Tenant.

27. SUBORDINATION. Tenant's interest in the premises shall be subordinate to any encumbrances now or hereafter placed on the premises, to any advances made under such encumbrances, and to any extensions or renewals thereof. Tenant agrees to sign any documents indicating such subordination that may be required by lenders.

28. SURRENDER OF PREMISES. At the expiration of the term of this lease, Tenant shall immediately surrender the premises in as good condition as at the start of this lease.

29. LIENS. The estate of Landlord shall not be subject to any liens for improvements contracted by Tenant.

30. SMOKE DETECTORS. Tenant shall be responsible for keeping smoke detectors operational and for changing battery when needed.

31. ABANDONED PROPERTY. By signing this Agreement the Tenant agrees that upon surrender or abandonment, the Landlord shall not be liable or responsible for storage or disposition of the Tenant's personal property.

32. MISCELLANEOUS PROVISIONS. _____

_____

_____.

WITNESS the hands and seals of the parties hereto as of this _____ day of _____, _____.

LANDLORD: TENANT:

_____   _____

_____   _____

This page intentionally left blank.

RENTAL AGREEMENT

LANDLORD: _____   TENANT: _____

_____   _____

PROPERTY:_____

IN CONSIDERATION of the mutual covenants and agreements herein contained, Landlord hereby rents to Tenant and Tenant hereby rents from Landlord the above-described property under the following terms:

1. TERM. This Rental Agreement shall be for a month-to-month tenancy which may be cancelled by either party upon giving notice to the other party at least 15 days prior to the end of a month.

2. RENT. The rent shall be $_____ per month and shall be due on or before the _____ day of each month. In the event the rent is received more than three (3) days late, a late charge of $_____ shall be due. In the event a check bounces or an eviction notice must be posted, Tenant agrees to pay a $15.00 charge.

3. PAYMENT. Payment must be received by Landlord on or before the due date at the following address: _____ or such place as designated by Landlord in writing. Tenant understands that this may require early mailing. In the event a check bounces, Landlord may require cash or certified funds.

4. DEFAULT. In the event Tenant defaults under any terms of this agreement, Landlord may recover possession as provided by Law and seek monetary damages.

5. SECURITY. Landlord acknowledges receipt of the sum of $_____ as the last month's rent under this lease, plus $_____ as security deposit against rent or damages. In the event Tenant vacates the premises without giving proper notice, said amounts are non-refundable as a charge for Landlord's trouble in securing a new tenant, but Landlord reserves the right to seek additional payment for any damages to the premises.

6. UTILITIES. Tenant agrees to pay all utility charges on the property except: _____ _____.

7. MAINTENANCE. Tenant has examined the property, acknowledges it to be in good repair, and in consideration of the reduced rental rate, Tenant agrees to keep the premises in good repair and to do all minor maintenance promptly (under $_____ excluding labor) and provide extermination service.

8. LOCKS. If Tenant adds or changes locks on the premises, Landlord shall be given copies of the keys. Landlord shall at all times have keys for access to the premises in case of emergencies.

9. ASSIGNMENT. This agreement may not be assigned by Tenant without the written consent of the Landlord.

10. USE. Tenant shall not use the premises for any illegal purpose or any purpose that will increase the rate of insurance and shall not cause a nuisance for Landlord or neighbors. Tenant shall not create any environmental hazards on the premises.

11. LAWN. Tenant agrees to maintain the lawn and shrubbery on the premises at his expense.

12. LIABILITY. Tenant shall be responsible for insurance on his own property and agrees not to hold Landlord liable for any damages to Tenant's property on the premises.

13. ACCESS. Landlord reserves the right to enter the premises for the purposes of inspection and to show to prospective purchasers.

14. PETS. No pets shall be allowed on the premises except: _____ and there shall be a $_____ non-refundable pet deposit.

15. OCCUPANCY. The premises shall not be occupied by more than _____ adults and _____ children.

16. TENANT'S APPLIANCES. Tenant agrees not to use any heaters, fixtures, or appliances drawing excessive current without consent of the Landlord.

17. PARKING. Tenant agrees that no parking is allowed on the premises except: _____. No boats, recreation vehicles, or disassembled automobiles may be stored on the premises.

18. FURNISHINGS. Any articles provided to tenant and listed on attached schedule are to be returned in good condition at the termination of this agreement.

19. ALTERATIONS AND IMPROVEMENTS. Tenant shall make no alterations to the property without the written consent of the Landlord and any such alterations or improvements shall become the property of the Landlord.

20. ENTIRE AGREEMENT. This rental agreement constitutes the entire agreement between the parties and may not be modified except in writing signed by both parties.

21. HARASSMENT. Tenant shall not do any acts to intentionally harass the Landlord or other tenants.

22. ATTORNEY'S FEES. In the event it becomes necessary to enforce this agreement through the services of an attorney, Tenant shall be required to pay Landlord's attorney's fees.

23. SEVERABILITY. In the event any section of this agreement shall be held to be invalid, all remaining provisions shall remain in full force and effect.

24. RECORDING. This agreement shall not be recorded in any public records.

25. WAIVER. Any failure by Landlord to exercise any rights under this agreement shall not constitute a waiver of Landlord's rights.

26. SUBORDINATION. Tenant's interest in the premises shall be subordinate to any encumbrances now or hereafter placed on the premises, to any advances made under such encumbrances, and to any extensions or renewals thereof. Tenant agrees to sign any documents indicating such subordination that may be required by lenders.

27. SURRENDER OF PREMISES. At the expiration of the term of this agreement, Tenant shall immediately surrender the premises in as good condition as at the start of this agreement.

28. LIENS. The estate of Landlord shall not be subject to any liens for improvements contracted by Tenant.

29. SMOKE DETECTORS. Tenant shall be responsible for keeping smoke detectors operational and for changing battery when needed.

30. ABANDONED PROPERTY. By signing this Agreement the Tenant agrees that upon surrender or abandonment, the Landlord shall not be liable or responsible for storage or disposition of the Tenant's personal property.

31. MISCELLANEOUS PROVISIONS. _____
_____.

WITNESS the hands and seals of the parties hereto as of this _____ day of
_____, _____.

LANDLORD: TENANT:

_____   _____

_____   _____

This page intentionally left blank.

Disclosure of Information on Lead-Based Paint and/or Lead-Based Paint Hazards

Lead Warning Statement

Housing built before 1978 may contain lead-based paint. Lead from paint, paint chips, and dust can pose health hazards if not managed properly. Lead exposure is especially harmful to young children and pregnant women. Before renting pre-1978 housing, lessors must disclose the presence of known lead-based paint and/or lead-based paint hazards in the dwelling. Lessees must also receive a federally approved pamphlet on lead poisoning prevention.

Lessor's Disclosure

(a) Presence of lead-based paint and/or lead-based paint hazards (check (i) or (ii) below):

  (i) _____ Known lead-based paint and/or lead-based paint hazards are present in the housing (explain).

  _____

  _____

  (ii) _____ Lessor has no knowledge of lead-based paint and/or lead-based paint hazards in the housing.

(b) Records and reports available to the lessor (check (i) or (ii) below):

  (i) _____ Lessor has provided the lessee with all available records and reports pertaining to lead-based paint and/or lead-based paint hazards in the housing (list documents below).

  _____

  _____

  (ii) _____ Lessor has no reports or records pertaining to lead-based paint and/or lead-based paint hazards in the housing.

Lessee's Acknowledgment (initial)

(c) _____ Lessee has received copies of all information listed above.

(d) _____ Lessee has received the pamphlet *Protect Your Family from Lead in Your Home.*

Agent's Acknowledgment (initial)

(e) _____ Agent has informed the lessor of the lessor's obligations under 42 U.S.C. 4852(d) and is aware of his/her responsibility to ensure compliance.

Certification of Accuracy

The following parties have reviewed the information above and certify, to the best of their knowledge, that the information they have provided is true and accurate.

Lessor	Date	Lessor	Date
Lessee	Date	Lessee	Date
Agent	Date	Agent	Date

This page intentionally left blank.

NOTICE OF HOLDING SECURITY DEPOSIT

To: _____

From: _____

Pursuant to New York law, this notice is to advise you that your security deposit is being held as follows:

1. The account is at the following depository: _____
_____

2. The funds are:
   ❐ in a separate account solely holding security deposits
   ❐ in an account commingled with landlord's funds

3. The account is:
   ❐ interest-bearing
   ❐ not interest-bearing

This page intentionally left blank.

AGREEMENT REGARDING ABANDONED PROPERTY

This agreement is made between _____

as Landlord and _____ as

Tenant of property described as _____.

The undersigned Landlord and Tenant agree that BY SIGNING THIS AGREEMENT THE TENANT AGREES THAT UPON SURRENDER OR ABANDONMENT, AS DEFINED BY THE NEW YORK STATUTES, THE LANDLORD SHALL NOT BE LIABLE OR RESPONSIBLE FOR STORAGE OR DISPOSITION OF THE TENANT'S PERSONAL PROPERTY.

Date: _____   Landlord:

_____

_____

Tenant:

_____

_____

This page intentionally left blank.

INSPECTION REQUEST

Date:

To:

It will be necessary to enter your dwelling unit for the purpose of _____ _____ _____. If possible we would like access on _____ at ____o'clock ___.m.

In the event this is not convenient, please call to arrange another time.

Sincerely,

_____

Address:

Phone:

This page intentionally left blank.

STATEMENT FOR REPAIRS

Date:

To:

It has been necessary to repair damage to the premises that you occupy, which was caused by you or your guests. The costs for repairs were as follows:

This amount is your responsibility under the terms of the lease and New York law and should be forwarded to us at the address below.

Sincerely,

_____

Address:

Phone:

NOTICE OF CHANGE OF TERMS

Date:

To:

Dear _____

You are hereby notified that effective _____ the terms of your rental agreement will be changed as follows:

If you elect to terminate your tenancy prior to that date kindly provide 30 days notice as provided by law.

Sincerely,

_____

Address:

Phone:

This page intentionally left blank.

AMENDMENT TO LEASE/RENTAL AGREEMENT

The undersigned parties to that certain agreement dated _____, _____ on the premises known as _____, hereby agree to amend said agreement as follows:

WITNESS the hands and seals of the parties hereto this ____ day of _____, _____.

Landlord: Tenant:

_____   _____

_____   _____

This page intentionally left blank.

LETTER—CONTINUATION OF TENANCY

Date:

To:

Dear _____

    This letter is to remind you that your lease will expire on _____. Please advise us within _____ days as to whether you intend to renew your lease. If so, we will prepare a new lease for your signature(s).

    If you do not intend to renew your lease, the keys should be delivered to us at the address below on or before the end of the lease along with your forwarding address. We will inspect the premises for damages, deduct any amounts necessary for repairs, and refund any remaining balance as required by law.

    If we have not heard from you as specified above we will assume that you will be vacating the premises and will arrange for a new tenant to move in at the end of your term.

        Sincerely,

        _____

        Address:

        Phone:

This page intentionally left blank.

NOTICE OF TERMINATION OF AGENT

Date:

To:

    You are hereby advised that _____ is no longer our agent effective _____. On and after this date he or she is no longer authorized to collect rent, accept notices or to make any representations or agreements regarding the property.

    Rent should thereafter be paid to us directly unless you are instructed otherwise by in writing.

    If you have any questions you may contact us at the address or phone number below.

                      Sincerely,

                      _____

                      Address:

                      Phone:

This page intentionally left blank.

NOTICE OF APPOINTMENT OF AGENT

Date:

To:

    You are hereby advised that effective _____, our agent for collection of rent and other matters regarding the property will be _____. However, no terms of the written lease may be modified or waived without our written signature(s).

    If you have any questions you may contact us at the address or phone number below.

Sincerely,

_____

Address:

Phone:

This page intentionally left blank.

NOTICE OF NON-RENEWAL

_____

_____

_____

_____
(Tenant's Name and Address)

Dear _____:
        (Tenant's Name)

You are notified that your tenancy will not be renewed at the end of the present term. You will be expected to vacate the premises on or before _____, _____. In the event that you do not vacate the premises by said date, legal action may be taken in which you may be held liable for rent, court costs, and attorney fees.

_____
(signature)

Landlord's Name_____

Address _____

Phone Number _____

This page intentionally left blank.

DEMAND FOR RENT

To: _____   From: _____

_____   _____

_____   _____

Dated: _____

Re: Lease dated _____ by and between _____ (landlord), and _____ (tenant), regarding the premises located at:

_____, Apt. #____

_____-_____

PLEASE TAKE NOTICE, that you have failed to pay the rent specified in the lease totaling $_____ due for the period(s) as follows:

Period   Amount due each period

_____, _____ $_____

_____, _____ $_____

_____, _____ $_____

_____, _____ $_____

Total amount due: $_____

You are required to pay the total amount due on or before _____, that being more than three (3) days from the date of the service of this notice, or surrender possession of the premises to the landlord. If you default on this notice, the landlord will commence a summary proceeding against you according to the laws of the state of New York.

_____

Name of Landlord

_____

Signed By

This page intentionally left blank.

DEMAND FOR PAYMENT OF DISHONORED CHECK

Date:

To: _____
        Name of Drawer
_____
_____

_____
Last Known Residing Address or Place of Business

❏ 1ST NOTICE

❏ 2ND AND FINAL NOTICE

WARNING:
You may be sued 30 days after the date of this notice if you do not make payment

Your check, in the amount of $_____ dated _____ payable to the order of _____ has been dishonored by the bank upon which it was drawn, because

_____ You had no account with that bank.

_____ You had insufficient funds on deposit with that bank.

If you do not make payment, you may be sued under Section 11-104 of the General Obligations Law to recover payment. If a judgment is rendered against you in court, it may include not only the original face amount of the check, but also additional liquidated damages, as follows:

❏ If you had no account with the bank upon which the check was drawn, an additional sum that may be equivalent to twice the face amount of the check or seven hundred fifty dollars, whichever is less; or

❏ If you had insufficient funds on deposit with the bank upon which the check was drawn, an additional sum that may be equivalent to twice the face amount of the check or four hundred dollars, whichever is less.

Please make payment in the amount of $_____ to:

_____
Name of Payee

_____

_____

_____
Address to which Payment Should Be Delivered

This page intentionally left blank.

NOTICE OF DEFAULT

To: _____ ,

at the address _____ ,

and to any and all persons occupying the premises as hereinafter more fully described.

Re: the premises: _____

     PLEASE TAKE NOTICE that you are violating a substantial obligation of your lease

dated _____ by and between _____, landlord

and _____, tenant(s).

Specifically, you have (nature of violation):

_____

_____ in

violation of paragraph number _____ of the lease, as follows (description of acts):

_____

_____

     PLEASE TAKE FURTHER NOTICE that you are required to cure the violation

within _____ days from the date of this notice by doing the following:

_____

_____

     PLEASE TAKE FURTHER NOTICE, that if you fail to cure the violation on or before

_____, that being at least _____ days (number required) from

the date of service of this notice upon you, your tenancy will be terminated and you will

be required to remove from and surrender possession of the premises to the landlord.

Dated: _____

                              _____(landlord)

                              _____(address)

                              _____

This page intentionally left blank.

TEN-DAY NOTICE TO QUIT

To: _____ (tenant(s))

Re: the premises: _____

    PLEASE TAKE NOTICE, that you and all other persons occupying the subject premises are required to quit and vacate the premises on or before _____ (10 days after service of notice) because (check as many as apply):

❏ you (or the person whom you have succeeded) have intruded into, or squatted upon, the subject premises without the permission of the undersigned landlord who is the person entitled to possession, and your occupancy has continued without permission (or after permission has been revoked and notice of revocation given to you).

❏ you are in possession of the premises as a licensee of _____ _____ (tenant(s)), and your license to occupy the premises has expired or has been revoked by _____ (tenant(s)).

❏ the premises have been sold in foreclosure and a deed (or a certified copy of the deed) delivered to the purchaser pursuant to the foreclosure sale has been exhibited to you.

❏ your tenancy has been terminated due to: _____ _____ _____ and you have no legal right to possession of the premises.

    PLEASE TAKE FURTHER NOTICE, that unless you quit and vacate the subject premises on or before _____, the undersigned will commence summary proceedings against you to remove you from the subject premises.

Dated: _____   _____(landlord)

_____, New York

This page intentionally left blank.

NOTICE OF TERMINATION

To: _____(tenant(s)) residing at

_____

Re: the premises:

_____

_____

    PLEASE TAKE NOTICE, that the undersigned Landlord elects to terminate your tenancy of the subject premises, now held by you.

    PLEASE TAKE FURTHER NOTICE, that unless you remove from the subject premises on or before _____ (_____ days after service of notice), the day on which your term expires, that being more than _____ days from the date of service of this notice upon you, the Landlord will commence summary proceedings to remove you from the subject premises for the holding over after the expiration of your term and will demand the value of your use and occupancy of the subject premises during such holding over.

Dated: _____   _____(landlord)

_____, New York   _____ (address)

                                            _____

This page intentionally left blank.

NOTICE OF PETITION—NEW YORK STATE CITY COURTS

CITY COURT OF _____

_____)	
Petitioner,)	
Address_____)	**HOLDOVER**
_____)	**NOTICE OF PETITION**
-against-)	{Commercial/Residential}
)	Index No. _____
_____)	{L & T}
Respondent{s},)	
Address_____)	
_____)	

To the Respondent(s) _____, above named and described, in possession of the premises herein described or claiming possession thereof:

PLEASE TAKE NOTICE that a hearing at which you must appear will be held at the City Court of the City of _____, _____ District, to be held at _____, City of _____, County of _____, on the _____ day of_____, _____, at _____{AM/PM}, which asks for a final judgment of eviction awarding to the Petitioner the possession of premises designated and described as follows:

_____
_____;

and further granting to the Petitioner such other and further relief as is demanded in the Petition which you must answer.

TAKE NOTICE, also that a demand is made in the Petition for judgment against you, the Respondent, for the sum of $_____, with interest thereon from _____.

TAKE NOTICE also that your answer may be made at the time of the hearing specified above unless the Notice of Petition is served upon you on or before the _____day of _____, _____, in which event you must answer at least three (3) days before the Petition is noticed to be heard, either orally before the clerk of the court at his or her office, or in writing by serving a copy thereof upon the undersigned attorney for the Petitioner, and by filing the original of such written answer with proof of service thereof in the office of the clerk at least three (3) days before the time the Petition is noticed to be heard; in addition thereto, you must appear before the court at the time and place hereinabove set forth for the hearing.

TAKE NOTICE, that your answer may give any defense or counterclaim you may have against the Petitioner, unless such defense or counterclaim is precluded by law or agreement of the parties.

TAKE NOTICE also that if you should fail at such time to give any defense that you may have to the allegations of the Petition, you may be precluded from asserting such defense or the claim on which it is based in any other proceeding or action.

TAKE NOTICE, that your failure to appear and answer may result in a final judgment by default for the Petitioner in the amount demanded in the Petition.

Dated: County of _____

_____ day of _____, _____

Petitioner_____

Address_____

_____

Telephone Number_____

_____
Clerk of the Court of the City

of _____

NOTICE OF PETITION—NEW YORK CITY CIVIL COURT

CIVIL COURT OF THE CITY OF NEW YORK
COUNTY OF _____

_____)
                    Petitioner,)
Address_____)
_____)   **HOLDOVER**
        -against-   )   **NOTICE OF PETITION**
)   {Commercial/Residential}
_____)   Index No. _____
        Respondent{s}-Tenant{s},))
Address_____)   {L & T}
_____)

To the Respondent(s) _____,
in possession of the premises herein described or claiming possession thereof:

PLEASE TAKE NOTICE that a hearing at which you must appear will be held at the Civil Court of the City of New York, _____ Part to be held at _____ County of _____, on the _____ day of _____, _____, at _____ {AM/PM}, which asks for a final judgment of eviction awarding to the Petitioner the possession of premises designated and described as follows:

_____
_____
_____

and further granting to the Petitioner such other and further relief as is demanded in the Petition which you must answer.

TAKE NOTICE, also that a demand is made in the Petition for judgment against you, the Respondent, for the sum of $_____, with interest thereon from _____.

TAKE NOTICE, that your answer may give any defense or counterclaim you may have against the Petitioner, unless such defense or counterclaim is precluded by law or agreement of the parties.

TAKE NOTICE that you will be required to post rent or use and occupancy accrued from the date the petition and notice of petition are served upon you, pursuant to RPAPL § 745(2), upon your second adjournment request, or thirty days after the first appearance, whichever is sooner, unless you can establish one of the defenses in RPAPL § 745(2)(a).

TAKE NOTICE also that if you should fail at such time to give any defense that you may have to the allegations of the Petition, you may be precluded from asserting such defense or the claim on which it is based in any other proceeding or action.

TAKE NOTICE that your failure to appear and answer may result in a final judgment of eviction by default for the Petitioner in the amount demanded in the Petition.

Dated: County of_____
The_____day of_____,_____.

_____
Clerk of the Civil Court of the
City of New York

Petitioner _____
Address_____
_____
Telephone_____

NOTICE OF PETITION—NEW YORK STATE DISTRICT COURTS

CIVIL COURT OF THE STATE OF NEW YORK
COUNTY OF _____

_____)
                       Petitioner,)
Address_____)
)
_____)   **HOLDOVER**
          -against-)   **NOTICE OF PETITION**
)   {Commercial/Residential}
_____)   Index No. _____
          Respondent{s}-Tenant{s},)   {L & T}
Address_____)
_____)

     To the Respondent(s) _____,
in possession of the premises herein described or claiming possession thereof:

     PLEASE TAKE NOTICE that a hearing at which you must appear will be held at the District Court for the County of _____,_____ District, Part to be held at _____, Town of _____, County of _____on the _____ day of _____, _____, at _____ {AM/PM}, which asks for a final judgment of eviction awarding to the Petitioner the possession of premises designated and described as follows:

_____

_____

and further granting to the Petitioner such other and further relief as is demanded in the Petition which you must answer.

     TAKE NOTICE also that a demand is made in the Petition for judgment against you, the Respondent, for the sum of $_____, with interest thereon from _____, _____.

     TAKE NOTICE also that your answer may be made at the time of the hearing specified above unless the Notice of Petition is served upon you on or before the _____ day of _____, _____, in which event you must answer at least three (3) days before the Petition is noticed to be heard, either orally before the clerk of the court at his or her office, or in writing by serving a copy thereof upon the undersigned attorney for the Petitioner, and by filing the original of such written answer with proof of service thereof in the office of the clerk at least three (3) days before the time the Petition is noticed to be heard; in addition thereto, you must appear before the court at the time and place hereinabove set forth for the hearing.

TAKE NOTICE that your answer may give any defense or counterclaim you may have against the Petitioner, unless such defense or counterclaim is precluded by law or agreement of the parties.

TAKE NOTICE also that if you should fail at such time to give any defense that you may have to the allegations of the Petition, you may be precluded from asserting such defense or the claim on which it is based in any other proceeding or action.

TAKE NOTICE that your failure to appear and answer may result in a final judgment by default for the Petitioner in the amount demanded in the Petition.

Dated: County of _____, the   _____
_____ day of _____, _____   Clerk District _____

Petitioner _____
Address _____

_____
Telephone Number _____

NOTICE OF PETITION—CITY COURTS OUTSIDE NEW YORK CITY

CITY COURT OF _____

_____)
                    Petitioner,)
Address_____)
_____)
          -against-   )
)
_____)
               Respondent{s},)
Address_____)
_____)

**NOTICE OF PETITION
(NONPAYMENT)**
{Commercial/Residential}
Index No. _____
{L & T}

To the respondent(s) _____,
in possession of the premises herein described or claiming possession thereof:

PLEASE TAKE NOTICE that a hearing at which you must appear will be held at the District Court for the County of _____,_____ District, Part to be held at _____, Town of _____, County of _____on the _____ day of _____, _____, at _____ {AM/PM}, which asks for a final judgment of eviction awarding to the Petitioner the possession of premises designated and described as follows:

_____
_____
_____
_____
_____,

and further granting to the Petitioner such other and further relief as is demanded in the Petition which you must answer.

TAKE NOTICE also that a demand is made in the Petition for judgment against you, the respondent, for the sum of $_____, with interest thereon from _____.

TAKE NOTICE also that your answer may be made at the time of the hearing specified above unless the Notice of Petition is served upon you on or before the _____ day of _____ in which event you must answer at least three (3) days before the Petition is noticed to be heard, either orally before the clerk of the court at his or her office, or in writing by serving a copy thereof upon the undersigned attorney for the Petitioner, and by filing the original of such written answer with proof of service thereof in the office of the clerk at least three (3) days before the time the Petition is noticed to be heard; in addition thereto, you must appear before the court at the time and place hereinabove set forth for the hearing.

TAKE NOTICE that your answer may give any defense or counterclaim you may have against the Petitioner.

TAKE NOTICE also that if you should fail at such time to give any defense that you may have to the allegations of the Petition, you may be precluded from asserting such defense or the claim on which it is based in any other proceeding or action.

TAKE NOTICE, that your failure to appear and answer may result in a final judgment by default for the Petitioner in the amount demanded in the Petition.

Dated: County of _____,
the _____ day of _____, _____

Petitioner _____
Address _____
_____
Telephone Number _____

_____
Clerk of the Court of the City
of _____

NOTICE OF PETITION—NEW YORK CITY CIVIL COURT

CIVIL COURT OF THE CITY OF NEW YORK
COUNTY OF _____

_____)
                  Petitioner,)

Address_____)

_____)

            -against-)

)

_____)

           Respondent{s},)

Address_____)

_____)

)

_____)

**NOTICE OF PETITION
(NONPAYMENT)**
{Commercial/Residential}
Index No. _____
{L & T}

To the respondent(s) _____,
in possession of the premises herein described or claiming possession thereof:

PLEASE TAKE NOTICE that the annexed Petition of _____
(landlord), verified the _____ day of _____, asks for a final judgment
of eviction, awarding to the Petitioner possession of premises described as follows:

_____

_____

_____

_____

as demanded in the Petition.

TAKE NOTICE also that demand is made in the Petition for judgment against you
for the sum of $_____, with interest from_____.

TAKE NOTICE also that within five (5) days after service of this Notice of Petition
upon you, you must answer, either orally before the clerk of this Court at
_____, County of _____, City and State of New York, or
in writing by serving a copy thereof upon the undersigned attorney for the Petitioner,
and by filing the original of such answer, with proof of service thereof, in the Office of the

Clerk. Your answer may give any defense or counterclaim you may have against the Petitioner. On receipt of your answer, the Clerk will fix and give notice of the date for trial or hearing which will be held not less than three (3) nor more than eight (8) days thereafter, at which you must appear. If, after the trial or hearing, judgment is made against you, the issuance of a warrant dispossessing you may, in the discretion of the Court, be stayed for five (5) days from the date of the judgment.

TAKE NOTICE, that you will be required to post rent or use and occupancy accrued from the date the petition and notice of petition are served upon you, pursuant to RPAPL § 745(2), upon your second adjournment request, or thirty days after the first appearance, whichever is sooner, unless you can establish one of the defenses in RPAPL § 745(2)(a).

TAKE NOTICE also that if you fail to give any defense that you may have to the allegations of the Petition, you may be precluded from asserting such defense or the claim on which it is based in any other proceeding or action.

In the event you fail to answer and appear, final judgment by default will be entered against you, but a warrant dispossessing you will not be issued until ten days following the date of the service of this Notice of Petition upon you.

Dated: City of New York, County of _____,

_____
Clerk of the Civil Court of
the City of New York

Petitioner _____
Address _____
_____
Telephone Number _____

NOTICE OF PETITION—DISTRICT COURT

DISTRICT COURT OF THE STATE OF NEW YORK

COUNTY OF _____

_____)	
Petitioner,)	
Address_____)	**NOTICE OF PETITION**
_____)	**(NONPAYMENT)**
-against-)	{Commercial/Residential}
)	Index No. _____
_____)	{L & T}
Respondent{s},)	
Address_____)	
_____)	

To the respondent(s) _____,
in possession of the premises herein described or claiming possession thereof:

PLEASE TAKE NOTICE that a hearing at which you must appear will be held at the District Court for the County of _____,_____ District, Part to be held at _____, Town of _____, County of _____on the _____ day of _____, _____, at _____ {AM/PM}, which asks for a final judgment of eviction awarding to the Petitioner the possession of premises designated and described as follows:

_____

_____

_____

_____

_____,

and further granting to the Petitioner such other and further relief as is demanded in the Petition which you must answer.

TAKE NOTICE, also that a demand is made in the Petition for judgment against you, the respondent, for the sum of $_____, with interest from _____.

TAKE NOTICE also that your answer may be made at the time of the hearing specified above unless the Notice of Petition is served upon you on or before the____day of ____, _____ in which event you must answer at least three (3) days before the Petition is noticed to be heard, either orally before the clerk of the court at his or her office, or in writing by serving a copy thereof upon the undersigned attorney for the Petitioner, and by filing the original of such written answer with proof of service thereof in the office of the clerk at least three (3) days before the time the Petition is noticed to be heard; in addition thereto, you must appear before the court at the time and place hereinabove set forth for the hearing.

TAKE NOTICE, that your answer may give any defense or counterclaim you may have against the Petitioner.

TAKE NOTICE also that if you should fail at such time to give any defense that you may have to the allegations of the Petition, you may be precluded from asserting such defense or the claim on which it is based in any other proceeding or action.

TAKE NOTICE, that your failure to appear and answer may result in a final judgment by default for the Petitioner in the amount demanded in the Petition.

Dated: County of _____,
the _____ day of_____, _____

_____
Clerk
District _____

Petitioner _____
Address _____
_____
Telephone Number _____

_____COURT OF THE STATE OF NEW YORK
COUNTY OF _____

_____
                                        Petitioner,

Address:_____

_____

        -against-

_____,
                                Respondent(s),

Address(es):_____

_____

_____

Holdover Petition
{Commercial/Residential}

Index No. _____

(L & T)

Petitioner landlord, _____, hereby swears that:

1. Petitioner, _____, is the landlord of the premises described below.

2. ❏ Respondent(s)-tenant(s) _____ is/are
    the tenant(s) of record pursuant to a rental agreement made _____,
    between Respondent(s) and the Petitioner beginning _____ and
    originally ending _____.

                        or

    ❏ Respondent(s) _____ entered into
    possession of the Premises under a license which has expired or been revoked.

                        or

    ❏ Respondent(s) _____ intruded into or
    squatted upon the Premises without permission, and the occupancy has continued
    without permission. Permission has been revoked and notice of the revocation duly
    given to the Respondent.

                        or

    ❏ Respondent(s) _____ entered into
    possession of the Premises as an incident of employment, and that the time agreed
    upon for such possession has expired and the employment has been terminated.

    ❏ Respondent(s)-Undertenant(s) _____/
    "JOHN DOE" and "JANE DOE" are the undertenant(s) of the Respondent(s).

3. Upon information and belief, respondent(s) is/are not in the military service of the United States.

4. Respondent(s) entered into possession on _____ date and continue(s) in possession of the premises.

5. The premises from which removal is sought were rented for residential/commercial purposes and are described as follows:

   _____

   _____

   _____.

6. Said premises are situated within the jurisdiction of this Court.

7. At least _____ days before the expiration of the term, Respondent(s) was/were served in the manner provided by law with a notice in writing, a copy of which is annexed hereto (with proof of service) and made a part of this Petition, that the landlord elected to terminate the tenancy (or 'occupancy'), and unless Respondent(s) moved from the premises on the day the expired, Landlord would commence summary proceedings under the statute to remove the Respondent(s) from the premises.

8. Respondent(s) continue in possession of the premises without permission of the Landlord after the expiration of the term.

9. (In New York City):

   ❏ The premises is rent-controlled and the dwelling is subject to the New York City Rent and Rehabilitation Law and the premises are registered with the New York State Division of Housing and Community Renewal, and the rent demanded in this petition does not exceed the maximum rent prescribed by the New York State Division of Housing and Community Renewal.

   or

   ❏ The premises is rent-stabilized and the dwelling is subject to the Rent Stabilization Law of 1969, as amended, and the premises are registered with the New York State Division of Housing and Community Renewal, and the owner is in compliance with the Rent Stabilization Law and Code; the rent demanded in this petition does not exceed the lawful stabilized rent permitted the owner under the law and appropriate Rent Guidelines Board Order as registered with said agency.

   or

❏ The premises is a cooperative unit occupied by a non-rent-regulated Tenant(s) and the dwelling is not subject to the New York City Rent and Rehabilitation Law or the Rent Stabilization Law of 1969, as amended, because the dwelling is owned as a cooperative unit and is not occupied by a "non-purchasing tenant" as defined under section 352-eeee of the General Business Law and Rehabilitation Law or the Rent Stabilization Law of 1969, as amended, because the dwelling is owned as a condominium unit and is not occupied by a "non-purchasing tenant" as defined under section 352-eeee of the General Business Law.

or

❏ The premises is a two-family home and as such is not subject to the New York City Rent and Rehabilitation Law or the Rent Stabilization Law of 1969, as amended, because the dwelling is in a two-family house occupied, in part, by the owner.

or

❏ The premises is a commercial premises and is not subject to the City Rent and Rehabilitation Law or the Rent Stabilization Law of 1969, as amended, because it is rented for business purposes.

10. (In New York City)

❏ The premises is not a multiple dwelling.

or

❏ The premises is a multiple dwelling and pursuant to the Housing Maintenance Code, Article 41, there is a currently effective registration statement on file with the office of Code Enforcement in which the owner has designated the managing agent named below, a natural person over twenty-one years of age, to be in control of and responsible for the maintenance and operation of the dwelling:

(1) Multiple Dwelling Registration Number: _____

(2) Registered Managing Agent:_____

(3) Business Address:_____

_____

(4) Telephone Number:_____

11. Petitioner lacks written information or notice of any address where the Respondent(s) reside(s), is/are employed, has/have a place of business in New York, other than the premises sought to be recovered and _____

_____.

12. Under the terms of the governing rental agreement, Respondent(s) agreed to pay rent for the Premises at the rate of _____ per month, together with such other lease-related costs, such as attorney's fees which might be incurred by Petitioner in any action or proceeding to enforce the Petitioner's rights under the rental agreement.

13. No funds for rent and/or "use and occupancy" have been received or accepted for the period after _____.

14. In addition, the value of Respondent's(s') use and occupancy of the premises after _____ is at the rate of at least $_____ per month.

15. Under the terms of the governing rental agreement, Petitioner is entitled to recover from Respondent(s) such costs, disbursements, and attorneys' fees incurred by the Petitioner.

16. Petitioner has and will incur such costs and fees, the total amount of such costs and fees to be determined by the Court at a hearing or trial, but believed to be at least $_____.

WHEREFORE, Petitioner requests a final judgment awarding Petitioner:

❏ possession of the premises with the issuance of a warrant to remove respondent(s) from possession of the premises,

❏ a money judgment against Respondent(s) for rent arrears through _____ totaling $_____ with interest from _____, together with an award for the use and occupancy of the premises from _____ in an amount to be determined by the Court, attorney's fees no less than $_____, and, for the costs and expenses of this proceeding.

Dated: _____, New York

Petitioner _____

Address _____

_____

Telephone Number _____

_____COURT OF THE STATE OF NEW YORK
COUNTY OF _____

_____
                                                Petitioner,

Address:_____

_____   **Nonpayment Petition**

              -against-   {Commercial/Residential}

_____,
                              Respondent(s),   Index No. _____
Address(es):_____   (L & T)

_____

_____

Petitioner landlord, _____, hereby swears that:

1. Petitioner, _____, is the landlord of the premises described below.

2. Respondent(s)-Tenant(s), _____,
   occupy(ies) the premises pursuant to a rental agreement made on _____
   between Respondent and the Petitioner beginning _____ and
   ending _____, whereby Tenant(s) agreed to pay to Landlord rent
   each month in advance on the _____ day of each month.

3. Respondent(s)-Undertenant(s), _____, are
   the undertenants of the Tenant.

4. Tenant(s) [and respondent(s)-undertenant(s)] entered into possession and continue in
   possession of the premises.

5. The premises from which removal is sought was rented for {residential/commercial}
   purposes and is described as follows:

   _____

   _____

6. This premises is situated within the jurisdiction of this Court.

7. Under the rental agreement dated _____ between landlord
   and tenant(s) beginning on _____ and expiring on
   _____, there was rent due to the Landlord from Tenant(s) rent as
   follows:

Month/Date/Year	Description	Amount
_____	_____	_____
_____	_____	_____
_____	_____	_____

8. Said rent has been demanded orally, by service of a written three-day demand (a copy of which is attached to this Petition with proof of service) from the Respondent(s)-Tenant(s) after the amount became due.

9. Respondent(s)-Tenant(s) have/has defaulted in the payment of said rent, pursuant to the agreement under which the premises is held.

10. Respondent(s) hold(s) over and continue(s) in possession of the premises without Landlord's permission after the default and the demand.

11. Upon information and belief, the tenant(s) is/are not in the military service of the United States.

(In New York City):

12. Select the appropriate sections if the premises is rent-regulated:
    ❏ The premises is rent-controlled and the dwelling is subject to the New York City Rent and Rehabilitation Law and the Premises is registered with the New York State Division of Housing and Community Renewal, and the rent demanded herein does not exceed the maximum rent allowed by the New York State Division of Housing and Community Renewal.

    or

    ❏ The premises is rent-stabilized and the dwelling is subject to the Rent Stabilization Law of 1969, as amended, and the premises is registered with the New York State Division of Housing and Community Renewal, (DHCR) and the owner is in compliance with the Rent Stabilization Law and Code; the rent demanded herein does not exceed the lawful stabilized rent permitted the owner under the Law, Code, and appropriate Rent Guidelines Board Order as registered with the DHCR.

    or

    ❏ The premises is commercial and as such is not subject to the New York City Rent and Rehabilitation Law or the Rent Stabilization Law of 1969, as amended, because the subject premises are rented and used for business purposes only.

or

❑ The premises is a cooperative unit occupied by a non-rent-regulated tenant and as such is not subject to the New York City Rent and Rehabilitation Law or the Rent Stabilization Law of 1969, as amended, because the dwelling is owned as a cooperative unit and is not occupied by a "non-purchasing tenant" as defined under section 352-e of the General Business Law.

or

❑ The premises is a condominium unit occupied by a non-rent-regulated tenant and as such is not subject to the New York City Rent and Rehabilitation Law or the Rent Stabilization Law of 1969, as amended, because the dwelling is owned as a condominium unit and is not occupied by a "non-purchasing tenant" as defined under section 352-e of the General Business Law.

or

❑ The premises is a two-family home and is occupied in part by the owner and as such is not subject to the New York City Rent and Rehabilitation Law (rent control) or the Rent Stabilization Law of 1969, as amended.

(In New York City only):

13.❑ The premises is not a multiple dwelling.

or

❑ The premises is a multiple dwelling and pursuant to the Housing Maintenance Code, Article 41, there is a current registration statement on file with the office of Code Enforcement in which the owner has designated the managing agent named below, a natural person over twenty-one years of age, to be in control of and responsible for the maintenance and operation of the dwelling:

    (1)   Multiple Dwelling Registration Number: _____

    (2)   Registered Managing Agent: _____

    (3)   Business Address: _____

                 _____

    (4)   Telephone Number: _____

14. Under the terms of the rental agreement, Petitioner is entitled to recover from Tenant(s) costs, disbursements, and attorney's fees incurred by the Petitioner, the total amount of such costs and fees to be determined by the Court at a hearing or trial, but believed to equal to or exceeding $_____.

WHEREFORE, Petitioner requests a final judgment awarding Petitioner:

(a) possession of the premises with the issuance of a warrant to remove respondent(s) from possession of the premises;

(b) a money judgment against Tenant(s) for rent in arrears for $_____ with interest thereon from_____;

(c) an award of Petitioner's attorney's fees, costs, and disbursement in an amount to be determined by the Court but believed to be no less than $_____, and such further relief the Court deems just and proper.

Dated: _____,

_____
Petitioner

Petitioner _____

Address _____

_____

Telephone Number _____

VERIFICATION

STATE OF NEW YORK   )
) ss.:
COUNTY OF   )

_____, being duly sworn, deposes and says:

1. I am the Petitioner identified and named in the within Petition.

2. I have read the foregoing Petition and know the contents thereof to be true to my own knowledge, except as to those matters therein stated to be alleged upon information and belief, and as to those matters your deponent believes to be true.

_____
Petitioner

_____
Signature

Sworn to before me
This _____ day of
_____, _____

_____
Notary Public

This page intentionally left blank.

SUPREME COURT OF THE STATE OF NEW YORK
COUNTY OF _____

---X

                      Petitioner(s)   Index No:_____

-against-

                    Respondent(s)   **AFFIDAVIT OF SERVICE**

---X

STATE OF NEW YORK, COUNTY OF _____ ss.:

_____ being duly sworn, says:

1.   I am not a party to the action, I am over 18 years of age and reside at:

_____

2.   On _____, _____, at ____a.m./p.m. at _____
_____ I served the within _____
on _____, the Respondent named in
the _____, by delivering a true copy of the
_____ to the Respondent by the following method:
_____
_____
_____
_____

3.   I knew the person so served to be the person described in the _____
as the Respondent. My knowledge of the Respondent and how I acquired it is as follows:
(select one)

☐   I have known the Respondent for _____ years and _____
_____
_____

OR

☐   I identified the Respondent by a photograph annexed to this affidavit and which was given to me by the Petitioner

OR

☐   Petitioner accompanied me and pointed out the Respondent.

OR

☐   I asked the person served if he/she was the person named in the _____ _____ and Respondent admitted being the person so named.

5.   Deponent describes the individual served as follows:

<u>Sex</u>	<u>Height</u>	<u>Weight</u>	<u>Age</u>	Color of <u>Skin</u>	Color of <u>Hair</u>
☐ Male	☐ Under 5"	☐ Under 100 Lbs.	☐ 14-20 Yrs.	Describe color:	☐ Black
☐ Female	☐ 5'0"-5'3"	☐ 100-130 Lbs.	☐ 21-35 Yrs.	_____	☐ Brown
	☐ 5'4"-5'8"	☐ 131-160 Lbs.	☐ 36-50 Yrs.	_____	☐ Blond
	☐ 5'9"-6'0"	☐ 161-200 Lbs.	☐ 51-65 Yrs.	_____	☐ Gray
	☐ Over 6"	☐ Over 200 Lbs.	☐ Over 65 Yrs.	_____	☐ Red
					☐ White
					☐ Balding
					☐ Bald

Other identifying feature, if any: _____.

6.   At the time I served the Respondent, I asked him/her if he/she was in the military service of this state or nation or any other nation, and the Respondent responded in the negative.

Dated: _____   _____

                                                 Server

Sworn to before me on

_____, _____

_____

Notary Public

_____ **COURT OF THE STATE OF NEW YORK**
COUNTY OF _____

```
_____     )
                 Petitioner, )
Address_____ )
                              )
  _____   )      STIPULATION SETTLING
       -against-              )      HOLDOVER PROCEEDING
                              )      {Commercial/Residential}
_____     )      Index No. _____
             Respondent{s},)
Address_____ )     {L & T}
  _____   )
```

The parties hereby agree and stipulate to settle this proceeding as follows:

1. Respondent(s) consent(s)to the jurisdiction of this Court, waive(s) any and all jurisdictional defenses, and withdraw(s) any counterclaims with prejudice.

2. ❑ Respondent(s) consent(s) to the entry of a final judgment of possession in favor of the Petitioner, warrant to issue forthwith, with execution stayed subject to the terms set forth herein.

    ❑ Respondent(s) agree(s) to voluntarily vacate the subject premises on or before _____, _____, and agree(s) to return all keys to the subject premises to the Petitioner, and to leave the premises in broom clean condition, empty of all persons and property. Any furnishings or personal property left by Respondent(s) after such date will be deemed abandoned by Respondent(s), and may be removed from the premises at the sole cost and expense of the Respondent(s).

    ❑ Respondent(s) agree(s) to pay Petitioner the sum of $_____ per month, which represents the fair and reasonable value of Respondent's(s') use and occupancy of the premises, for the following periods:_____ _____ due on the following dates:_____.

    ❑ In the event of Respondent's(s') failure to pay any one or more of the foregoing installments, Petitioner may enter judgment in the amount of $_____/may move to restore the proceeding the calendar for a determination of the money judgment to be awarded to Petitioner.

6. In the event that Respondent(s) fail(s) to vacate the premises on the date set forth above, or fail(s) to make an installment of the use and occupancy payments as set forth above, the warrant of eviction shall execute forthwith, without any further notice other than service of a 72-hour notice of eviction by the marshall/sheriff/constable.

Dated:_____

_____   _____
Petitioner   Respondent

_____ COURT OF THE STATE OF NEW YORK
COUNTY OF _____

_____)
                    Petitioner,)
Address_____)
)
  _____)   **STIPULATION SETTLING**
          -against-   )   **HOLDOVER PROCEEDING**
)   {Commercial/Residential}
  _____)   Index No. _____
                 Respondent{s},)   {L & T}
Address_____)
  _____)

The parties hereby agree and stipulate to settle this proceeding as follows:

1. Respondent(s) consent(s) to the jurisdiction of this Court, and waive(s) any and all jurisdictional defenses and withdraw(s) any counterclaims with prejudice.

2. Respondent(s) consent(s) to the entry of a final judgment of possession in favor of the Petitioner, with a warrant to issue forthwith, and execution stayed subject to the terms set forth herein.

3. On or before _____ (*date*), Respondent(s) agree(s) to do the following:

_____

_____ and further agree(s) to comply with all the terms and conditions of the lease forthwith, including the payment of unpaid rent or use and occupancy in the sum of $_____, which shall be paid to the Petitioner on or before _____ (*date*).

4. Should the Respondent(s) fail to fully or timely comply with the terms of this stipulation, the warrant of eviction shall execute forthwith, without any further notice other than service of a 72-hour notice of eviction by the Marshall/Sheriff/Constable.

Dated:_____

_____   _____
Petitioner

                                        _____
                                        Respondent(s)

This page intentionally left blank.

_____ **COURT OF THE STATE OF NEW YORK**

COUNTY OF _____

_____)	
Petitioner,)	
Address_____)	
_____)	**STIPULATION SETTLING**
-against-)	**NONPAYMENT PROCEEDING**
)	**WITH FINAL JUDGMENT**
_____)	{Commercial/Residential}
Respondent{s},)	Index No. _____
Address_____)	{L & T}
_____)	

The parties hereby stipulate and agree to settle the proceeding as follows:

1. The Petition is amended to include all rent owed through _____.

2. ❑ Respondent(s) consent(s) to the jurisdiction of this Court, waive(s) any and all jurisdictional defenses, and withdraw(s) any counterclaims.

   ❑ Respondent(s) consent(s) to the entry of a final judgment of possession in favor of the Petitioner, with a warrant to issue and execution stayed subject to the terms as set forth herein.

   ❑ Respondent(s) consent(s) to the entry of a money judgment in favor of Petitioner in the amount of $_____, representing unpaid rent for the period from _____ through _____ at a rate of $_____ per month.

   ❑ Respondent(s) agree(s) to pay the arrears by certified check, bank check, or money order: _____.

6. In the event Respondent(s) default(s) in the payment of one or more of the installments due under this stipulation, a warrant of eviction shall be issued, without any further notice other than service of a 72-hour notice of eviction by law enforcement.

7. ❑ Repairs are not needed.

or

❑ Petitioner agrees to inspect and repair, as necessary, the following conditions:

_____

_____

or

❑Respondent(s) agree(s) to grant Petitioner access to the premises for the inspection and completion of repairs on _____ between the hours of _____ and _____.

9. In the event of Petitioner's default or non-compliance with this stipulation, Respondent may restore the case to the calendar on _____ days' written notice to Petitioner.

10. Upon timely payment of all arrears as required in this stipulation, the proceeding shall be deemed discontinued.

Dated:_____

_____

Petitioner

_____

_____

Respondent(s)

_____ COURT OF THE STATE OF NEW YORK
COUNTY OF _____

_____)
                 Petitioner,)
Address_____)
_____)
       -against-   )
)
_____)
       Respondent{s},)
Address_____)
_____)

**STIPULATION SETTLING
NONPAYMENT PROCEEDING**

{Commercial/Residential}
Index No. _____
{L & T}

The parties do stipulate and agree that this proceeding shall be settled as follows:

1. The Petition is hereby amended to include all rent due through the date of this stipulation, _____.

2. Respondent(s) consent(s) to the jurisdiction of this Court, waive(s) any and all jurisdictional defenses, and withdraw(s) any counterclaims.

3. The parties agree that Respondent(s) owe(s) a total of $_____ in arrears for rent for the months of _____ through _____ at a rate of $_____ per month.

4. Respondent(s) agree(s) to pay the arrears by bank check, certified check, or money order as follows: _____.

5. ❑ Repairs by Petitioner are not needed.
                 or
❑ Petitioner agrees to inspect and repair, as necessary, the following conditions:
_____
_____
_____.
                 or
❑ Respondent(s) agree(s) to grant Petitioner access to the premises for the inspection and completion of repairs on _____ between the hours of _____ and _____.

6. In the event of either party's default, the case may be restored to the trial calendar on _____ days' written notice to the defaulting party.

Dated: _____

_____   _____
Petitioner

                                     _____
                                     Respondent(s)

_____ **COURT OF THE STATE OF NEW YORK**
COUNTY OF _____

_____)
                Petitioner,)
Address_____)   **NOTICE OF MOTION FOR**
_____)   **SUMMARY JUDGMENT**
        -against-   )
)   {Commercial/Residential}
_____)   Index No. _____
                Respondent{s},)   {L & T}
Address_____)
_____)

To the above named Respondent(s):

Please take notice that the Petitioner will move this court for Summary Judgment, based upon the attached Affidavit and supporting documents on _____, _____, at _____ AM/PM at the courthouse located at _____ _____, in part _____.

Dated:_____

Petitioner _____
Address _____
_____
Telephone Number _____

AFFIDAVIT OF PETITIONER

State of New York:
City/Town of _____:
ss:

_____, being duly sworn, swears as follows:

1.   I am the Petitioner and landlord in this matter and hereby reassert and realledge all allegations contained in the Petition for this matter.

2.   I am the owner of the property located at _____ _____, which is the subject of this proceeding.

3.   Respondent(s) signed a lease on _____, which expires on _____.

4.   Respondent(s) has/have breached the lease/failed to pay rent as follows:
_____
_____

5.   The following notice(s) were served upon the Respondent(s), _____ _____, on the following date(s)_____ by the following method(s) _____.

6.   This action is based on the following incidents which occurred as indicated: _____
_____
_____.

7.   Respondent(s) has/have failed to appear or respond, having been served with the following on the following dates and Affidavit of Service being herein attached:
_____
_____.

Based upon the above there is no triable issue of fact in this matter and summary judgment should be granted to Petitioner with the following relief:_____ _____, along with such other and further relief that to the Court may seem just and proper.

Sworn to before me this
_____ day of _____, _____

_____
Notary Public

_____
Petitioner

_____ **COURT OF THE STATE OF NEW YORK**
COUNTY OF _____

_____)
                    Petitioner,)
Address_____)
       _____)
         -against-)
)
_____)
            Respondent{s},)
Address_____)
       _____)

MOTION FOR DEFAULT JUDGMENT

{Commercial/Residential}

Index No. _____

{L & T}

Petitioner moves this court for Default Judgment based upon the attached Affidavit and supporting documents on _____, _____, at _____ AM/PM, at the courthouse located at _____, in part _____.

Dated: _____

Petitioner _____

Address _____

_____

Telephone Number _____

AFFIDAVIT OF PETITIONER

State of New York:
City/Town of _____:
ss:

_____, being duly sworn, swears as follows:

1.   I am the Petitioner and landlord in this matter and hereby reassert and realledge all allegations contained in the Petition for this matter.

2.   I am the owner of the property located at _____ _____, which is the subject of this proceeding.

3.   Respondent(s) signed a lease on _____, which expires on _____.

4.   Respondent(s) has/have breached the lease/failed to pay rent as follows:
_____
_____

5.   The following notice(s) were served upon the Respondents(s), _____ _____, on the following date(s)_____ by the following method(s) _____.

6.   This action is based on the following incidents which occurred as indicated: _____
_____
_____.

7.   Respondent(s) has/have failed to appear or respond, having been served with the following on the following dates and Affidavit of Service being herein attached:
_____
_____.

Based upon the above, default judgment should be granted to Petitioner with the following relief:_____
_____, along with such other and further relief that to the Court may seem just and proper.

Sworn to before me this
_____ day of _____, _____

_____
Notary Public

                              _____
                              Petitioner

_____ **COURT OF THE STATE OF NEW YORK**

COUNTY OF _____

_____)

                Petitioner,)

Address_____)

_____) **JUDGMENT**

      -against-)

) {Commercial/Residential}

_____) Index No. _____

          Respondent{s},) {L & T}

Address_____)

_____)

A Petition having been filed by the Petitioner dated _____ seeking the following relief:_____
in a _____ proceeding and the Respondent(s) having been served on _____ by _____ and Respondent(s) having appeared/not appeared on _____ and a hearing/inquest having been held on _____, it is hereby ordered, adjudged, and decreed:

_____
_____
_____
_____
_____
_____
_____
_____
_____
_____
_____
_____
_____.

Dated:_____

_____

Hon. _____

This page intentionally left blank.

72-HOUR NOTICE OF EVICTION

THIS IS AN EVICTION NOTICE

To: _____

Address: _____

_____

    PLEASE TAKE NOTICE by virtue of a Warrant to Remove issued out of the _____ Court on the date _____ signed by the Honorable Judge _____ to me directed and delivered:

_____ (Title of type of Officer)
_____ (Address)
_____

    I hereby give you seventy-two (72) hours' notice to vacate the premises.

    In the event that you fail to move out of the premises within such seventy-two (72) hours, I legally have the authority to evict you immediately.

Dated: _____   _____
                                             {Signature of Officer}
_____, New York

This page intentionally left blank.

_____ **COURT OF THE STATE OF NEW YORK**
COUNTY OF _____

_____)
              Petitioner,)

Address_____)

_____)

        -against-   )

)

_____)

         Respondent{s},)

Address_____)

_____)

         WARRANT OF EVICTION

         {Commercial/Residential}
         Index No. _____
         {L & T}

THE PEOPLE OF THE STATE OF NEW YORK

     To the Sheriff of the County of _____, or the Marshall of the City of _____, or any Constable of the Town of _____:

     WHEREAS, _____ (Petitioner) commenced a summary proceeding pursuant to Article 7 of the Real Property Actions and Proceedings Law in this court to remove _____ (Respondent(s)) from the following premises described as follows:_____ _____(as described in the Petition) by the service of a Notice of Petition and verified Petition upon _____ (Respondent(s)) on the date _____; said Petition having been heard before the Honorable Judge _____ on _____ (date Judgment was issued).

     WHEREAS, the respondent(s) having appeared and interposed a defense/the respondent(s) having failed to appear, a final judgment was issued and entered on _____, awarding delivery of possession of said premises to Petitioner, _____.

     THEREFORE, YOU ARE COMMANDED TO REMOVE _____ _____ (Respondent(s)) from said premises and put the Petitioner in full possession thereof.

Dated: _____

                             _____

                           Judge, _____ Court

This page intentionally left blank.

_____ COURT OF THE STATE OF NEW YORK
COUNTY OF _____

_____)
              Petitioner,)
Address_____)
_____)
     -against-)
)
_____)
          Respondent{s},)
Address_____)
_____)

STIPULATION AFTER WARRANT

{Commercial/Residential}
Index No. _____
{L & T}

The parties do stipulate and agree as follows:

❏   1.   The parties hereby agree to reinstate the lease under the following terms, which include an agreement that Landlord withdraws the warrant ordering Tenant(s) to vacate the premises: _____

_____

❏   2.   The parties agree that Tenant(s) shall pay to Landlord the sum of $_____, which shall be in satisfaction of past rent due. The parties agree and understand that the payment and acceptance of this amount shall not impact Landlord's judgment of possession and the warrant issued by the court.

Dated: _____

_____   _____
Petitioner   Respondent

                                        _____
                                        Respondent

This page intentionally left blank.

_____ **COURT OF THE STATE OF NEW YORK**
COUNTY OF _____

_____)
                Petitioner,)
Address_____)
     _____)
       -against.-)
)   **NOTICE OF APPEAL**
_____)
          Respondent{s},)
Address_____)   Index No._____
     _____)

PLEASE TAKE NOTICE, that Petitioner hereby appeals to the _____ _____ Court, from an Order of the _____ Court (Hon. _____), entered in the _____ Court Clerk's Office on _____, and from each and every part thereof (and from each and every intermediate Order therein entered).

DATED: _____

                _____ Petitioner
                _____ Address
                _____

TO: Court Clerk:_____
      Respondent(s):_____

This page intentionally left blank.

_____ **COURT OF THE STATE OF NEW YORK**
COUNTY OF _____

_____,
Petitioner,

_____
_____
Address

vs.   **SATISFACTION OF JUDGMENT**

_____,   Index No._____

Respondent.

_____
_____
Address

_____/

   This document is signed by _____, (individually/as agent of Petitioner corporation) on _____, _____ (date).

   Petitioner, _____, acknowledges full payment of the judgment signed by the Hon. _____, on _____, _____. Petitioner agrees that Respondent(s) do(es) not owe the Petitioner any more monies for the judgment.

_____
(Petitioner)

Sworn to before me this _____
day of _____, _____.

_____
Notary Public

This page intentionally left blank.

WINDOW GUARD RIDER

<u>WINDOW GUARDS REQUIRED</u>

LEASE NOTICE TO TENANT

<u>You are required by law</u> to have window guards installed if a child 10 years of age or younger lives in your apartment.

<u>Your landlord is required</u> by law to install window guards in your apartment:

- if you <u>ask</u> him to put in window guards at any time (you need not give a reason)

OR

- if a child 10 years of age or younger lives in your apartment.

<u>It is a violation of law</u> to refuse, interfere with installation, or remove window guards where required.

CHECK ONE
❏   CHILDREN 10 YEARS OF AGE
      OR YOUNGER LIVE IN MY APARTMENT

❏   NO CHILDREN 10 YEARS OF AGE OR
      YOUNGER LIVE IN MY APARTMENT

❏   I WANT WINDOW GUARDS EVEN
      THOUGH I HAVE NO CHILDREN
      10 YEARS OF AGE OR YOUNGER

_____

TENANT (PRINT)

_____

TENANT SIGNATURE

FOR FURTHER INFORMATION CALL:
Window Falls Prevention Program
New York City Department of Health
65 Worth Street, 5th Floor
New York, NY 10013
(212) 334-7771

This page intentionally left blank.

(Form CO 1 – Rev 9/04)

THE CITY OF NEW YORK
DEPARTMENT OF HOUSING PRESERVATION AND DEVELOPMENT
DIVISION OF CODE ENFORCEMENT

CARBON MONOXIDE DETECTOR – CERTIFICATE OF INSTALLATION

Premises Address: _____ _____

In accordance with the provisions of Section 27-2046.1 and 27-2046.2 of the Administrative Code of the City of New York and the rule promulgated by the Department of Housing Preservation and Development (DHPD) to implement those sections, the owner of the above premises must file with DHPD's Division of Code Enforcement Borough Office, in the borough in which the property is located, a certification of satisfactory installation of carbon monoxide detecting devices within 10 days after such installation.

I hereby certify that one or more approved and operational carbon monoxide detecting device has been installed in each dwelling unit of the above premises as prescribed in the rules of the Department of Buildings and DPHD, with the exception of those locations listed below which have not yet been equipped with carbon monoxide detecting devices for the reasons indicated.

Total number of dwelling units:

_____

Total number of dwelling units in which one or more approved and operational carbon monoxide detecting device has been installed:

_____

Carbon Monoxide Detecting Device Not Installed:

Date	Location (story, apt. #)	Reason
_____	_____	_____
_____	_____	_____
_____	_____	_____
_____	_____	_____
_____	_____	_____
_____	_____	_____

(If additional space is needed, please attach another sheet.)

OWNER: _____   _____
                         Signature   Date

ADDRESS: _____   _____
                                                           Telephone

CODE ENFORCEMENT OFFICES

Manhattan: 560 West 133 Street, 1st Floor, New York, NY 10027
Bronx: 1932 Arthur Avenue, 3rd Floor, Bronx, NY 10457
Brooklyn: 701 Euclid Avenue, Brooklyn, NY 11208
Queens: 120-55 Queens Boulevard, 1st Floor, Kew Gardens, NY 11424
Staten Island: Borough Hall, 2nd Floor, St. George, NY 10301

FOR DEPARTMENT USE ONLY

Department Certification
By:_____   Date:_____

This page intentionally left blank.

Form for Notices for Carbon Monoxide Alarms

The following is a sample form for providing notice to occupants about carbon monoxide alarms.

NOTICE

The owner, _____, of this building located at
_____ is required by law to post this notice advising tenants that the owner is required by law to provide a CO alarm in each apartment in this building within 15 feet of the primary entrance to each room lawfully used for sleeping. The law further makes the tenant of each apartment responsible for the maintenance and repair of the alarms installed in the apartment and for replacing any or all alarms that are stolen, removed, missing, or become inoperable during the occupancy of the apartment. The law also provides that the occupant of each Class A apartment in the building in which a CO alarm is provided and installed shall pay the owner $25.00 per alarm for the cost of such work. The occupant has one year from the date of installation to make such payment to the owner.

This page intentionally left blank.

(Form CO/SD-1 rev. 9/04)

THE CITY OF NEW YORK
DEPARTMENT OF HOUSING PRESERVATION AND DEVELOPMENT
DIVISION OF CODE ENFORCEMENT

SMOKE & CARBON MONOXIDE DETECTOR – CERTIFICATE OF INSTALLATION

Premises Address: _____

In accordance with the provisions of Section 27-2045, 27-2046, 27-2046.1 and 27-2046.2 of the Administrative Code of the City of New York and the rules promulgated by the Department of Housing Preservation and Development (DHPD) to implement those sections, the owner of the above premises must file with DHPD's Division of Code Enforcement Borough Office, in the borough in which the property is located, a certification of satisfactory installation of smoke and carbon monoxide detecting devices within 10 days after such installation.

I hereby certify that one or more approved and operational smoke and carbon monoxide detecting device has been installed in each dwelling unit as prescribed in the rules of the Department of Buildings and DHPD, with the exception of those locations listed below which have not yet been equipped with smoke and/or carbon monoxide detecting devices for the reasons indicated.

Total number of dwelling units: _____

Total number of dwelling units in which one or more approved and operational smoke detecting device has been installed: _____

Total number of dwelling units in which one or more approved and operational carbon monoxide detecting device has been installed: _____

Smoke & Carbon Monoxide Detecting Devices Not Installed:

Date	Location (story, apt. #)	Device (circle device(s) not installed)	Reason
_____	_____	Smoke/ Carbon Monoxide	_____
_____	_____	Smoke/ Carbon Monoxide	_____
_____	_____	Smoke/ Carbon Monoxide	_____
_____	_____	Smoke/ Carbon Monoxide	_____
_____	_____	Smoke/ Carbon Monoxide	_____
_____	_____	Smoke/ Carbon Monoxide	_____
_____	_____	Smoke/ Carbon Monoxide	_____

(If additional space is needed, please attach another sheet.)

OWNER: _____   _____
                          Signature   Date

ADDRESS: _____   _____
                                                                                                    Telephone

---

FOR DEPARTMENT USE ONLY
Department Certification
By:_____   Date:_____

This page intentionally left blank.

Owner
Property Name
Owner Address
City, State, Zip Code

Current Occupant
Apartment Number
Property Address
City, State, Zip Code

Keep the top part of this form for your records.

Annual Notice to Tenant or Occupant in Buildings with 3 or More Apartments
Protect Your Child from Window Falls and Lead Poisoning

You are required by law to complete and return this form to your landlord before **February 15** each year. If you do not return the form, your landlord is required to visit your apartment to find out the ages of children living with you. Call **311** for more information on preventing window falls and lead poisoning.

Window Guards

- Your landlord is required by law to install window guards in all your windows if a child age **10** years or younger lives with you, **or** if you ask for them (even if no children live with you). However, windows that open to fire escapes and windows on the first floor used as fire exits should not have window guards.

- Window Guards should be installed so there is no space greater than 4 ½ inches above or below the guard, on the side of the guard, or between the bars.

- It is against the law for you to refuse, interfere with installation, or remove window guards where they are required.

The above requirements apply to <u>all</u> buildings with 3 or more apartments regardless of when they were built.

Peeling Lead Paint

- Your landlord is required by law to inspect your apartment for peeling paint and other lead paint hazards at least once a year if a child age **6** years or younger lives with you.

- Always report peeling paint to your landlord. If a child age **6** years or younger lives with you, your landlord must inspect your apartment. Your landlord must provide you with the results of these paint inspections.

- Your landlord must use safe work practices to repair all peeling paint and other lead paint hazards.

- If you have a baby or if a child age **6** years or younger comes to live with you during the year, you must notify your landlord in writing.

The above requirements apply to buildings with 3 or more apartments built before 1960, or built between 1960 and 1978 if the landlord knows that lead paint is present in the building.

Fill Out and Detach the bottom part of this form and return in envelope.

Please check YES or NO:

1. A child age **10** years or younger lives in my apartment:	□ YES	□ NO
IF NO: I want window guards even though no children age 10 years or younger live in my apartment:	□ YES	□ NO
IF YES: A child age **6** years or younger lives in my apartment:	□ YES	□ NO
2. Window guards are installed in all windows as required:	□ YES	□ NO
3. Window guards need maintenance or repair:	□ YES	□ NO

Current Occupant
Apartment Number
Address
City, State, Zip Code

Name of Tenant/Occupant (Print): _____
Tenant/Occupant Signature: _____
Date: _____

Return to:

Owner
Property Name
Address of Owner
City, State, Zip Code

Instructions for Landlords:
Annual Notice to Tenant or Occupant in Buildings with 3 or More Apartments
Protecting Children from Window Falls and Lead Poisoning

Landlords in multiple dwellings (buildings with 3 or more apartments) are legally required to send a notice to tenants or occupants every year to inquire about the ages of children living in the building. The notice contains a form that tenants must return. The notice also contains information about window guards and peeling lead paint.

Where can landlords find the annual notice?
Landlords must use a form approved by the Department of Health and Mental Hygiene (DOHMH). Landlords can obtain a copy of the form by calling 311 or visiting http://www.nyc.gov/html/doh/pdf/win/win-wf013-appendixb.pdf

When should the annual notice be sent to tenants?
Landlords are required to send the annual notice to tenants no earlier than January 1 and no later than January 15 each year.

The notice may be delivered to tenants by:
1. First Class mail, addressed to the occupant of the dwelling unit,
2. Hand delivery to the occupant of the dwelling unit, or
3. Enclosure with the January rent bill, if such rent bill is delivered after December 15th but no later than January 16th.

What if tenant/occupant does not return the form?
If the landlord does not receive the completed form by February 15th, the landlord must inspect the occupant's apartment, giving reasonable notice and at reasonable times, to determine if a child of applicable age lives in the apartment. If there is a child 10 years or younger living in the apartment, the landlord must inspect the apartment to determine if window guards are installed and are in good repair. If between February 16th and March 1st, the landlord has made reasonable attempts but has been unable to gain access to apartment, the landlord must notify DOHMH.

What must the landlord do with the returned form?
The landlord must review the returned form to ascertain if a child of applicable age lives in apartments covered by window guard and/or lead paint laws. If a child of applicable age lives in a unit, the landlord must take appropriate actions, which may include inspecting the apartment, installing or repairing window guards, and/or fixing lead paint hazards using safe work practices. Landlords are also required to keep the completed form for a period of ten years.

Where can a landlord get more information?
For more information about the annual notice, windows guards, or lead paint, please call 311.

To: Tenant   From: Landlord
Date:

ANNUAL NOTICE

PROTECT YOUR CHILD FROM LEAD POISONING AND WINDOW FALLS

New York City law requires that tenants living in buildings with 3 or more apartments complete this form and return it to their landlord before February 15, each year. **If you do not return this form, your landlord is required to visit your apartment to determine if children age 10 years or younger (under 11) live in your apartment.** If young children live in your apartment, the law requires your landlord to inspect for and properly install window guards and to inspect for and safely repair peeling paint.

Peeling Lead Paint	Window Guards
By law, your landlord is required to inspect your apartment for peeling paint and other lead paint hazards at least once a year if a child age 6 years or younger (under 7) lives with you.	**By law,** your landlord is required to install window guards in all your windows IF a child age 10 or younger (under 11) lives with you, OR if you request them (even if no children live with you).
▪ You must notify your landlord in writing if a child under 7 comes to live with you during the year.	▪ ONLY windows that open to fire escapes, and one window in each first floor apartment when there is a fire escape on the outside of the building, are legally exempt from this requirement.
▪ If a child under 7 lives with you, your landlord must inspect your apartment and provide you with the results of these paint inspections.	▪ **It is against the law** for you to interfere with installation, or remove window guards where they are required. Air conditioners in windows must be permanently installed.
▪ *Always report peeling paint to your landlord. Call 311 if your landlord does not respond.*	
▪ Your landlord must use safe work practices to repair all peeling paint and other lead paint hazards.	▪ Window guards should be installed so there is no space greater than 4½ inches above or below the guard, on the side of the guard, or between the bars.
These requirements apply to buildings with 3 or more apartments built before 1960. They also apply to buildings built between 1960 and 1978 if the landlord knows that lead paint is present.	These requirements apply to all buildings with 3 or more apartments, regardless of when they were built.

Fill out and detach the bottom part of this form and return it to your landlord.

------------- ✂ ---

Please check all boxes that apply.

☐ **A child age 6 years or younger (under 7) lives in my apartment.**

☐ **A child age 10 years or younger (under 11) lives in my apartment and:**
  ☐ Window guards are installed in all windows as required.
  ☐ Window guards need installation or repair.
  ☐ Window guards are NOT installed in all windows as required.

☐ **No child age 10 years or younger (under 11) lives in my apartment:**
  ☐ I want window guards installed anyway.
  ☐ I have window guards, but they need repair.

Last Name		*First Name*		*Middle Initial*	
Street Address	*Apt. #*	*City*	*State*	*Zip Code*	*Telephone Number*
Signature			*Date*		

Return form to: Name and address of landlord or managing agent.
Call 311 for more information on preventing window falls and lead poisoning.

Index